That Reminds Me of a Funny Story

That Reminds Me of a Funny Story

*A Memoir, How-To, and Compendium
of Yankee Humor*

Rebecca Rule

HOBBLEBUSH BOOKS
Concord, New Hampshire

Copyright © 2019 by Rebecca Rule

All rights reserved. No part of this work may be used or reproduced in any manner whatsoever without written permission from the publisher, except in the case of brief quotations embodied in critical articles and reviews.

Composed in Adobe Caslon Pro with Just Another Hand and Macho display at Hobblebush Books (www.hobblebush.com)

Printed in the United States of America

Cover illustration by Todd Kramer (ToddKramerArt.com), based on a photograph by Kathleen Bailey

Author photo by Michael Sterling

"Why We Have Six Cats" and "Solstice" first appeared in *NH Home* magazine

ISBN: 978-1-939449-21-4

Library of Congress Control Number: 2019948333

Hobblebush Books
PO Box 1285
Concord, New Hampshire 03302
www.hobblebush.com

Contents

What to Expect on These Pages   1

WHY TELL STORIES
Good Stories and Good Songs   10
The Audience is Right There   14
Take Your Chances and Hope for the Best   16
Stories Tell Us Who We Are   21
There's Some Good and Bad in Everything   27
Many Reasons to Tell Stories   30
I Choose the Funny Ones   33
Trust the Stories; They Won't Let You Down   36

HOW TO TELL STORIES
Doin' What Comes Naturally   42
Gestures   44
Movement, Microphones, and Three Horror Stories   46
Facial Expressions   57
Props   59
Repetition, Rhythm, and Rhyme   64
Vocals   68
Above All, Find Your Territory and Trust Your Voice   76

A STORYTELLER'S LIFE
School: It Was the Best of Times and So Fawth   88
Make the Mistakes You Need to Make and Move On   90
Stories Are Puzzles   96
What Doesn't Kill You May Eventually Make You Laugh   100
A Skosh Askew   103
Under the Influence   106
They Just Keep Coming   110
Through the Window   115
Loss Shapes Us   117
Kindred Voices   118
Embrace Evolution   122
Choices   128
Honoring Ways of Life   132
Let Stories Tell Themselves   139
A Kind of Immortality   140
How Do You Get to Carnegie Hall?   143

As Popeye Said, I Yam What I Yam   145
  I Want to See the Ocean   153
  Money Is a Concept   156
  Bits and Pieces   160
  Stories That Stick   164
  Always Something New   169
  Trust Your Material, Your Audience, and Yourself   174
  A Particular Sense of Humor   183
  Natural Inclinations   187
  Shaping a Session   189
  Flexibility is Key   192
  When Your Inner Child Channels Your Inner Grown-up   195
  Didn't Go as Well as Expected   197
  The Prime Directive   200
  Secrets   203
  Whatever You Do, Make It a Good Story   208
  Smile When You Can   211

STORIES BY THE DOZEN
  Character and Characters   217
  Commerce and Frugality   224
  Common Sense   228
  Directions and Travel   230
  Family Dynamics   236
  Farming, Gardening, Working the Land, and Working in the Woods   242
  Ghosts and Cemeteries   245
  Holidays   248
  Ingenuity   251
  Kids   253
  The Law   257
  Liars and Tall Tales   262
  Lobster and Other Edibles   265
  Misunderstandings and Miscommunication   269
  Natives   272
  Politics and Town Meeting   275
  Small Towns and Neighbors   289
  Water and Waterways   295
  Weather and Fashion   298
  Wildlife, Hunting, and Fishing   302
  Yankee Attitude and Wisdom   308

  Acknowledgments   315
  About the Author   316

For Levi Silver, who loves stories

What to Expect on These Pages

Ideas about what makes a good story and how to tell it.

Stories about telling stories.

Yankee humor classics.

Stories collected over a lifetime (so far) of listening and telling and listening some more.

Stories to read and share.

Instruction in yankee-speak.

Real names and locations (when I can recall them).

Attribution when possible. Stories come to us from all directions. Some seem to live in the ethers. Some seem to rise from the earth itself. Those are the best ones.

PART I
Why Tell Stories

At a storytelling course for seniors, one of the participants, Jane Ramsay, said we'd met before. She said, "I told you the one about the Cockermouth River."

Knock me over with a feather. It must be a decade since I first heard that story. And I've probably told it 300 times. Here's Jane, in the flesh, back in my life just as I am back in hers—for the eight weeks of this course anyhow. What goes around comes back to you.

This time around Jane filled in a few details. The story about the Cockermouth came to her from Neil Davis, an elderly man chock-full of stories. She had the presence of mind as a young woman to listen and remember and pass on Neil's stories.

He was a memorable character. One day, she said, he made a point of admiring her umbrelli, that's what he called it. He asked where she got it, how much it cost, and would she get him one just like it. She said she would.

Not long afterward, she got a call. "Don't get me that umbrelli," Neil said.

"Why not?"

"I might die," he said. "If I die with that umbrelli, I'll have to figure out who to leave it to."

Neil did die eventually, without the burden of having to figure out who would inherit his umbrelli. But his stories live on.

Scaly Buggahs
Neil Davis via Jane Ramsay

The Cockermouth River runs through Hebron into Newfound Lake. Years ago, according to locals, the salmon ran so heavy up the Cockermouth in the spring that you could practically walk across the river on their backs. They were running upstream to spawn. It's illegal to fish during spawning season. Wouldn't be fair. The salmon have their minds on other things.

One day, Nancy—out back of her house hanging laundry—heard gunshots down by the river. When you hear gunshots in some parts of the country, you go the other way. But around here, in those days, when you heard gunshots, you headed out to investigate. *What the heck's going on? It ain't deer season.*

Nancy dropped her laundry basket and walked cross-country through the field and woods. On the bank of the river, she found her neighbor, Charlie, sitting cross-legged with his .22 across his knees. "What you doing?" she asked.

"Shootin' muskrats."

Nancy looked. Beyond Charlie in the ferns she spotted five large salmon all laid out, not looking too lively.

"Muskrats, huh."

"Yup," Charlie said. "Scaly buggahs, ain't they?"

For the last twenty-five years, give or take, I've travelled town-to-town telling stories. Wherever I go, people tell me stories. I write them down in my little book and tell them in the next town. It's a total racket. Sometimes they find their way into published books—a dozen so far. It's my mission to preserve as many stories as I can. They are precious and ephemeral. They teach us about ourselves. They reflect our culture. They connect us.

There are a few different versions of "Scaly Buggahs," so I'm convinced it has a lot of truth to it. Most stories do. What the heck, all stories have some truth to them. In this case, at some point a lawbreaker got caught shooting fish. In one version, Nancy is a game warden and poor Charlie gets nabbed, loses his fishing license (if he had one), and has to pay a fine. In most versions, Charlie doesn't say "scaly buggahs," he says, "scaly bastids." I've softened that for younger audiences and churchgoers.

Sometimes the softer version is as funny as the off-color one. Buggahs versus bastids seems like a draw to me. Other times, the off-color word is more effective. Dick Wakefield has a treasure trove of Fodd Boody stories. Fodd was a hermit up Moultonborough way. The off-color version of "Fodd Boody's Tall Mother" is, to my ear, the funniest. Though when I tell it to kids or in churches, I'm apt to change one word.

If you were to compare my current telling to Dick's version from a few years back, they'd be different. That's the way it is with stories. They evolve teller to teller, telling to telling, though the kernel—the heart of the story—remains the same.

Fodd Boody's given name was Forrest, but everybody called him Fodd. At a Ladies' Tea at Geneva Point Farm, now a conference center, a Moultonborough native said when she was little, her mother would scold her by saying, "Now you're acting just like Fodd Boody."

In other words, don't act like Fodd Boody unless you are Fodd Boody.

Fodd Boody's Tall Mother
Dick Wakefield (sort of)

Fodd Boody was a hermit. Lived in the woods all by himself. Once in a blue moon he'd walk into town, do some work for ready money at Geneva Point Farm, buy provisions, and disappear again.

Fodd always wore a broad-brimmed straw hat, overalls, and a tattered flannel shirt. His gray beard reached his belly button. His toes poked out through his shoes. At the general store, a new kid was clerking. Fodd lays his purchases on the counter to be added up and bagged. The kid looks the old man over and says, kinda sassy, "Hey, Mistah, what stands between you and a damned fool?"

Fodd says, "At the moment, it's a counter."

Fodd was a tall man, but it was said he inherited his height from his mother. Fella says, "Fodd, exactly how tall was your mother?"

Fodd looks the fella over. He looks him up and down. He says, "Stand on that chair."

Fella stands on the chair. Fodd looks the fella up and down. He grabs a thick phone book. He says, "Stand on this phone book on the chair." The fella does. Fodd looks him up and down. He says, "Stand on your tippy toes and reach as high as you can with your right arm." The fella does.

"Ayuh," Fodd says, "you could just about touch the dear old lady's ass."

Note to irritated grammarians: This story begins in the past tense and moves into the present tense between these two lines: "At the general store, a new kid was clerking. Fodd lays his purchases on the counter to be added up and bagged." One of the traditions of yankee storytelling is to move from past (what was) to present (what is). The story is remembered and so begins in the past, but when the action starts, the present tense zooms in. Two rules of thumb: past tense is more believable; present tense is more immediate. A teller tries to balance the two without confusing the listener.

Ayuh: Exclamation. Informal. Accent on the first syllable, or the second, or both. An all-purpose New England expletive. I don't use it much, but my father did some, and my grandparents certainly did. It can express approval, disapproval, surprise, dismay, or concern. It can mean yes, no, or maybe. Variations include—ayum (skeptical) or ayup (in agreement).
"Town meetin's Tuesday."
"Ayuh." (Yes it is; I'm aware of it.)
"You going?"
"Ayum." (Don't know, don't really want to, probably should.)
"Town meetin' ain't what it used to be."
"Ayup." (Yes, it ain't.)

As for "the dear old lady's ass," you can substitute other words, but "bum," "butt," "derriere," "rump," "rear," "tush," or "sit-down" lack the panache of "ass." I like the French "fesses," but not everybody speaks French even a little bit. Case in point, our French friend Béatrice instructed her American kindergarten class to sit on their "fesses." They thought she was telling them to sit on their faces. The obedient little mites tried, but they just weren't limber enough.

For me, "Hey, Mistah, what stands between you and a damned fool" will always be associated with Fodd Boody, though it is a classic yankee humor setup, like "How do you get to Millinocket?" Answer: "You can't get theyah from heeyah," or "Don't you move a goddamn inch." These two wry comebacks were made famous by Marshall Dodge and Bob Bryan, but I'm pretty sure they'd been part of the canon for decades before the first Bert & I record dropped in 1958. "You can't get theyah from heeyah" can, no doubt, be traced to the first time somebody from away asked a Maine-ah for directions and the Maine-ah decided to have some fun.

"Ayuh," said the Maine-ah, "You could take Mountain Road up as far as the red bahn, well, the cawnuh where the red bahn used to be.... No, that's a dead end. What you should do, probly, is take the left a quartah mile before you get to the cawnuh where the red bahn used to be.... No, that won't work. Bridge went out in the big stawm of nineteen aught eight and the town's too damn cheap to replace it. Your best bet is to head back toward the highway, cross over onto the River Road and where it splits.... No, that'll take you into the gulf and this time of ye-ah, the gulf is nawthin' but a mud hole...."

However long the story goes, however many twists and turns it takes, the punch line is always, "Come to think of it, you can't get theyah from heeyah," as existential a theorem as there ever were.

> **Maine-ah:** Noun. Someone from the state of Maine. In yankee-speak, the "r" is often dropped at the ends of words or in the middle. Corner becomes cawnuh, barn becomes bahn, year becomes ye-ah, storm becomes stawm. Because yankees are frugal, we hate to waste those dropped "r's," so they're apt, in some dialects, to turn up in unexpected places, especially at the ends of words ending in "a." The name Maria becomes Marier, banana is bananer, algebra is algebrer, and so on.

Dodge and Bryan didn't invent yankee humor, but they respected it, interpreted it, and popularized it. These two young Ivy Leaguers collected stories from the old-timers, the clam diggers, lobster fishermen, and islanders of Down East Maine. They mastered the dialect and delivery. They sold a ton of records. As a kid, I listened to Bert & I along with the hymns of Tennessee Ernie Ford and the Irish ballads of Burl Ives—my mother's favorites. I wouldn't be telling stories today if it weren't for Bert & I. Come to think of it, those hymns were stories set to music ("The Little Brown Church") as were the ballads of Burl Ives ("Nell Flaherty's Drake"). I can recite every one of them to this day.

It's likely I paid more attention to the stories told in the family because of Bert & I, which proved that homey stories in the yankee vernacular were worth saving and passing on. A rhyme passed down through the family goes: Old Rob, Young Rob, Rob's Rob and Curly Bob. Those were four of my relations, all named Robert and all living in the same town. The rhyme helped distinguish one from another.

Another one goes:

Emma, Tamar, Etta, Scott
Rosa, Mollie, May and Dot
And Dot was Ned
But Ned didn't rhyme.

Those are the names of my great-great aunts and uncles in the Ford (pronounced Foe-uhd) family. Cousin Sheree found a family story in a clipping from a magazine, probably *Yankee*. The source—author unnamed—is *The History of Slab City—Grafton, NH*. It's about George Nelson Ford, our Great-Great-Grandfather, dad to the aunts and uncles of the rhyme. What a find!

Great-Great-Grampa George Ford's Story from a Book

One day, George Ford, a farmer who lived on the edge of the valley, came to my father's with a sow to mate with his boar. Father asked him "why he came here" [*sic*] when George Dean, a near neighbor, had a boar. His reply was, "By Goddy, Jeff, if George Dean had the last boar and I had the last sow, there would be no more pigs."

This story and those rhymes link the generations. This is our family. Some of us are stubborn to the core just like Great-Great-Grampa George.

When my dad said that a person's "brains rattled around like a BB in a box car," I wrote the expression down in a notebook of funny sayings—just like the notebook I keep today, little things people say that are worth remembering. At six years old, I was already a collector. In that same notebook I wrote my first poem:

April showers
Bring May flowers
And now that it's May
Happy Mother's Day.

I read it out loud at a family party and received my first applause.

More than fifty years later, I drove my dad to the hospital for his final stay. "Last trip," he told my mother when we bundled all that was left of him into the car. He'd been saying it all morning, she said—"last trip, last trip, last trip." Our first stop was at the cancer wing to check in with his oncologist. The nurses knew Dad well from chemo sessions and welcomed him warmly. The doctor took one look at him and said he needed to be admitted right away. On his way to the elevator in the requisite wheelchair, Dad regaled us with a poem from childhood:

> The boy stood on the burning deck
> His feet all full of blisters
> He had no britches of his own
> So he had to wear his sister's.

Then he said with exaggerated dignity: "Some applause might be in order." We applauded. Dad took a bow.

GOOD STORIES AND GOOD SONGS

In 2008, to celebrate the fiftieth anniversary of the first Bert & I record, Islandport Press published their stories on CD. Storytellers gathered at L.L. Bean in Freeport, Maine—the mothership—for an afternoon of nothing but Bert & I stories. Present were Bob Bryan (himself!), Fred Dodge (brother to Marshall who died young), Kendall Morse, John McDonald, Tim Sample, and me.

We performed two sets because we couldn't fit all the listeners into the cleared-out camping section at once. I noticed that as each teller spoke, members of the audience mouthed the words. They knew the stories by heart.

Good stories are like good songs—they stick with you. People don't mind hearing them over and over. In fact, they like it. The more you hear a story or a song, the more it becomes your own, as Tommy Makem, Irish folksinger and songwriter, reminds us:

> Sing me the old songs of laughter and pleasure
> Sing me the old songs of sorrow and pain
> Sing from the heart, sing of love without measure
> The good times, the bad times, the sunshine, the rain.

When someone asks, "Have you heard this before?" I say no, because even if I've heard it a hundred times, I've never heard your particular version. When you share it with me, it becomes ours. That's what happened at L.L. Bean in Freeport, Maine. People who loved Bert & I came together to tell, listen, laugh, remember, and make new memories. A veteran said when he told Bert & I stories while stationed overseas some of his colleagues were annoyed, but the soldiers from New England couldn't get enough. Those stories meant home.

At sessions, I ask audiences, "Who remembers Bert & I?" People smile and nod. Others look puzzled. Those familiar with the stories swap a few. You can't explain a Bert & I story—or any good story for that matter—you just have to tell it. We tell stories so we don't have to explain. In the telling we bring others into the circle of what we know, what we understand, how we are.

Listen to words, notes, and rhythms of traditional Cajun, Appalachian, French-Canadian, Mexican, or Caribbean music—you'll hear the similarities. Rooted in the earth, they trace their origins to simpler times and reflect the lives of those who came before.

A few years ago, I attended a Gipsy Kings concert at the Portsmouth Music Hall. Our seats were as far back in the auditorium as they could be. But those rhythms, those lyrics—in Andalusian Spanish performed by Frenchmen descended from Gypsies—made me feel the way I felt in a pub on the coast of Ireland singing along at a midnight pick-up session. I feel much the same when drumming with my friends at a community center among the trees overlooking a frog pond in New Hampshire. Picture ten pale women of a certain age playing djembes and djun-djuns and shaking our maracas. Sometimes when we get going, we can hear singing soft and far away. And it's not us.

"Fanga Alafia," a West African chant and invocation, is a favorite. I've sung and drummed Fanga at senior centers, assisted living facilities, and nursing homes. The seniors sing and drum, too. A woman joined our circle. The nurse said Althea was a hundred and six years old, deaf and blind. Yet she tapped the rhythms on the arm of her wheelchair. She must have felt the vibrations.

At one point, I cupped my hand over hers. We tapped together. She said: "I can't hear you or see you, but I'm enjoying the music."

These rhythms live within us. As my friend Mary Lamenzo—teacher, drummer, and wise woman—often said, "Each of us has a drum inside. It's called the heart."

Read the folk tales of any culture and you see the sameness. These are our shared roots. At the most basic level, these are stories of human nature.

Kindness is a universal theme. We show it in different ways, but even the smallest kindness deserves a story. This one takes place in the North Country years ago. It's a family story told by the daughter of a game warden who spent many early mornings on patrol in remote locations under harsh weather conditions.

The Game Warden and the Salty Salt

Seven AM on a foggy, dismal morning. The warden shivered as he filled the tank of his state-owned vehicle. This was in the days when gas stations sold just one thing—gas. On the other side of the pump stood an old guy—an old salty salt, the daughter said, though how he got so salty in the White Mountains, I don't know. Maybe it was the roads. Or maybe he come across from Maine.

The old salty salt had a beater truck. His worn cap pulled low, he was smoking one of those stubby black pipes old-timers used to smoke. This was before gas pumps sported signs saying "Don't smoke here or you might blow up."

As they were filling their respective tanks and staring into soggy space, the warden said out loud, kind of plaintive: "I wonder where a fella could get a good cup of coffee around here this time of day?"

The old salty salt takes a puff. Pulls the pipe out of his mouth and sets it on the roof of the truck. "Well," he says. "I guess you'll just have to come home with me."

Mark Winkley's friends and family showed him great kindness in this next story. I like to think Mark would get a kick out of the story being included here. By all accounts, he was a man with a well-honed sense of humor. Plus, he loved Model Ts.

Mark Winkley's Model T

At the Annual Meeting of the New Hampshire Model T Club, several members, including Mark Winkley's son, contributed to this story.

Mark loved his Model T. He loved to drive it. All over. His son complained, "Dad, that car's going to be all worn out by the time I inherit it." Mark said that wouldn't be a problem, since he planned to be buried in it.

"Why's that, Dad?"

Mark said: "Because I never saw a hole a Model T couldn't get out of."

He didn't get the chance to be buried in his Model T because it burned in a barn fire.

His friends rallied. One donated an engine. Another donated a chassis. Another donated wheels and tires. The Model T Club built a whole "new" Model T from spare parts for Mark Winkley.

When he died, a procession of Model Ts escorted his coffin to the graveyard. The coffin itself was carried in one. Mourners observed he would have gotten a kick out of how his feet were hanging out the back.

Storytelling is not a profession that calls many people. Yet it called me, despite the fact that I was a shy child, a shy adolescent, a shy young adult, virtually nonverbal in school, and as socially paralyzed as they come. In our high school year book, I was named "Quietest" and photographed behind a drum set. It was not a compliment. My shyness was a crutch I had to discard. The stories demanded it.

I tell stories because the telling makes me happy and so do the stories. I want to pass that happiness on. "I can't remember when I laughed so hard," people say. "My face hurts from laughing," they say. "I haven't had much to laugh about lately, but tonight I laughed." The hope is that each listener takes a few stories home and shares them, and their listeners share them, and so on—until (and this happens) they return to me, to be enjoyed all over again.

Stories have the power to push troubles clean out of our heads. A room full of people absorbed in the same story is a sacred space. A room full of people laughing together is communion.

THE AUDIENCE IS RIGHT THERE

One of the joys of storytelling is how physically close tellers can get to the audience. With a portable mic, I can move around the room, forward and back, side-to-side. I can walk the aisles and—this is so much fun—hand the mic to an audience member with a comment or a question or a story to tell. It's interactive and unpredictable. The stories flow among us. We play off each other like jazz musicians.

My friend Susan Poulin—actress, writer, storyteller, and "the funniest woman in Maine"—and I discussed the difference between acting and telling. Actors, we concluded, stand on a stage bathed in light. They interpret lines. They interact with other actors. The audience sits in the dark taking it all in. It's spectacle.

Storytellers, on the other hand, share the light with listeners. We get right up close. The audience becomes part of the story. It's reciprocal.

Sometimes I get so close to listeners I have to apologize for spitting. Once my mouth gets in gear, who knows what's going to fly out? If I can't see my audience, I lose rhythm and connection. The telling suffers. The reactions of listeners fuel the stories. Their reactions light the way to the next line and the next story and the one after that.

Often there's one person, arms crossed, straight-faced, who challenges me: *Make me laugh if you can. I dare you.* If I can just make that person meet my eye, if one line coaxes a grin, or a chuckle, the evening is a success. These folks are like butternuts—pronounced buttnuts in yankee-speak—slow to ripen and hard to crack. But their reactions—if and when they come—are so sweet they're totally worth the effort.

It's easy to misinterpret audience reaction. The grim-faced family of four (mother, father, preteen son and daughter) stymie me. Later, the organizer reveals the family is Russian, new to this country, with limited English skills. They weren't scowling. They were concentrating.

At a library, three women in the back of the room looked pained. Later, I mention this to the librarian. She says, "Oh, that was a misunderstanding. They thought they were here for next week's program."

"What's next week's program?"

"Medicinal Herbs for Menopausal Women."

Just because somebody looks asleep doesn't mean they are. Some people listen better with their eyes closed. If a person is snoring, chalk it up to a long day or a medical condition. If a person squirms on the seat, he might suffer from hemorrhoids. Someone who looks dead serious on the outside might very well be feeling a lightness of spirit inside. You never know what will touch somebody's funny bone—or their heart. One lady said her favorite part of the evening was the word *dite*. "My mother used to say dite," she said. "I haven't heard that word in years." Now I try to include it in every performance. Just in case.

Dite: Noun. A little bit. Not very much.

Crosscut is a program my husband, John Rule, and I have developed about the paper industry in Berlin, NH, illustrated with vintage photographs. One woman said of a photograph of about thirty women in 1940s garb posed at their workstations: "When I got up this morning, I never thought I'd see my mother." Yet there she was in that old picture projected on the wall. And here we were sharing stories of what it was like to be a woman working in the mills at that time.

If somebody rushes out mid-story, I never take it personally. That person might have an urgent need for the bathroom. Or an appointment.

And, of course, there are the Vermonters.

During one season I told stories along the Connecticut River in several different towns. At three of these sessions a man stood in the back, arms crossed, unsmiling. Could not coax a smile out of him. Not a twitch.

At the end of the third session I accosted him—not pissed off, just curious. "Noticed you in the back at three of these *humor* sessions. Noticed you never once cracked a smile."

"I'm a fifth generation Vermonter," he said. "We don't."

TAKE YOUR CHANCES AND HOPE FOR THE BEST

Storytelling requires improvisation. I never know what somebody's going to come out with during a session—including me. That's the fun of it. Once, as I told a story in which a horse "drops dead in the furrow, something he'd never done before," a listener quipped, "and would never do again." Now when I tell that story I include that line. It's a cockah.

> **Cockah:** Noun. Spelled *corker* in the dictionary. An astonishing person or thing. A lot of stories are interesting, thought-provoking, funny, but cockahs are rare.

My husband, John, and I love to visit the Caribbean. It's so different from New England. Especially in winter. For one thing, it's wahm. A few years ago, John and I witnessed an interaction between an innkeeper and her employee that literally stopped us in our tracks. The employee's comeback was a cockah. It earned a place in my collection of snappy comebacks, along with "That's right, too," "You coulda knocked me over with a feather," and "Ain't that a kick in the head."

Judith and Michael Reach an Understanding

On our trip to St. Lucia, John and I came around a green, steamy corner to find the narrow path from the beach to our B&B blocked. Our British hostess, Judith, was reaming out Michael, the gardener—a tall, handsome St. Lucian about three times her size. She was displeased with the work he and his crew had done the day before and said so. Several times. In colorful ways. Michael and his crew would do better, she said, or else!

He stood before her, straight and stoic. Then he smiled a beatific smile and said in a charming Caribbean lilt, "Madame, you always bring out de best in me."

If you cut "Madame" and get rid of the lilt, it's quintessential yankee humor, as is this story from Dan Allen about a famous New London character named Ira Littlefield, whose sense of humor was as dry as Lake Sunapee is wet.

The Boathouse

The one-eyed ragman, often seen about town on a motorcycle with a side car, got into a bitter conflict with his neighbor. The neighbor accused the ragman of violating the line between their lakefront properties with a boathouse. The ragman insisted that his boathouse was entirely on his own property and hired surveyor Ira Littlefield to prove it.

When the survey was complete, he found the ragman in his cottage paring his toenails and delivered the bad news. The ragman's boathouse was, indeed, partly over the line.

"What'm I gonna do?" said the ragman.

"You got but two choices," Ira said. "You can either move the boathouse or move the line."

The Two Doctors Clough

Dan Allen also tells about two other local characters, Old Dr. Clough and Young Dr. Clough. Ira Littlefield always did his doctoring with the elder, but there came a time when Old Dr. Clough called a halt to that. "I can't see patients anymore," he told Ira. "You'll have to go see my boy."

Ira did. Young Dr. Clough gave Ira a thorough exam and prescribed belladonna pills for his ailments.

Ira went home and looked the medicine up in the medical books left behind by Dr. Anna Littlefield. He called Old Dr. Clough all worked up. "Your boy prescribed me belladonna. It says in the book that's for pregnant women. You and I both know I ain't pregnant."

"How many's he got you on," asked Old Dr. Clough.

"Five a day."

Old Dr. Clough says, "He's got me on eight."

Other storytellers say, "What if you invite somebody in the audience to share a story and it's long and boring?"

That's the chance you take. When you open a door, you never know who will walk through. In my experience, it's worth the risk.

A fair question would be, "What if somebody in the audience is funnier than you?"

Loads of people are funnier than me. The more stories, the funnier the stories, the better. Don't much matter who tells them. Occasionally I have to pry the microphone from the hand of an audience teller with a lot on his mind. Occasionally I have to interject, summarize for the hard of hearing, or gently guide a story to conclusion. This takes skill—more skill, maybe, than telling itself. I'm getting better at it. To maintain a semblance of control, I give a short speech at the beginning of each session: "One story leads to another," I say. "That's the tradition. If something reminds you of a story, feel free to tell it. All I ask is that the story not be too long, too boring, or too off color."

Then I tell about the time I forgot to include the off-color part. A lady at the Greenfield Women's Club volunteered to speak. She ceremoniously walked from her seat to the front of the hall, then pulled a piece of paper from her pocket and carefully unfolded it. (Pretty sure she'd found this particular tale on the internet.)

She said, "Rebecca, I've got a story to tell. But before I tell it, you should know that my name is Estalyn Williams. I'm ninety-eight years old. And my story might be a little off-color."

I said, "Estalyn, you go right ahead and tell it."

And she did.

And it was.

And they're still talking about it at the Greenfield Women's Club.

Estalyn lived to be 102. No doubt her sense of humor was among the qualities that sustained her.

Sometimes, when an audience is particularly receptive and mature, I repeat Estalyn's joke as a treat. The story lies not in the joke itself, but in the fact that Estalyn told it at the Greenfield Women's Club to a proper group of older ladies who laughed their proper asses off. It's a small story, but somehow Estalyn managed to stretch it out.

What Estalyn Said

A wife was in the kitchen ironing her bra. Her husband said, "I don't know why you bother ironin' your bras. You got nothin' to put in them."

The wife replied, "I iron your shots, don't I?"

Shots: Noun, plural. Another word for underpants, one of the funniest words in the English language. But what Estalyn said was shots, so shots it is.

Shot, the singular, is tricky if you have a yankee accent. I used to be able to turn the accent on and off. Thought I could. Bragged that I was bilingual. Not so much anymore. I can pronounce the "r" in the middle of some words, like farm, harm, or purloin, but it hurts. To me, farm is fahm, harm is hahm, and so fawth. I recently had a close encounter of the son-of-a-gun kind with a lawyah named Cairns. I made the mistake of calling him by his first name—on the stand, during a trial. "Call me Mister Cairns," the son-of-a-gun said.

I couldn't. Just could not get my mouth around it. The closest I could come was Mistah Cay-uns. So I didn't call him anything at all. Luckily our time together was shot, i.e., not very long.

Shot can mean diminutive as well as struck by a bullet.

"Gladys had a hahd time running the machines in the towel room at the paypah mill," I explained to an audience. "She was shot."

The crowd got real quiet.

Uh-oh.

"Not shot," I said, "*shot*. Not very tall."

Reading the crowd is an acquired skill. If you confuse or upset listeners, you've got to straighten them out before proceeding. Otherwise they'll be too busy picturing poor Gladys dead on the factory floor to absorb what comes next. A confused audience is not an amused audience. A confused audience will not laugh, except hesitantly at their own discomfort.

Random thoughts will pop up in the middle of a story. This may sound strange, but every time I tell a story, it is new to me. Not the whole story, of course, but some aspect of it. Has to be. Otherwise, I'd bore myself into a coma. Words frequently come out of my mouth before they've passed through any kind of filter. The more responsive the audience, the more I trust them, the more I'm apt to wing it. When I'm on a roll, I literally do not know what I'm saying until I hear myself say it. It's an out-of-body experience. At the Auburn Historical Society, I blurted something off color. My filter—too late—said, *Oh-oh*.

"I'm sorry," I told the listeners. "I hope I didn't offend anybody."

David Griffin, town patriarch, said, "If they's offended, they can just go home."

It's true. People will be offended. But it's not the end of the bleepin' world. Humor that's completely inoffensive has no bite and it's not very funny. My friend Dana would call it flan. Edible but not particularly interesting. I take David Griffin at his word. If offended, "they can just go home." At the end of the day, we can all just go home.

David's observation inspired a woman to tell a tale on her husband, Emerson Heald, seated next to her, leaned back in his folding chair, arms crossed. Impassive. My husband, she told us, is known for his colorful language. Out in the barn, he banged his thumb good with a hammer. Returned to the house for medical attention and sympathy. "Emerson," she said, "when you banged your thumb good with that hammer out in the barn, what did you say?"

"Didn't say nothin'. Nobody around to hear it."

So big-mouth-me said something that might have been offensive, which led David Griffin to wax eloquent on what offended people are free to do, which led to a story about Emerson, which prompted Emerson to say: "Didn't say nothin'. Nobody around to hear it." Emerson's insight was totally worth the trouble.

STORIES TELL US WHO WE ARE

In stories, local characters like Estalyn Williams, David Griffin, Sore-Thumb Emerson, Fodd Boody, Ira Littlefield and Drs. Clough are immortalized. Through oral history we recognize how these characters enrich our communities and our lives.

Years ago, at a nonprofit board retreat, the leader asked us to fill in the blank: "I come from a people who . . ." That got me thinking. Who are my people? What are they like? How am I like or unlike them? Stories help us fill in the blanks.

My daughter, just a little girl back then, asked a question that revealed quite a lot about the people she and I come from. She said, "Mum, why do Grampa Bud's stories always end the same way?"

I said, "How do they end?"

She said, "And then I shot it."

My dad, her grandfather, took after his father, who often ended his own stories with "And then I shot it." Runs in the family. But not in me. Or her. We choose not to shoot things—animate or inanimate. Dad tried to teach me to shoot. My mother claimed I was a good shot when I was a kid. I don't remember. Didn't like the noise. Didn't like the heft of the gun or the oiliness. Didn't like the idea that if the gun were accidentally loaded and accidentally pointed at somebody and accidentally the safety was off and accidentally it discharged, somebody could get killed. Did not go for that at all. Didn't like the time when, for a joke, Dad set me up with a 30 ought 6 and it knocked me ass ova teakettle.

Ova: Preposition. The opposite of undah.

Near as I can tell from genealogy, my ancestors were a Scots-Irish-English mix, with a soupçon of Jew. (I'm talking about you, Great-Grammie Ada Wellman.) I don't need a family tree to confirm the yankeeness of the clan. They looked like yankees, talked like yankees, and acted like yankees—every stinkin' one of them. With the exception of my immigrant grandmother, Elizabeth Moynihan Barker, who came over on the boat from Galway, her clay bean pot in her arms. This was, near as I can figure, around 1919 or '20. I still have the pot, bake beans in it once every couple of years, and wish I'd known her better. She died in a county nursing home when I was little. Mostly I remember her black hair against a white pillow and above her, nailed to the wall, a crucifix. Whenever I visited the home, I spent most of my time at the foot of the bed being horrified by Jesus on the cross wearing nothing but a diaper. I still have the crucifix. In a box. Under my desk.

Every once in a while, my dad would say, "That's a song my mother used to sing," or "When you wear your hair in a bun like that you remind me of my mother." He said she planted the Johnny jump-ups that popped up every spring along the foundation of the old house. I feel deeply connected to that short, stout, Irish woman who left a Down Syndrome child behind in Lahile Woodford, a child who died before he could join her in America. Big sorrow. That's what my dad always said when something really bad happened. I say it too. Big sorrow. Sometimes he used it sarcastically, in response to a small problem made out to be big. "Dick's Moto-Ski broke down. Again. Left him on the trail. Big sorrow." I never use the phrase sarcastically. When I say it, I mean it, because it reminds me of my dad and how much I miss him. Near the one-room house where my father and his sister, Florence, grew up, where Elizabeth Moynihan Barker and Bill Barker raised them, stands a huge granite rock, not as big as the house itself, but close. In the family story, a salesman stops by to try to sell something to Elizabeth. During their chitchat he asks how that big rock came to sit where it did, so close to the house. "I don't know," she famously said. "'Twas here when I arrived."

That true story reminds me of one of the first yankee classics I learned—from Michael Caduto. We were sitting in rockers on a wraparound porch at a hotel in the mountains at an arts conference, shooting the breeze. Michael said a newcomer to rocky old New England was puzzled by the boulders dotting the landscape. "Where'd they come from?" he asked.

The local said, "Glacier brought 'em."

"Where's the glacier now?"

"Guess it went back for another load."

Michael's a Vermont writer who specializes in nature, the environment, and Native American lore. Remembering his glacier story brings him back to me. I can see him. I can see us. I remember that chilly but sunny day on that wraparound porch in the mountains. The experience is unspoken but embedded in the story. Or maybe the story is embedded in the experience. The glacier story brings to mind a classic pig story as told by my friend Charter Weeks, with all the fixings. Charter's version was so specific I was sure (until the very end) that it was absolutely true and had happened to him. He fooled me! Went something like this:

The Neighbor's Big Pig

Neighbor down the road raises pigs. He's a great old guy. Walked down to visit him the other day. It took a while, but eventually I located him down below the second barn. Feeding a massive pig. Musta gone five, six hundred pounds. The funny thing was, he had a pail of slop and he was feeding it to the pig one teaspoon at a time. Never saw anything like it. So I says to him, "Don't it take an awful long time to feed that big pig with a teaspoon?"

"Ayuh," the neighbor said. "Time don't mean nawthin' to a pig."

In another version the farmer holds a sow up over his head so she can eat apples from a tree. "Don't it take a long time to feed that pig one apple at a time?" Same response, "Time don't mean nawthin' to a pig."

> **Nawthin'**: Noun. Less than nothing. As in: "That chainsaw I sold to Beanie—all I could squeeze out of that cheap son-of-a-gun was five bucks. If it run, it'd be worth at least $50.00. Beats nawthin', I guess."

Mandatory Classic Chainsaw Story

When the topic of chainsaws comes up, somebody is bound to tell this story. Usually it's attributed to a French Canadian logger, but it can also be about a generic woodsman or a yankee or a Norwegian. As my friend Ola Olsen said of those who worked in the woods along the Androscoggin: "The Norwegians came first. The French, they came later."

"Oh," said his mother, Norma. "The woods were full of 'em."

It's said in the North Country that within weeks after the first chainsaw was introduced, everybody had one—a vast improvement over the labor-intensive crosscuts. Larry bought himself a chainsaw. Tried it out but didn't like it one bit. Took it back to the Berlin General Store. "Nawthin' wrong with this saw," the clerk said. And pulled the starter cord.

Larry jumped. "What's that noise?"

Great-Grammie Ada Wellman Barker was known for her extreme jealousy. The family legend is she and her husband, Willie, moved from the city (somewhere in Massachusetts or New York) to the isolated town of Danbury, NH, so she could keep a better eye on him. In the family, the word "psychotic" is sometimes whispered, and that's not a word we bandy about. She had to know where her husband was and exactly what he was doing every minute of every day. She kept track of every penny spent and what it was spent on. Every minute. Every day. Every penny. Come to think of it, my mother was the same way with my dad. Maybe it wasn't the Barker women who had a problem, but the men. Maybe the women needed to keep a tight rein.

Among my Grampa Bill Barker's treasures, I found an envelope containing a lock of hair. "This was my mother's hair," he wrote. "She was black-headed until the day she died."

I like to think the storytelling gene came from his wife, Elizabeth Moynihan Barker, known as Lizzie. One of the best compliments I ever received came from a man at a senior center luncheon. "You remind me so much of my Irish grandmother," he said, "when she was drunk."

Growing up among yankees, I'm drawn to stories that reflect the collection of traits identified as yankee: frugal, laconic, practical, reserved. Definitely not warm and huggy. An unexpected hug sends me into penguin mode. My arms drop to my sides. I stiffen, unsure where my head should be. Or my ear. I don't dislike hugs, sometimes I even initiate them; it's just that I've yet to figure out how they're supposed to work. That's the yankee in me. On the other hand, I'm quick to laugh and just as quick to cry. That's the Irish in me.

Yankees are, generally, slow to express emotion. The first time my grandfather, Bill Barker, and my father, Lewis Bud Barker, told me they loved me was on their respective death beds. My mother, on the other hand, expressed her love every day for the last two years of her life. Dementia dissolved an emotional wall and allowed her to be more herself than she'd been since childhood—sweet, kind, and appreciative. She thanked me for the simplest things like putting whipped cream on her strawberries or combing her hair. She said "I love you" every night as I tucked her into bed. And I said it right back—an un-yankee-like thing to do. Yankees have feelings. We just don't make a big deal out of them.

Gosh, my mother was funny, especially toward the end of her life when she finally relaxed. She found humor even in dire circumstances, like being confined to a wheelchair in a house that is not your own. She didn't want to leave her home in Boscawen, but there came a time when she could no longer live alone. A shoe dropped—old age is all about waiting for the next shoe to drop—and she had to abandon her old house to live in ours. It wasn't easy for her or for us. But we found a way to enjoy each other and our altered circumstances. Laughter sustained us.

One night she insisted on wearing her glasses to bed. "Why do you want to wear your glasses to bed, Ma?" I said.

"I might want to see something."

She rang a bell when she needed help at night. Ninety pounds of attitude, she rang it with gusto. A one-bell night was good for sleeping because the household was awakened just the once. A five-bell night? Let's just say we were all zombies the next day.

One night she rang her bell at about 2:00 AM. "There's a mouse in here," she said.

She could tell I was skeptical. "There *is* a mouse in here," she said and shone her flashlight.

Sure enough. A mouse hunkered between the bed and the desk, trying to blend into the floorboards. We alerted the cats and went back to bed. Don't know what happened to the mouse. Never found its carcass. Guess it took the hint and vacated the premises.

One morning I made omelettes for breakfast—a special treat. I noticed Ma was feeding quite a lot of it to the chihuahua.

"Shall I get Chico his own fawk?" I said.

"Don't need it."

Fawk: Noun. Companion to a knife and spoon. Cindy told about her father who ate ice cream with a fawk. One evening, on the couch eating ice cream with a fawk as usual, he dropped his fawk. It stuck into the top of his foot and drew blood.

His wife come in from the other room, "What have we learned from this?"

"When I eat ice cream I should wear my shoes."

This story prompted a fella to say: "I eat my ice cream with a fawk, too. But usually there's a pie underneath."

Fawk can also refer to a split in the road. In Maine you'll find a lot of peninsulas as well as fawks in the road. In the yankee classic, the lost tourist pulls over at the point where the road fawks dramatically. She hollers to a lobsterman setting on his lawn repairing his traps. The tourist says, "How far to Harpswell?" The lobsterman, says, "If you take the left fawk, it's about ten miles."

The tourist says, "What if I take the right one?"

"You'll be swimming."

THERE'S SOME GOOD AND BAD IN EVERYTHING

"There's some good and bad in everything," said Jenny Parent of Berlin, NH. Jenny was in the hospital being treated for pneumonia when we met. She was coming up on 102 years old. For forty-eight years, she worked in the paper mills. Never married or had children, because if you married or had children, she said, you lost your job. "People say, 'Jenny, why you work so hard in the mills all those years?' I say, 'For the money, like everybody else!'"

Those mills, as Jenny lay dying, were being torn down, brick by brick. The end of an era. The beginning, maybe, of a new era. Many in town cried when the smoke stacks, symbols of pollution and prosperity, were blown to smithereens. Others cheered.

There's some good and bad in everything.

Jenny's words come back to me when I think of my mother. Ma died of lung cancer but didn't know she was sick. "I'd be all right," she said, "if I could just get rid of this damn cough." The dementia protected her from knowing death was at hand. Home hospice care kept her comfortable. She was happy and very much a part of the world until a few days before the end. The spoonful of chicken noodle soup (Campbell's, the good stuff) tasted good, but she was too tired to get out of bed. She closed her eyes and, sometime in the night, stopped breathing mid-breath.

Yankee humor is dry. Often you don't know if a yankee is being deadpan funny or deadly serious. The delivery is exactly the same. "Ma," I said, "you have a cat on your head."

"I know," she said. "Get it off."

She often reminded me how ridiculous I am. She's in her wheelchair, warming herself in front of the wood stove, door open so she can see the flames. I put a log on the fire. It's too long so the end sticks out over the cast-iron lip. Ma points at the sticking-out log. As soon as part of the log has burned, I plan to push the sticking-out part back so it won't fall off the lip onto the hearth rug, catch the rug on fire, and burn the house down.

With that in mind, I say, "Ma, don't worry. I know what I'm doing."

She says, "Sometimes I don't think so. And this is one of those times."

Was she being funny? Maybe. She delivered the line without inflection. That's the essence of yankee humor.

Welcome to the Dump

Maxwell moved into a small town in Northern New England. Could be yours. Could be mine. He came from New York State and still had New York plates on his station wagon. The first week he put his trash out at the end of this driveway. Nobody picked it up. A neighbor let him in on the secret: No trash pickup here. People take their trash to the dump on Wednesday or Saturday.

The following Saturday, Maxwell loaded his station wagon and headed to the dump, a.k.a. transfer station. There were signs for metal, plastic, glass, furniture, compost. Signs with arrows pointing every which way. It was confusing. He stopped to ask the man in the orange vest for help. "How does this work?" Maxwell asked. "What do I do first?"

The fella looked him over. Looked the station wagon over. He said, straight-faced and without inflection, "Drive around the circle, go past the lagoon, keep a-goin' past the 'Municipal Transfer Station' sign, get back onto the main drag, and go back where you come from."

I tell stories to remember people I love and keep them close. Old photographs make me cry. Old stories make me smile. During one of Ma's hospitalizations, a nurse, fussing with tubes by the bed, said, "Your mother is such a sweet lady."

I said, "She kin be."

That bald statement of truth made Ma laugh. Me, too. The nurse, pretty sure, didn't know what to make of it.

Ma never traveled far from home. She grew up in Danbury—population around a thousand now, half that then. She never rode on a plane in all her life, but once took a trip to New York City with a couple of girlfriends. This was shortly after she graduated high school. The girls had a friend in a Broadway play. They rode the train from Danbury to Concord to Boston to New York.

One evening as they waited for their friend at the stage door, who should appear but Yul Brynner. He stopped to chat.

"What did he say, Ma?"

"Oh, he asked a lot of stupid questions."

"Like what?"

"He wanted to know where we were from. We said New Hampshire.

He wanted to know where in New Hampshire. So I said Concord. Didn't want him to think we was total hicks."

I asked if she'd gotten his autograph. "Oh no," she said. "I didn't want to bother him."

A year or so after she died I told the story at the Concord City Auditorium. It's a big venue, so I projected photographs on the screen behind me to illustrate some of the stories. When I told the Yul Brynner story, Ma's high school graduation photograph appeared. Dark hair. Dark, wide-apart eyes. White high-collared shirt with a velvet bow. A week later I received this handwritten letter:

Dear Rebecca,

I attended your performance at the Concord City Auditorium. I enjoyed it very much. The best part, for me, was when you did the story about your mother.

I recognized her immediately. Jean and I worked together at the NH Association for the Blind. We became friends. I was the one that went to NYC to see the play, *The King and I*. Her cousin was in it and took us backstage. Wonderful memories.

Nancy D. Minery

MANY REASONS TO TELL STORIES

We tell stories to connect. Person to person, generation to generation, heart to heart.

We all tell stories. It's human nature. We tell them to amuse ourselves and to entertain others. We tell them to persuade or dissuade. Sometimes we tell them to make ourselves look good. That's called bragging. We tell them to make others look bad. That's called gossip. We tell them to hold onto memories. We tell them to figure things out. Bottom line: to tell a story is to shape a chaotic series of events into a beginning, middle, and, by gosh, an end. Even painful experiences become less painful when you talk them out. We tell stories because we can't not tell them. Stories don't change what happened, but they help us put experiences into perspective.

Years ago, I corresponded with a man named Tae Hyok Kim. In his youth, Tae had been detained by the South Korean military and accused of being a spy. He had left his home in North Korea to seek work in the South. He was no spy, and at the time of his incarceration—when he was beaten, shocked with electricity and forced to live in a small cell with many other men and a pail for a toilet—he was seventeen years old and weighed eighty-eight pounds.

He later immigrated to the United States. In the process of writing his memoir, he sent me drafts for comment and encouragement. He said, "I never knew writing stories could be medicinal." Writing about his troubled life felt like healing. It was healing.

This I have learned: If you can tell the story, you can make some sense of the experience. You can contain the experience. And telling stories over and over is, as Tae says, medicinal.

This I have learned: The deepest wounds never heal completely. They just don't. But to tell a story is to move in the direction of understanding what happened and what it means.

To tell a story is to exert control.

To tell a story is to preserve memories and moments.

Stories about a life honor that life.

Stories about a way of life celebrate it.

Stories of a region highlight the uniqueness of that region.

Stories are our identity. Or, translated into yankee-speak: Stories ah ah identity.

Why We Have Six Cats

We started with two—Pocket and Mini. Two seemed about right.

Then came Shadow, who turned up one night and left her paw prints in the snow on the steps. We put out food. She ate it. We'd sit by the window and watch for her, my mother and I.

Shadow would eat, but we couldn't get near her. Ma was just home from rehab after a fall and confined to a wheelchair. Watching for Shadow through our glass kitchen door kept her occupied. The cat gave her something to think about. Gave us all something to think about.

It was a long, snowy winter. Shadow survived. She even grew fat but declined our invitation to come inside.

We tried to trap her in a Havahart. Caught two big male cats we'd never seen before. Got them neutered and adopted. They were nice boys. Not too wild. We also caught three raccoons. Or one not-too-bright raccoon three times.

Shadow fell for none of it, but four of her kittens did. One kitten's tail was stripped of fur. The tail later fell off. Close encounter with some kitten-eating predator—maybe a fox. We're pretty sure a couple siblings didn't make it. We named the little one without a tail Colin Feral at the suggestion of a punny friend, Priscilla Merrill, who figured it would be good for the little guy's self-esteem.

When the kittens were big enough we got them fixed, found homes for two, and kept two. Wild kittens do better in pairs, we were told. So that made four. Pocket, Mini, Colin Feral and his brother Godzilla—a big lovely orange boy who bore a striking resemblance to those adult males from the Havahart.

Shadow continued to eat on the steps. A month passed. Or two. Or three. Spring crept in. The daffodils came into their own. Ma would sit on the ramp by the steps in her wheelchair enjoying the sun. Shadow would creep to her food dish, almost close enough to touch.

By then we had hospice nurses and LNAs helping daily. We saw signs that Shadow had produced another litter and hidden them somewhere, but darned if we could find them. She'd take food in her mouth and disappear in the woods. We worried when she stopped coming to eat. Sara, one of the LNAs, said the cat hadn't looked healthy last time she'd seen her. Rheumy eyes.

Ma asked every day: "Where's my kitty?" We were really worried about Shadow and her new litter.

She'd moved the kittens from the woods to the woodpile and later into the insulation under the porch, but we didn't figure that out until later. One evening they came out from under the porch and played under the outside light. Six of them. Six bouncy little fur balls. But no sign of Shadow.

Sara made it her mission to catch those kittens. And she did. One by one over several days. She was unrelenting. We called her the kitten ninja.

Ma loved Shadow's kittens. They considered her wheelchair, her afghan, and her self their personal jungle gym. When they got tired, they'd curl up in her lap and sleep.

We never saw Shadow again. But we were grateful—we will always be grateful—that she trusted us enough to leave her kittens for us to care for, just when we needed them the most.

To finish off the math, we found good homes for four of the little ones Sara rescued. We kept two. So we had our two original cats, two from the first litter, and two from the second —that's Pocket, Mini, Colin Feral, Godzilla, Maple, and Elizabeth, who looks exactly like her mother.

And that is why we have six cats.

I CHOOSE THE FUNNY ONES

Before I started telling stories professionally, I published them in collections. Each short story worked through a question, conflict, or a hurtful incident. I used stories to try to make sense of what I didn't understand—like why my dad loved to kill the wild animals he seemed to admire, like why my parents seemed to hate each other even though they also loved each other, like why people in our small town were so mean to each other over the most trivial differences. Though the stories were serious, they always included humorous elements, because that's the way life is, and because the stories we write and tell reflect our true natures.

Comedy and tragedy—two sides of the same nickel. I prefer the comedy. It's how I see the world. I was a laughing baby. A laughing toddler. A laughing child. In an early memory I'm sitting with my legs tucked under me in a white wicker rocker at my grandparents' house laughing so hard at Laurel and Hardy on the TV that Grampa Stewart (my mom's dad), engrossed in a jigsaw puzzle, looked up from his labors and said to Grammie Stewart something like, "What's so damn funny? What's that kid laughing at?"

He was a kind man. Dry as kindling, but easily irritated. He suffered crippling arthritis, so he was probably in pain all the time. He seemed ancient, though he died in his early sixties—younger than I am now. How he hated it when the cat jumped on his jigsaw puzzle and sent the pieces flying—"goddamcat!" How he loved the Red Sox. He called them the "goddamredsox" when they messed up, which they did a lot in those days. The family story, often told, was of Grampa Stewart's younger days. His four children were squirming, fighting, and whining at the dinner table. He laid into them about having some "goddammanners" and illustrated his point with a dramatic sweep of his arm. Knocked over the pitcher of milk.

The kids didn't dare laugh.

Or maybe they did.

I inherited his round oak puzzle table and have become as big a Red Sox fan as he was, as my mother was. While working on a puzzle, fending off cats, watching the "goddamredsox" on TV, I feel Grampa Stewart and Ma with me. Is that weird? I feel as though they are watching, too.

Science (that's right, *science*) tells us toddlers laugh upwards of three hundred times a day, but adults fewer than twenty. We'd all be better off on the toddler end of the spectrum. My favorite stories, by far, are the funny ones, although as Maine storyteller Tim Sample says regarding the slow boil of yankee humor, "Sometimes you don't laugh until the next day."

Yankee humor has a lot in common with the dry humor of the British comedies on PBS, a tradition that goes back to the famous Yorkshire humor. Here's a classic example:

The Proposal

A couple sits on a park bench. They've been dating for thirty-seven years. She says to him, "Don't you think it's time we married?"

He says, "I do. But who would 'ave us?"

Yankee humor has a lot in common with the Yorkshire humor in rhythm, style, attitude, and subject matter. Both dissect family dynamics to the bone. These are close-to-home stories. In them we see ourselves. In them we see those we know or have known, those we love or have loved. And we smile.

Bungy Comes to Breakfast

Nelson in Hudson fondly recalled the little farm on the side of Reservation Road where his grandma lived with a cousin named Bungy, who was known as a big eater, but was not particularly energetic, ambitious, or clever. The family loved him all the same, as families do. Nelson and his parents lived just down the road, walking distance, from Grandma and Bungy.

One day, Bungy showed up early in the morning, just in time for breakfast. He saw the pile of pancakes and tucked in.

After a spell, Mother asked, "What you doing out so early in the mornin', Bungy?"

"Oh," Bungy said. "Almost forgot. Mum sent me down to tell ya the house is on fire."

Bachelor Brothers

Cliff and Art were bachelor brothers who lived up on Old Mountain Road in the family homestead. They were known for being deliberate in all things. One morning, Cliff was in the kitchen putting on his socks and boots one foot at a time like always. He was about halfway through the operation when Art came clumping down the stairs.

"Bettah hurry up with them boots," Art said.

"Why's that, Brother?" Cliff said.

"House afire."

The fire was extinguished without too much damage, but sadly the brothers, some time later, come to a parting of the ways. They were settin' on their porch one afternoon watchin' the world go by. Hoss and buggy passed. Cliff said, "That's one fine lookin' black hoss."

A week later, settin' on the porch, Art remarks, "That wa'n't a black. That was a bay."

A week after that in the afternoon, Cliff comes down the stairs with a suitcase.

"Where you going?" Art says.

"Moving out," Cliff says. "Can't stand all this bickering."

Hoss: Noun. Horse. Also pronounced huss in some parts of the Northeast and in some families. Pronunciations are not only regional but familial—you say things the way your parents said them and their parents before them and so fawth.

TRUST THE STORIES; THEY WON'T LET YOU DOWN

At a nursing home, with an hour to spare between sessions, the activities director suggested I tell stories to about a dozen residents in a common room. It was a long, well-lit room with folding tables, a wide-screen TV (mercifully turned off), and several vinyl recliners lined up along one wall, full of customers. This was the place to be between breakfast and lunch—reading, doing puzzles, coloring, folding, visiting, napping, or just sitting.

In I went. What could possibly go wrong?

Without the benefit of an introduction beyond "Hello," I stood as close to the middle of that rectangular room as I could get and started to tell stories. Several residents looked up, mildly interested. After a couple of quick tales, I launched into a story about a snapping turtle who'd taken possession of a station wagon. Each time the wagon's owner tried to remove the turtle, he'd be thwarted.

I was just getting to the exciting part when Laura rolled in, keening and moaning. I'd seen her in the hallway earlier. A nurse had explained that keening, moaning, and wheeling around in her chair was what she did all day. Pay no attention.

Laura wheeled up to within a few inches of me and stopped. She looked up, directly into my eyes as if to say, *I see you. Do you see me?* I met her gaze, *I see you, Laura*, and continued the story. I demonstrated the action with wide arm gestures. I hissed like the turtle, my fingers pinched together like a turtle head, hands opening and closing with each hiss. The turtle hissed at Laura. She seemed startled, but not scared. She stopped keening and moaning. She watched. She listened. She may not have understood a word, but something caught and held her attention.

When the story ended, she wheeled away. I could hear her keening and moaning as she wheeled down the hall.

This is why I tell stories and, maybe, why you should too. Sure, they help me work out my angst and insecurities. They help me know who I am and who I come from. Sometimes they might even provide a clue to where I'm headed. Sure they make me happy in the telling. But it's the listener who matters most. I tell stories for Laura.

It has become my life's work to record and remember as many, mostly funny, stories as possible about rocky old New England and the people (and turtles) who inhabit this place. It has become my life's work to pass these stories on so others can tell them, too. The late and greatly missed Peter Brodeur, also known as Bearded Turtle, told Native American stories. He said he told them so they wouldn't be lost. I'm with you, Bearded Turtle. Let the stories be found and treasured. Let them live on. If all goes well, they will outlive us all.

Lindsay, Joe, and the Huge Snapping Turtle

Joe and Lindsay are neighbors. On a summer Saturday morning they were outdoors doing what men do on summer Saturday mornings. Lindsay was mowing his lawn. Joe was washing his car. When Joe moved his car down the driveway to get close to the spigot, he noticed on the pavement where the car had been parked lay a huge snapping turtle. Must have crawled under the car for the shade.

Joe's kids and a couple of neighbor kids were playing in the yard. They spotted the turtle. Joe figured he better get it out of the way before somebody got hurt. But he wasn't sure how to do it. He hollered over to Lindsay, who shut off his mower and came over. Everybody stood in a circle around the turtle staring. The turtle paid no attention.

Finally, Lindsay says, "Joe, you got a snow shovel?"

Joe found one in the garage. Lindsay slid the shovel under the turtle. The turtle paid no attention. Now what?

Joe says, "Lindsay, you got a big laundry basket?"

Lindsay did and ran home to get it. Joe lay the basket on its side next to the turtle. Lindsay levered the turtle into the basket with the snow shovel. There the turtle lay. On its back. In the basket. Paying no attention. Each man took a handle of the basket and loaded it into the hatchback of Joe's Subaru.

The gathering of kids applauded as did a few other neighbors who'd come out to watch the operation.

"Good job, Lindsay," Joe said. He patted his friend on the back. "That was a great idea you had about the snow shovel."

Lindsay patted his friend on the back. "The basket was your idea, Joe. Without the basket we'd never have got him into the car."

"Hurrah," said the crowd.

The two proud men grinned, jumped into the Subaru, waved to the admiring throng, and off they went in the direction of the pond. They had almost reached their destination when they heard a scrabbling and scratching in the back of the car. Somehow that turtle had righted itself, climbed out of the basket, scrabbled and scratched its way into the back seat, and now it was trying to climb into the front seat with them.

Joe pulled to the side of the road. Both men jumped out, slamming the doors behind them.

They looked at each other.

How are we gonna get that enormous turtle out of the car?

Joe approached the front of the car. The turtle was right there, *hisssss-ing* and clawing at the window. Lindsay approached the right side of the car. The turtle was right there *hissssing* and clawing at the window. Same with the left side. *Hisssss*. Same with the back. *Hisssss*. The turtle had commandeered Joe's Subaru.

Joe and Lindsay sat on the stonewall beside the road. They weren't grinning. They weren't congratulating themselves. They were, more or less, contemplating their places in the universe and wondering how to get that turtle out of the car without being shredded.

After a while a kid on a bike comes down the road. She sees Joe and Lindsay. Stops. "What are you guys doing?"

They explain how the huge snapping turtle has taken control of the Subaru and they didn't know what to do. She says, "I know how to get that turtle out of there."

In the woods she finds a stout stick, about as big around as your arm and a bit longer. She says, "Pop the hatchback."

Lindsay pops the hatchback. She pushes the stick into the crack. The turtle grabs ahold. Once a snapper grabs onto something he *doesn't let go*.

The girl drags the turtle from the car and down the road. She leaves it near the water. The turtle smells the water, unclenches its jaw, slides into the pond and swims away.

The girl walks back to the car. She gets on her bike and pedals off, waving a cheery goodbye.

Lindsay looks at Joe. Joe looks at Lindsay. They get into the car. They drive back toward the house. Joe says to Lindsay, "We shall never speak of this."

Lindsay agrees.

And they never did.

The moral of the story is: If you ever buy a Subaru, be sure and get a stick.

PART II

How to Tell Stories

In each story, the teller chooses—consciously or unconsciously—what listeners need to know when. The teller (or writer) designs a pattern of revelation. In "Lindsay, Joe, and the Huge Snapping Turtle," we discover right away that Lindsay and Joe are neighbors and they like to do man stuff on Saturday mornings. We learn about the turtle. It's a big turtle—as big as the teller wants to show with outstretched arms. We see that Joe and Lindsay have a couple of good ideas of which they are proud. They like the admiration of the crowd that has gathered. This is a story about ego and problem solving.

One piece of information—that listeners probably already know—is saved for later. Snappers are famous for closing their jaws and holding tightly to whatever they've grabbed. That bit of information must be revealed at just the right time for the girl on the bike to save the day.

The story unfolds one relevant detail at a time. If the detail doesn't move the story forward, leave it out to make room for the details that do. It matters, for example, that the turtle is a snapper, and that the car is a hatchback. Those details move the story forward. It does not matter that Lindsay has blue eyes or Joe's wearing overalls. These details do not move the story forward, so they must go.

As for the moral—it was suggested by a guy named Lindsay the first or second time I told the story. I named the character after him. And thank him for that ending. People grumble when they hear it. They think it's corny. But I think it's pretty cute.

My friend Ada Hatch tells a story, coming up, that demonstrates what a difference order can make. What do you clue listeners into first, second, third and so forth? What do you reveal last or next to last?

It often takes many tellings to find out what pattern works best. I use "Why We Have Six Cats" as a title to frame the story of Shadow and her kittens. It tells listeners where the story is headed. I repeat the phrase at the end to pull all the pieces together and snap the story shut like a pocketbook.

When you pull back the curtain on a scene, which side do you start from? What do listeners or readers need to know for the story to move forward at a good clip? You want to hook them and invite them in, but you can't reveal everything at the beginning. That would be a lump of exposition. Too much to take in. Better to infuse stories with key information a little at a time.

Ada Checks Things Out

Ada and her husband, Urban, own a camp across the pond from ours. She said, "Becky, did you see all those canoes and kayaks heading up the pond Friday evening?"

"I did. I noticed a bunch of them. And some of them had big blue barrels."

"Those weren't barrels," Ada said. "They were kegs."

She and Urban were curious where the group was headed. They jumped in their boat and followed them to where they'd set up camp on Sand Beach. Ada and Urban anchored off shore. Pretended to be fishing.

"You wouldn't believe it, Becky," she said. "They were drinking and playing music real loud. They were smoking—and not just tobacco. They were dancing around the campfires. Playing volleyball." She said, "Once them nudists get going, you don't know what's going to happen." ~

If Ada had revealed that the campers were nudists at the beginning or in the middle, it would be a completely different story and not nearly as surprising.

The pattern of revelation is critical and so is using the right word. One time, telling Ada's nudist story I lost the word *keg*. I pictured the blue barrels (could see them clearly in my mind's eye) and described them as casks. The story fizzled on the spot. Casks? Caskets? Castanets? The audience looked puzzled. The pieces did not fit. Nobody brings a cask of wine camping. *Keg.* The word is *keg.* Now my trigger words for that story are "Ada, nudists, kegs."

DOIN' WHAT COMES NATURALLY

Storytelling is as natural as falling off a mossy log. A professional storyteller gets paid to do something anybody can do. We tell stories to each other from the moment we learn to speak until the moment we die. We don't have to be taught that they matter. We just know. We don't have to be taught to love them. We just do. We learn to love them snuggled in our parents' arms. Lullabies are stories that soothe us to sleep.

Just as listening to stories comes naturally, so does telling. And it doesn't take much to get started:

How was your day?
What did you learn in school?
How'd you break your arm?
Did you ever take care of that woodchuck problem?
Are cowboy boots comfortable?
Where'd you get that hat?
Since when do you have a pilot's license?
How do you know George Bush's house in Kennebunk is unheated?
Did you work for Community Action in the '70s? You look familiar.

A simple question primes the pump. We want to tell our stories to one another. We build relationships on those stories.

Scrappy's Pants

Scrappy had a terrific work ethic. He worked harder and faster than any other person on the town crew. Not just a little harder and faster, but ten times harder and faster. He was a dynamo!

After he died, his wife gave his old clothes to the local swap shop. A few weeks passed, and something strange happened. The crew boss couldn't believe it. Bungy, known for moving slow and doing as little as possible, suddenly perked up. He was patching holes in the tar, cutting brush, and digging ditches at lightning speed. Word got back to Scrappy's wife, who upon hearing of Bungy's transformation got a little emotional.

"Oh my goodness," she said. "Bungy's wearing Scrappy's pants." ～

The world has many names for storytellers: *seanachie* (Celtic), *griot* (African), *bard* (British). In Lascaux, France, 35,000 years ago, cave paintings preserved the stories of the people who lived there. Stories carry our history and our culture. They bind us, inform us, entertain us. Native Americans told stories around campfires—philosophical stories of how human beings fit in the universe as well as practical ones about hunting and fishing, where to find the most game, the hungriest fish. We still tell stories around campfires. We try to scare each other with gruesome tales of hook-handed murderers and ghostly hitchhikers. Think of the lessons in Aesop's fables or the horrors of the Brothers Grimm. Think of Mother Goose. Be careful carrying water up the hill, or you may end up tumbling down like Jack and Jill. If you go to church, what do you hear? Parables. If you turn on the six o'clock news, what do you hear? News stories. What is history if not his-story? Or hers?

The earth rests on the back of a giant turtle, the wise man says. The child says, "What's the turtle rest on?"

"Another turtle."

"But what does *that* turtle rest on," the child says.

The wise man says, "It's turtles all the way down."

It's stories all the way down, cradle to grave. We live in our stories and they live in us. After we die we are remembered in stories.

Storytellers do, however, have a specialized set of tools that can be used to enhance stories. It's one thing to shoot the breeze with your buddy Todd in the backyard after a shot of single malt, but if you're trying to hold the attention of fifty strangers in a stuffy, poorly-lit church basement on the hottest day of summer, your stories better be riveting. Practice keeps storytelling tools sharp. Experience helps us know which to use. These tools have come in handy for me:

- gestures
- movement
- facial expressions
- props
- repetition, rhythm, and rhyme
- vocals

You might want to try them. If they feel awkward, try them again. Find the variations that suit you. Apply as needed. It's empowering to know they're in your tool box and available when stories ask for them.

GESTURES

When you describe the fish that got away, you indicate its enormity with the space between your hands, one at the imaginary head, one at the imaginary tail. You just do it. If somebody's acting crazy, you draw spirals in the air in the vicinity of your brain. If a realization comes quick but late, you smack your forehead. With gestures, tellers reinforce action and emotion. A hand to the heart indicates love, sadness, longing, understanding. Hands pressed over the eyes say you're seeing something maybe you'd rather not. If you're reenacting the time you stepped in something the dog left behind, you might lift your foot and inspect the sole. Some tellers use big, dramatic gestures. For others, gestures are few, small, and all the more significant.

For the most part, gestures just happen. You're probably not even aware of them at first. But it's a good idea to note those automatic gestures when you're learning and practicing a story. If they make the story more vivid, they stay. The gestures help the audience and me envision the scene. The more the teller sees, the more the audience sees, too. To paraphrase a famous author—maybe Flaubert—you don't have to describe the whole garden. Just describe the fountain and the rest will come into focus. In my world, you don't have to describe the outhouse, just the moon on the door or the rich soil underneath.

Advice to writers often includes the old saw, "show don't tell," which puts storytellers in a pickle. Telling is what we do. Well, it's part of what we do. When telling "Fodd Boody's Tall Mother," I say, "Fodd looked the fella up and down" and show the action with a lift of my head. I look down at the imaginary fella's feet then slowly raise my eyes to the top of the fella's head. When I say, "Now, stand on tippy-toe and reach as high as you can with your right hand," I do it.

When I tell Delphis's story—below—I measure the size of his trophy with my hands. Some sessions the trophy is a foot tall. Sometimes, if I'm feeling magnanimous, it's three feet tall. Sometimes it's so heavy I can barely lift it.

Second Place in the Hoss Pulling Contest at the Lancaster Fair

Roland Aube tells a story about his father, Delphis, who once won second place in the hoss pulling contest at the Lancaster Fair. He got a trophy with his name on it and everything.

Delphis brought the trophy home and whenever company came he would tell the rather lengthy story of how he came to win second prize in the hoss pulling contest at the Lancaster Fair.

Until one day he went to get the trophy where he thought he left it. It was amongst the missing. Maybe it's in the attic or down cellar, he thought. Maybe Mother tucked it away in the cupboard.

Well, that trophy never showed up again. And after a while, Delphis stopped telling the story.

Years later, after Delphis died, Roland and his brother were taking down a shed on the property that had previously been an outhouse. They got the building down and the lumber cleared away. They were digging around in that rich soil underneath, when what do you know? Clink.

It was the trophy.

They brushed it off, took it up to the house. They said, "Mother, look!" She said, "Oh, you found it." ~

For this story, I say "Clink" once and gesture a shallow dip into rich, loose soil with the shovel. Another teller might do a lot of clinking and emphasize the digging. Maybe Roland and his brother had to dig deep to find the trophy after the initial clink. Maybe there were some tough old roots in the way. That's the teller's decision. Me, I'm not much of a digger, so with gestures—I give the trophy a shallow grave in soft soil with no pesky roots.

This story almost always comes with an addendum—the story behind the story. Roland told me his stories at his place of work, Isaacson Steel. He found a job there after being laid off from the mills—where he'd worked his whole adult life as had his father and grandfather before him. When we spoke, he was still sad about the lay off and sad, too, that the mills were being torn down. Berlin would no longer be a proud paper-making community.

I noticed he was wearing an onyx ring—a beautiful black ring—and commented on it. He said he'd inherited the ring from his father, from Delphis, and only wore it on special occasions.

I said, "Roland, you're wearing it today. What's the occasion?"

He said, "You asked me to tell my stories. When the mills closed, nobody asked us to tell our stories."

MOVEMENT, MICROPHONES, AND THREE HORROR STORIES

Gestures have to do mostly with head and hands—although you can also gesture with your foot or leg. Movement pertains more to the whole body, head to toe, including trunk and appendages. Being stuck behind a lectern with a fixed microphone limits movement. A standing microphone offers a little more freedom, but not much. A handheld mic restricts your gestures—one hand is always busy holding the mic—but allows for movement all over the stage or as far as the cord will reach, if there is a cord. Lapel mics or over-the-ear apparatuses that position the mic in front of your mouth allow for lots of movement, when they work properly, though it's distracting when they fall off and particularly distracting when you lose a lapel mic down your cleavage. This has happened to me. Twice. If you've got the money to buy your own audio set up and the muscles to carry it around, go for it. I'm a yankee. Frugal to the bone and sometimes to the point of absurdity, I take my chances venue to venue. If I wanted to lug around a lot of equipment, I'd join a band.

When offered a microphone, always accept it. It'll help the people hear better—especially those with hearing loss, those in the back of the room, and those with hearing loss who choose to sit in the back of the room. A mic also evens out the sound so people aren't straining to hear, even when a character decides to *whisper*. If you're one of those people (and I've been guilty of this) who says, "I have a loud voice. I don't need a mic," I have two words for you: "You're wrong."

One of the biggest mistakes I continue to make is failure to control the space in which I'm telling. Microphone limitations aside, most venues offer tellers at least a little leeway in terms of where to stand or sit, where the audience sits, lighting, background noise. Turn off the fans and close the outside door and the windows unless it's just too hot.

Some people simply will not perform outdoors. I should be one of them, but, you know, a job's a job. If, for example, you're asked to tell stories for forty-five minutes at an outdoor pie festival; if you're told, "We've put you under the tent," and the tent is open-air, 200 feet from a busy road, and between you and road is another tent where people are judging and sampling pies and conversing loudly; if most of the attendees are more interested in pie and friends than your stories; if all these things happen at once, it is almost impossible to control the space so interested parties can hear your stories. This happened to me.

Horror story #1. So I arrive at the festival a half hour before my scheduled performance time as usual and there's no microphone. Some pie eaters are sitting in chairs at the edge of the tent. Others are at picnic tables and on wooden benches outside the tent. The organizer announces that I'll be telling stories any minute. Nobody takes much notice. My heart sinks a little.

On the bright side, this is a challenge, and faced with a difficult situation, I up my game—project my voice, go BIG with gestures and movements, walk right up to some listeners, ask others where they're from and what kind of pie they are enjoying, make eye contact with anybody who'll meet my gaze. I tell to the front, to the side, and, at times, to two teenage girls sitting behind me. When the convoy of Harleys roars by, I pause and smile. When the fire truck goes by in full siren mode, I pause and laugh.

Instead of the prescribed forty-five minutes, I do thirty. I have books for sale. Nobody buys any. One lady flips through a picture book, then puts it back. The organizer brings me a piece of chocolate cream pie with Oreo crust. It is delicious. I chat with a few folks, then slip away and take the long walk to my car, parked a half mile down the road. I hope the check will be in the mail in a day or two. On the ride home, I think about what I should have done and come to a couple of conclusions.

First, I should have asked in advance, "Is there a mic?" instead of assuming one would magically appear. They usually do—especially for outside programs. Also, my session was to be preceded and followed by a "band." Bands, typically, use mics. Turns out the band was a woman with a guitar playing folk music. One child sat on a bench in front of her and clapped after each song. I clapped, too, and sang along. No doubt the lonely folksinger was as nonplussed as I was at the setup.

Also, upon seeing the situation, I should have—though it would have been awkward—grabbed a few chairs, pulled them into a tight circle in a corner of the tent (as far from the road as possible), and—in a loud voice—invited anybody who wanted to hear stories to join me in the corner. If nobody accepted the invitation, so be it.

I didn't do either of those things. The session was—to my mind—less than successful. That said, at least ten members of the scattered audience, including the teenage girls and a babe in arms, seemed to enjoy the stories. The baby didn't cry. I took that as a thumbs up. It wasn't entirely an exercise in futility. Also, I had a few lovely conversations with listeners after the fact. Two bakers (waiting for the results of the judging) told me stories. One man talked about his life in Hawaii and said his wife had recently died. Still, here he was, out and about with a group from the local assisted-living community, enjoying pie on a sunny day. I was glad to have had those interactions.

On the other hand, if I'd taken control of the space from the get-go, it might have been a better experience for all concerned. Instead, I let the space take control of me. Next time I'll know better.

Horror story #2. Another time at a fairly large venue—previously a movie theater—the sound guy didn't show. He'd had a death in the family, so his absence was entirely understandable. The problem was, nobody knew how to run the audio system. Couldn't locate all the pieces. Didn't know what to plug into what.

"You'll have to do it without a mic," the big boss said. He was not sympathetic. I was not happy, but the theater was already half full and it wasn't the audience's fault, so I blew out my voice trying to push the words to the back row. Not the best of circumstances. Not my best performance. But people laughed in all the right places. They clapped at the end. My talk was preceded by a bean supper, but they ran out of beans. Some in the crowd had to settle for corn bread and nothing more. I settled for nothing more. It was a night to remember.

Horror story #3. The Final Horror—as Michael Caine says in the hilarious movie *Noises Off.*

The Infamous Incident at the Pittsfield Balloon Rally

Once, just once, I was invited to tell stories at the Pittsfield Balloon Rally. If the weather cooperated, hot air balloons would soar in a dramatic and colorful display, and people could pay to ride in them. There were also, as I recall, helicopter rides. Plus, vendors selling ice cream, hot dogs, popcorn, fried dough, and lemonade. Plus, entertainment, including a clown driving a noisy little train. The Pittsfield Balloon Rally is a big event. I was flattered to be asked to perform.

The local mortician fronted a band. I don't remember exactly what kind of music the band specialized in. Golden oldies from one decade or another.

The plan was the band would play, I'd tell a couple of stories. The band would play some more. More stories. We'd go back and forth for maybe an hour.

A flatbed truck equipped with many microphones served as the stage. It sat in front of some bleachers. The stage did not face the bleachers—it faced a huge field, big enough to be a football field, though I'm not sure it was used for that purpose. It was a wicked hot day, sneaking up on a hundred degrees and humid. This combination of heat and humidity is the scourge of New England summers. It usually doesn't last long—a few days or a week—but when the dog days hit, we wilt. I was pretty well wilted before I set foot on the stage.

On account of the extreme heat, the rally was under attended. Also, those who did come were more interested in the balloons, balloon rides, fried dough, and the clown than in music and stories.

Our audience sat baking in beach chairs in the field, at least fifty yards away from us. I don't know why they sat so far away. There were five of them. Two were fans of the mortician's band—one was his girlfriend, I think. The other three were my husband, my daughter and her then-boyfriend-now-husband. The sun beat down on their heads.

The band played a set. The little audience applauded. The girlfriend may have whooped. When it was my turn, I told one story. Then another. Sweat dripped off my beak, but I carried on until I noticed that our little audience seemed uncomfortable. Not just melting-in-the-sun uncomfortable—it was more than that. They looked pained. They looked sick. My daughter tucked her chin and pulled the neck of her T-shirt over her nose. Others followed suit.

What the heck? This was not the way audiences usually responded to my story about the $16.00 picnic table.

I noticed the row of porta-potties to the left of the stage. Must have been a dozen of them. Also noticed the honey wagon. That's yankee-speak for sewage hauler. The great hose of the honey wagon was sucking effluent out of the porta-potty closest to the field. It wasn't, evidently, a closed system. A blue shimmer in the air confirmed escaping fumes. The slightest of breezes transported those fumes directly into the noses of our over-heated audience.

I kept a-goin'. Made it to the end of the story lickity-split. I said, "Thank you very much" and stepped away from the mic. Yup, I ended my set early and got the hell out of there, family in tow.

It was the right thing to do.

"The Infamous Incident at the Pittsfield Balloon Rally" lends itself to lots of movements to develop the scene—the round of the balloons and their rising, the clown honking an obnoxious horn as the little train chugs through, the mortician wailing on his electric guitar, the wiping of sweat from my beak, noticing and being taken aback by the bank of porta-potties, the sucking of the big round hose, and most dramatic of all, the pulling of the T-shirt over the mouth as the fumes waft.

It can also be told straight, with no gestures or movements at all. Well, except for the wiping of the beak and the pulling up of the T-shirt. Those two movements are all the story really needs to make an audience say, "eew" and recall their own experiences with extreme heat and effluents.

This next story, "The Ghost with the One Black Eye," is for kids. It's a joke really, but also a popular campfire tale that lends itself to big and small movements. Just as kids like to sing along, they like to tell along and move along. They like to be involved. With this story, you can get them repeating lines and repeating movements. This holds their attention and helps channel some of their energy. The younger the child, the harder it is for them to sit quietly and listen, so the more important it is to get them involved. Wise tellers find ways to engage them physically in stories. If they're not engaged, they'll let you know. Fifty unengaged kids crowded into a school library or, even worse, a gymnasium—this is the stuff of nightmares. Which is why I tell mostly to adult audiences. Since publishing a couple of children's books, I'm invited more often to schools to share stories. It's a tough crowd full of pint-sized critics, but I'm getting better at choosing and delivering stories they'll appreciate.

The Ghost with the One Black Eye
Many Tellers

Baby is in her high chair. She wants her apple juice. "I want my apple juice," she says.

Sister says, "I'll get your apple juice, Baby." The apple juice is in the cellar. So sister opens the cellar door (*creeeeek*) and down she goes. Ten steps—one, two, three, four, five, six, seven, eight, nine, ten. She starts to cross the room to the shelf where the apple juice is kept. Lo and behold, she sees a ghost.

The ghost says, "I am the ghost with the one black eye."

Sister runs up the stairs—one, two, three, four, five, six, seven, eight, nine, ten. "I forgot. I'm supposed to go to Susie's house to play. Brother, could you get Baby's apple juice?"

Brother says, "Why didn't you get it? Were you scared of something down cellar?" But Sister's already out the door.

Baby says, "I want my apple juice."

Brother says, "I'll get your apple juice, Baby." He opens the cellar door (creeeeek) and down the stairs he goes—one, two, three, four, five, six, seven, eight, nine, ten.

He starts to cross the room when, lo and behold, he sees a ghost.

The ghost says, "I am the ghost with the one black eye."

Brother runs up the stairs—one, two, three, four, five, six, seven, eight, nine, ten.

Mother says, "Brother, what's wrong? Did something scare you down in the cellar?"

Brother says, "I just remembered I have homework due. I better go do it. Right now." He runs to his room and shuts the door behind him. Mother says: "That's strange. Oh, well."

Baby says, "I want my apple juice."

Mother says, "I'll get your apple juice, Baby." She opens the cellar door (creeeeek) and down the stairs she goes. She meets the ghost. The ghost says, "I am the ghost with the one black eye." Mother runs up the stairs—one, two, three, four, five, six, seven, eight, nine, ten.

Uncle John has come to visit. He's standing in the kitchen. "Are you okay?" he says to mother. "You're white as a ghost."

Baby says, "I want my apple juice."

Mother says, "John would you mind getting Baby's apple juice down in the cellar?"

Uncle John says, "No problem." He opens the cellar door (creeeeek) and down the stairs he goes—one, two, three, four, five, six, seven, eight, nine, ten. He spots the shelf with the apple juice and starts to cross the cellar to get some for Baby when . . .

"I am the ghost with the one black eye."

He runs back up the stairs—one, two, three, four, five, six, seven, eight, nine, ten—and out the front door. "See you later," he calls over his shoulder.

Baby says, "I want my apple juice."

She hoists herself out of her high chair and toddles across the kitchen to the cellar door. She stands on her tippy toes to open the cellar door (creeeeek). Down she goes—one, two, three, four, five, six, seven, eight, nine, ten. She sees the ghost.

The ghost says, "I am the ghost with the one black eye."

Baby says, "I want my apple juice. Sister, Brother, Mama, and Uncle John all came down to get my apple juice but they didn't and I want my apple juice."

The ghost says, "I am the ghost with the one black eye."

Baby says, "If you don't get out of the way so I can get my apple juice, you'll be the ghost with the TWO black eyes."

With that, the ghost disappears and Baby gets her apple juice. ❧

This story can be short or long. It's adjustable: more detail, less detail; more repetition, less repetition; more movement, less movement. Come to think of it, all stories are adjustable, which is a significant advantage in a time crunch or with a group with other things on their minds—like snack.

Tellers usually pretend to walk down and run up the stairs for each of the characters in "The Ghost with the One Black Eye." Brother's and sister's steps are lighter, Mother's heavier. Uncle John clomps. When Baby toddles down the stairs, her progress is slow and precarious.

The movements can take up the whole stage or the teller can step in place. The creeeeek of the cellar door might include a movement to turn the knob and pull the door open along with the sound effect with the listeners joining in. Some tellers clap to indicate the movement—one, two, three, four, five, six, seven, eight, nine, ten—again with the audience clapping along. Some slap their thighs, fast or slow—one, two, three, four, five, six, seven, eight, nine, ten. The ghost can expand and move threateningly toward the hapless apple-juice seeker. When the ghost speaks, the teller might sway in a ghostly way or stretch ghostly arms toward Sister, Brother, Mother, Uncle, or Baby.

I've seen a storyteller sit through the whole story and—with slight body movements, gestures, eye movements, and sound—suggest that the story occupies the whole stage—kitchen, cellar door, stairs, cellar. It's amazing to watch how a scene, fully imagined, comes to life.

Joey Holmes of Grantham tells this next story about her husband

Alfred Holmes. It shows how words spoken at important events are seared into our memories.

Joey's story demonstrates how much town meetings—and the words people say at them—matter. It is my job as a storyteller to get those words exactly right—or as close to exactly right as possible. When someone tells me a story, I take quick, sloppy notes, but if there's an expression or a line that's unique and critical, I write it down exactly. Often I have to ask people to repeat that special line so I can record it word for word, then I repeat it to seal it in my memory. Sometimes only the exact wording will do.

The Irate Taxpayer and the Road Agent

At Grantham town meeting, a newcomer—only lived there ten or fifteen years—challenged the road agent's budget, saying, "You overspent your appropriated budget last year and I'd like to know why."

The road agent, Alfred Holmes—leaning into the wall at the back of the hall with his arms crossed the way the men do—sighed. He took the long slow walk down the center aisle to the microphone at the front, all eyes upon him. He sniffed. Adjusted his suspenders. Cleared his throat. Adjusted the microphone.

The newcomer repeated his request. "Mr. Holmes, why did you overspend your budget in the previous fiscal year?"

The road agent leaned into the microphone. He said, "It snowed."

And walked away. ∽

With this story if you have a microphone, you can use it as a prop and let the road agent (through you) speak into it. You can adjust your body to show the adjusting of the suspenders, the adjusting of the microphone, the tipping of the road agent's head as he listens to the newcomer's question before leaning in to the real or imaginary mic to deliver Alfred's final words on the subject: "It snowed."

At one point, I thought Alfred's final comment was just the one word "Snow." His wife, Joey, corrected me. "Actually, he said, 'It snowed.'" Joey's friend agreed, "That's right. I was there. I heard him." Which just goes to show, in moments of high drama like town meetings, people pay attention and remember what's said for decades.

Some stories beg for movement. In a story about an eagle, I spread my arms and swoop with my whole body. My feet are planted but my body imitates the pose of a moving bird, wings and all.

Be careful not to overdo the motions or the audience will think you're trying to be Marcel Marceau. Less is more. You're suggesting, not miming. Mime is an art unto itself—a whole different form of storytelling. If you ever get to see Antonio Rocha's unique combination of storytelling and mime, count yourself lucky. He's amazing!

This next story, "Where Selectmen Belong," started as a scene from a play but wanted to be its own story. The title is essential. I always say, "This story is called 'Where Selectmen Belong,'" as though that were critical information. Because it is. Without the title and the last line, the story is slapstick. With them, it's political commentary.

I'm particularly proud of the way this story traveled from Northwood, where I live, to the Maine/Canada border. Peter Farnsworth, who has a camp near ours on Donnell Pond in Franklin, Maine—about halfway up the long Maine coast—teaches in northern Maine. Somehow or other he got an audio tape of some of my stories. Pretty sure I gave it to him or his mother, Gina. He said that one student, not known for his public speaking skills, told "Where Selectmen Belong" to fulfill an assignment and enjoyed great success. It was the right story for the boy to tell and he told it well.

Stories are meant to be passed on. You never know who they'll find in their travels. You never know what connecting just-the-right-person to just-the-right-story will mean.

Where Selectmen Belong

One of the selectmen showed up at the dump kinda unsteady on his feet. Maybe it was mouthwash that made his breath so tangy. Maybe he had one of those inner ear infections that upset your balance. Coulda been. You hear different things.

Anyway, this selectman was heavin' a kind of a heavy bag into the compactor. Kermit the Dumpmaster calls it the crusher, because when a lot of bags get piled up he pulls the lever inside his little dumpmaster cottage, the steel slabs hydraulic together, and everything gets squished. Compacted.

This selectman got to swinging this kind of a heavy bag like a pendulum and when he worked up to the big swing to toss it, evidently he forgot to let go. He and the bag sailed over the railing. Down they went.

Luckily the crusher was pretty near full at the time. There he lay. Spread-eagled. His eyes were open but he didn't say anything. The bags puffed up around him.

Naturally, the customers gathered around wondering, *What is the best way to snag that selectman out of there?* Pretty soon Kermit emerges from his little dumpmaster cottage looking owly. He marches up to the rail. He peers down in. He says, "*What* are you doing in the crusher? Get out of theyah. Selectmen don't belong in the crusher. They belong over in compost."

Owly: Adverb. Grumpy.

When the notion strikes, I stop in the middle of this story, at the part where the word "compactor" comes up, and describe a delightful response from a listener at the Lin-Wood Senior Center, which serves the North Country towns of Lincoln and Woodstock. "So I got to the part about the 'compactor,'" I say, "and this woman waves her arm, all excited. She's got something to say. I call on her. 'I seen it,' she says, 'in Rumney.'" Evidently at that time in Lincoln and Woodstock, they didn't have compactors. You had to go to the metropolis of Rumney, population 1,500, to lay eyes on a compactor.

The swinging of the heavy bag like a pendulum calls for a dramatic motion of the arm, building up to the big swing until the inebriated selectman ... finally ... lets ... go. The rhythm of the sentence reflects the pendulum action of the bag: "This selectman got to swinging ... this kind of a heavy bag ... like a pendulum ... and when he worked up ... to the big swing ... to toss it ... evidently he forgot to let go."

Try it. You can feel the rhythm ... of the language ... in your body.

As the hydraulic slabs squish together, I press my hands together. When the unhappy selectman lies spread-eagle in the crusher, I spread my arms and legs. I trace the shape of the puffed-up bags in the air. Then, of course, I walk—one step, two steps, a quarter step depending on the space—to the railing of the crusher and peer down over.

The series of movements not only livens up the story, but helps me remember the sequence—hydraulic slabs, pendulum, sail over the railing, spread-eagle, puffed up bags, peer over the railing.

I know this story in my head and in my body. Maybe that's what people mean when they say you know something by heart.

During my brief, unsuccessful attempt at acting in community theater, the only lines I remembered were the ones that had definite movements associated with them. When I picked up the tea cup, I knew to say: "What are you doing here on this dreary afternoon, Patrick? I thought you were taking the train to Poughkeepsie." When I sank into the arm chair and settled my knitting basket at my feet, I knew to say, "The spirits are strong in this house. And they are restless and unhappy, my dears." However, in scenes with no definite movements attached to the lines (blame the director), I was adrift.

"Lindsay, Joe, and the Huge Snapping Turtle" has lots of room for both gestures and movement, as big or small as you like, but I like to go BIG. It's a snapper after all, and those beasts are prehistoric!

Do snapping turtles actually hiss? I don't know. If a snapper snapped at me I'd hear a hiss in my head, even if the turtle didn't actually vocalize it. Besides, I like saying "hisssss" as I poke my turtlehead hand in the direction of a listener. It certainly got Laura's attention.

To keep this story straight in my head, I need to have the names of our two hapless heroes and to get them situated in the scene. So I think: Lindsay = Lawnmower. The two L's. I picture Lindsay mowing, Joe—next door—washing the car, the turtle in the shade where the Subaru used to be parked. This trick gets the story going and once it's going, it goes until I get to the line: "Once a snapper grabs onto something . . ." That's where a pause for dramatic effect inevitably gets the audience to chime in "he *doesn't let go*." That's common knowledge, common ground, audience engagement. That's the point at which the story moves from "my story" to "ours."

FACIAL EXPRESSIONS

To my surprise, someone complimented me on my use of facial expressions. Apparently, as I told a story I made appropriate faces. Didn't know it. Didn't think about it. Never told a story in the mirror so I could see what my face was doing. The iconic straight-faced yankee storyteller? I ain't him. These guys (they're almost all guys) train themselves to stay expressionless. True yankees have been practicing the straight-faced delivery their whole lives. It's a joy to behold:

"Lived here all your life?"
"Not yet."

Or:

"Can I take this road to Charlestown?"
"You could, but if I was you, I'd leave it right where it is."

Or:

"You said you'd watch my hoss while I was in the stoah."
"I did. I watched it walk down the road and around the cawnah."

Showing no emotion on your face *is* a facial expression. And it's a hard one to maintain. Even the most stoic of New England storytellers show their feelings in their eyes. Look closely. You'll see a twinkle of amusement, a spark of anger, a chill of disapproval. Poker players, from what I hear, train themselves to reveal nothing, not even in their eyes. That's a feat and a half.

For most of us, emotions hopscotch across our faces. We can't hide them. When we tell a sad story, we look sad. When we tell a happy story, we look happy. When we're confused, we look confused, and companions say, "What?" The more clearly we imagine a story, the more we see, the more it's apt to show on our faces. The more deeply we feel a story, the more it shows on our faces and in our bodies, and the more deeply the listeners will feel it.

Is it an advantage for storytellers to have faces that reflect what's going on in their heads and hearts? I don't know. Maybe. It is hilarious when a true yankee storyteller delivers a funny line flat—offering no clue at all as to whether he, himself, sees the humor in it. Traditionally, this next yankee classic is delivered without a hint of irony or an iota of acknowledgment that it might, by some, be considered humorous.

The Dog at the General Store

Local sitting out in front of the general store, dog asleep at his feet. Fella from away comes by. "Your dog bite?"

"Nope."

Fella from away reaches down to pat the dog. Dog muckles onto his hand.

"I thought you said your dog didn't bite."

"Ain't my dog."

My face shows everything all the time, which is why I'm a useless liar, why I'll never make it as an actor, and why I can't pose for a decent head shot. The photographer says smile and I think, "My lips are sticking to my teeth. My teeth are crooked. Why didn't my parents spring for braces when I was eleven? Should I tilt my head? Maybe I should tilt my head. Don't blink. Jeez, I blinked. Don't squint. Don't make a face. Oh jeez, take the picture and get it over with." Every one of those thoughts shows on my face. The camera catches them all, and the photographer says, "Let's snap a few more, shall we?"

What?

I heard this story at a synagog in Bethlehem, New Hampshire. If you know Bethlehem, you know it's tucked into the White Mountains and most of the roads go uphill from the center of town. A mother and son were driving up one of those steep side roads when the little boy spotted a Hasidic Jew walking in their same direction. The boy had never seen a man dressed all in black with a bushy beard and side curls, topped with a broad-brimmed black hat. The boy stared.

The car and the Hasid arrived at the stop sign simultaneously. The boy was still staring. The man looked over at him and stared back. "What?" the man said. "You never saw a yankee before?"

PROPS

I don't use props much, but many tellers do. It's amazing what a skilled teller can do with, say, a scarf. A scarf can be used ten different ways in a single story: kerchief, mask, belt, cape, hankie, blanket, flag, tourniquet, sack, parachute. A scarf as a kerchief shows that one character is speaking. Used as a cape it turns the teller into a different character. The scarf transforms as the story progresses. I don't use scarves in my telling. I'm just not that clever. Props can enhance the telling but they also complicate it.

On second thought, I *do* use a prop. All the time. It's my little book, ever at hand and handy. It holds the list of stories to be told. It's a place to record stories people tell me. When I open my little book, the audience knows the session is about to begin. When I close it, the audience knows the session has ended. Tellers have to let the audience know what the heck is going on; they're not mind readers after all.

Some tellers use call and response to keep listeners up to speed. "Crick" the teller says. "Crack," the audience replies to let the teller know they're ready for a story. I usually say, "Hello," and the audience says "Hello" back. As a further check that I've got people's attention, I say: "Can you hear me in the back?" And wait for the answer. "Yes." Or sometimes, "No," which is pretty funny. Then I repeat, "Can you hear me in the back, as the moderator says at town meeting. And the fella says 'No.' The moderator says, 'Count your blessings.'" This usually elicits the first laugh of the evening. When we laugh together we're ready to share stories.

With kids—trust me on this—getting and holding attention can be challenging, so letting them know stories are about to begin is extra important. Listening takes a lot more energy than talking. Kids have loads of energy, but sometimes have difficulty channelling it into listening. These eager listeners can be so antsy, loud, and over-excited at the prospect of a story that they have a hard time settling down to actually hear it.

A visual cue like opening and closing my little book helps. A back and forth greeting or an invitation helps: *Are you ready to hear a story?* Some tellers use a singing or clapping game to harness the energies. The challenge is to get the little ones to pay attention. Once they are focused, a good story will hold that attention. It's getting them focused that takes skill. More skill than I have at the moment, but I'm working on it. Being able to effectively tell stories to four-year-olds for thirty minutes, that's my Moby Dick. Adult audiences are so much easier—especially if they've turned off their cell phones and the chairs are cushioned.

At the end of a session with children or adults I say, "Thank you!" and the audience applauds and, sometimes, says, "Thank you" back. Call and response. Storytelling is all about mutual engagement.

Once in a while I place a moose antler on a table. Antlers are magic—and they make nifty ice breakers. Before the program starts, folks come forward to examine the antler, touch it, ask about it, and tell stories. Lots of people have had notable encounters with moose or other wild animals, so the presence of the antler can get people thinking and talking. Sometimes, when I'm feeling impish, and somebody asks where I got the antler, I say: "I chased that moose through the woods and ripped it off the side of his head."

Then, of course, I have to complete the lie by saying the poor moose is still walking around with his head cocked sideways because he's got just the one antler left.

When invited to tell town meeting stories, I bring my gavel, another prop. And I'm not afraid to use it! I bang the gavel to open and close the session—or to bring the audience to order should they become unruly. It's fun and familiar. Anybody who's attended town meeting or any other gathering where Robert's Rules come into play knows the power of the gavel. A cousin-in-law of mine got gaveled at town meeting. Not only that, he got tossed out by the local constable. When I read about poor Todd's ejection in the paper, I called his wife: "Read in the paper that Todd got thrown out of the town meeting."

"Yup," Poppy said, "it was on his bucket list."

All hail the power of the gavel.

A puppet is a fancy kind of prop. Kids love puppets. I'm not skilled enough to use a puppet—it's all I can do to control my own mouth—but many tellers do to the delight of young audiences. Puppets have the power to grab the attention of even the most fidgety three-year-old.

If you have a prop that enhances your story, use it. Just be careful the prop doesn't steal the show. Keep your puppets in line. You are the boss of them.

Years ago, two poets—Diana Durham and Maren Tirabassi—and I did a spoken word program that featured a number of props, including a handmade rag doll. Once I'd used the doll for a story, I hid her away in a basket. Otherwise, our director told us, the audience would be focused on the doll instead of us. That doll was small but charismatic. Actors know if an apple is accidentally knocked to the floor during a scene, the audience will fixate on that apple until somebody picks it up and puts it back where it belongs.

It may seem counterintuitive, but you don't want to give your audience too much to look at. If you're on stage with an orange tree, a sawhorse, a giant panda and a whiskey bottle half full, people's attention will be all over the place. This is why, I think, tellers are apt to take the stage in dark clothes with just a glass of water on a small table and maybe a straight-backed chair. This is why we leave our glittering rings and tiaras at home. Unless we're performing in character—as a person who would wear glittering rings and tiaras. Lauretta Phillips puts on a floppy felt hat and transforms into "My Gal Sal," her alter ego. Steve Wood does a mean Abe Lincoln. The beard is not a prop, but the stovepipe hat is. When his wife, Sharon Wood, plays Mary Todd Lincoln, she dresses accordingly. Together they tell stories and create living history.

Bottom line: Use props deliberately and with care. Use them to catch and hold your audience's attention. Use them to give your story three dimensions. Remember to tuck props away when you're done with them.

Some gifted storytellers play the bodhran, harmonica, ukulele, guitar, or pipe to add music to their tales. Musical instruments are a special kind of prop, creating moods, moving action forward, building tension, distinguishing between parts of a story, or leading from one story to another. In the right hands, they enrich the experience for the audience. If you're musical, why not incorporate that gift into your telling? It's part of who you are. On the other hand, playing a bodhran, harmonica, ukulele, guitar, or pipe badly (as I would) doesn't enrich much of anything. It's just painful.

The Magic Antler

I love my antler for many reasons. Because my husband found it in the snow—just one little brown tip peeking out. Because it's solid and textured. Because it reminds me of many stories. It's a beautiful object, though I'm still looking for the perfect place to display it in our house. I've tried the piano, the dining room table, my desk, the bookcase. It's a wandering antler—never in one place for long. One of our dogs, Bob, would have happily chewed it up. But I couldn't allow that.

I love the antler because of what it brings out in people. Funny questions like: "What is it made of?" and, "Did you carve it?" One afternoon at a nursing home, I placed it on a table where two residents were sitting quietly as another resident played piano in the background.

Eula seemed surprised and fascinated by the antler. She ran her hands over it again and again. She began to talk about her childhood—about a little house on a hill. She told how, at dusk, she'd put out food for the wild animals and they'd come for it.

"What kind of animals?" I asked her.

"Deer," she said. The deer would come and eat in the evening at the little house on the hill. Her mother didn't like her feeding the animals, but this was not her mother's house, so Eula put out food for the deer and the deer would come.

She told the story several times. Her friend and I listened. With each telling a new detail emerged.

Later, an astonished nurse said she'd never heard Eula speak before.

I asked the friend about that. The friend said, "Eula *can* talk but she doesn't, not very often."

Inspired by the antler, Eula spoke at length that day. What a privilege it was to be invited into her beautiful childhood memory. ~

While I rarely use props when telling, I often use them when teaching. An old yellow ware bowl reminds people of a special kitchen where they spent time with loved ones. The scent of a pine cone takes them into the woods. A conch shell takes them to the beach. A pack of cigarettes, a skeleton key, a toy truck, a crisp dollar bill, a lit candle—almost any object will evoke memory or imagination and the stories will come. The stories want to come—they just need an excuse.

Once I put out a gnarled root—gray and brittle. I asked elementary school students to write what it reminded them of. One child said cancer. She wrote from personal experience and the power of her words grabbed us all by the heart.

Gerry and the Cherry Blossoms

At a nursing home, I had my basket of tricks—props to get people going. In it I carry art supplies, natural objects like shells and stones, old postcards. Gerry's in a reclining wheelchair, leaned way back, her legs elevated.

When prompted, she'll smile and say along with you, "Oh my goodness!" Other than that, she doesn't speak.

I pull out the postcards. She reaches for them and together we go through the pile one-by-one. When we come across a picture of the cherry blossoms in bloom by the Washington Monument, she presses the card to her face and kisses it.

One week later I'm back at the home. A family is sitting in the lobby and one woman recognizes me as a storyteller. She asks what I'm doing here. I explain I'm working with the residents. I ask what they are doing here. They're here because their mother just died. I ask the mother's name. It's Gerry.

I tell them the story of Gerry and describe the postcard she kissed. What was her connection to those cherry blossoms and that picture? Did she live in D.C.? Had she visited?

She had never lived in D.C. the daughter told me. She had never visited D.C. as far as anybody knew.

Then Gerry's son pulled out his phone. He scrolled through some photographs. "I visited D.C.," he said. "I showed her these pictures." There on his phone was the stock tourist photo of the cherry blossoms with the Washington Monument in the background.

When I tell Gerry's story, I'm back at the nursing home. I see her in her wheelchair. I hear her say, "Oh my goodness." I reach into my basket of tricks for the postcards. I feel them in my hand. I see her pallor and the slackness of her mouth. I see her knowing eyes. We look together at the cherry blossoms. I sense her spirit as her message is passed on to her grieving family—I love you—as if that were what she intended all along. ~

REPETITION, RHYTHM, AND RHYME

In "Second Place in the Hoss Pulling Contest at the Lancaster Fair," when I repeat the word "trophy," I repeat the gesture. "The Ghost with the One Black Eye" is mainly repetition. You can break it down to six repeated lines:

"I want my apple juice."
"I'll get your apple juice."
"Down the stairs."
"One, two, three, four, five, six, seven, eight, nine, ten."
"I am the ghost with the one black eye."
"Up the stairs."

By the third go-around, little listeners are telling along with teller.

Repetition is useful in general—whether it's words, gestures, movements, facial expressions, or silly voices. Picture book writers know that the littlest among us love repetition. Heck, we all love it. Who are we anyway but oversized five-year-olds with jobs and debt? Nursery rhymes rely heavily on repetition: "Humpty Dumpty sat on a wall. Humpty Dumpty had a great fall." Rhyme is repetition of sound.

Margaret Wise Brown, in her classic *Goodnight Moon*, repeats the word "goodnight" nineteen times—and there are only 132 words in the whole story. Think of your favorite line from your favorite song and how often it's repeated. Each time a repeated line or word comes up, it pulls you right back into the song, the poem, the story. You know it's coming. You sing along. You are engaged.

Rhythm and rhyme walk hand-in-hand with repetition. Some tellers (not me, not yet) memorize rhymed stories. Rhyme makes memorization easier. In *Goodnight Moon*, most of those 132 words rhyme with something—moon, balloon; bears, chairs; kittens, mittens. When the unrhymed word "whispering" pops up, it warrants special attention: "Goodnight to the old lady whispering 'hush.'" "Whispering"—what a beautiful word. It sounds like what it means. So does "hush." Call it an ideophone or onomatopoeia, "whisper" is a special word because you can't say it without *whispering*. "Hush" is special, too. You *can't* say it loudly. This is part of Margaret Wise Brown's genius. Bet you a buck, though, when she wrote that line she didn't think *onomatopoeia*. Bet she thought, *That sounds right*. With storytelling, a line *is* right when it sounds right.

If you tell a story often enough, you'll shape it until just about every line sounds right. Audiences recognize and appreciate a shapely story.

Repetition and rhyme create rhythm. They make rhythm obvious.

Da dum, da dum, da DUM. Da dum, da dum, da DUM. The jar is full of RUM. Drink up and don't be GLUM. My mother likes to DANCE. I hope she gets a CHANCE.

Every combination of words has rhythm. Each sentence in that last paragraph has rhythm. Together, they create another rhythm. Read them aloud. Clap along.

Try clapping to the Polly poem:

Polly put the kettle on,
Polly put the kettle on,
Polly put the kettle on,
We'll all have tea.

Did you clap twice for each of the Polly lines, and three times for the tea line? I did. If you found a different rhythm, good for you. The rhythms are on the page and in your ear.

Listeners may not clap along to the stories you tell, but they pick up on the rhythms. The rhythms of words in the air are even more obvious than on the page. After one of my first public readings—in graduate school (I was scared to death)—a famously acerbic poet said, "Your story was . . . rhythmic." It was not a great story, and I'm pretty sure he was trying to come up with something nice to say. But he was right. Even then, before the notion of being a storyteller was even an inkling of an idea, I was attentive to the rhythms of language.

Here's a yankee classic told two ways. Read them aloud and you'll hear how different they are. The story is the same. The words are almost exactly the same. Only the rhythms—created with punctuation and word placement—differ.

Unless You've Got Something to Say, Don't Say Nothin'
Version 1

The youngest boy, Pip, never spoke. He never said a word. He reached age two, three, three-and-a-half years old without speaking one word. Though Mother was concerned, the rest of the family—not so much.

The food, at suppertime, was passed around the table. Hand to hand.

Pip tucked in. He swallowed a mouthful of mashed potatoes. He put down his fork. "These potatoes are lumpy," he said, "and cold."

"Pip, you spoke!" Mother couldn't believe it. "You're almost four and never spoke before," she said. "Why now?"

"Mother," Pip said, "up until now, things were going right along smooth." ❧

Unless You've Got Something to Say, Don't Say Nothin'
Version 2

Pip, the youngest boy, never spoke. He got to be two, three, three-and-a-half years old, never said a word. Mother was concerned, but the rest of the family thought nothing much about it.

One suppertime, the food passed hand-to-hand around the table, Pip tucked into his mashed potatoes, swallowed a mouthful, then put down his fork and said: "These potatoes are lumpy and cold."

Mother couldn't believe it.

"Pip, you spoke! You're almost four years old and you never spoke before. Why now?"

Pip said, "Up until now, Mother, things were going right along smooth." ❧

One version is not necessarily better than the other but comparing them shows the many choices available. On the page, a paragraph break constitutes a break in rhythm. Translated into the air, the paragraph break becomes a pause, almost imperceptible sometimes, but still, a pause. Same with commas, periods, dashes, semicolons, colons and the ever powerful and mysterious . . . ellipsis.

Timing is rhythm. Rhythms within a story include repetition, the sentence structure, the way words play among themselves. Timing is more about audience manipulation and the power of the dramatic pause.

"Deering Selectman"—the shortest story I know—begs for a dramatic pause. In fact, the whole story depends on its two dramatic pauses.

Deering Selectman

Fella run for selectman once. (*dramatic pause*)
Unopposed. (*dramatic pause*)
And he lost. ❧

At the meetinghouse in Deering, I asked who had a Deering story to tell. Fella in the back said, "I guess I got one."

I said, "Go ahead. Tell it."

And he did.

Much later, Selectman J.P. Marzullo and Road Agent Peter Beard filled in some details. The fella who ran for selectman unopposed and lost was, in fact, the incumbent.

"What happened?" I asked.

Beard explained the unusual defeat in five words: "Pissed off the road agent."

VOCALS

We talk high, we talk low. We talk fast, we talk slow. Sometimes we whisper. Sometimes we shout. We draw words out. We clip them. We emphasize them. Our physical voices tell listeners what to pay attention to in the story. Characters speak differently so listeners can tell one from another. The old man speaks in a gravelly, shaky voice. The little girl speaks in a soft, high voice. Maybe she has a slight lisp because she's missing her front teeth. We paint an auditory picture with the range of our voices—dark to light, menacing to friendly, cold to sexy, growly to lilting.

I wrote "A New Friend" for a Halloween event. The assignment: Write a scary story that takes no more than five minutes to read. Nine writers read at the performance in Newmarket. Musicians provided spooky background music. I loved using my low, slow spooky voice for the narration, my happy child's voice for Gracie's invitations to Jonathan, and a hissing stage whisper for the surprise ending.

A New Friend

When the moon shines through the trees, the windows gleam on the house on the hill at the end of the road. *I'm not supposed to go there,* 'specially at night, but sometimes I do.

When the breeze ruffles the dry leaves on the oaks that guard the gravel drive to the house on the hill at the end of the road, it sounds like a hundred whispers. I press my hands to my ears as I pass, but the leaves still whisper.

Over the grand front door, somebody nailed a horse shoe that leaks rust in the rain.

Tonight there is no rain, no breeze. The trees are quiet. Fog rolls along the ground. The moon slides in and out of the clouds.

I'm not supposed to go into the house on the hill at the end of the road. It's not my house. But tonight I feel brave. I see a boy, about my age, silhouetted in the upstairs window.

It's Jonathan. I know his name because sometimes I hear his mother calling: "Jonathan, where have you gone? Jonathan come home! Oh, Jonathan." Sometimes she calls him by his two names: "Jonathan Albert."

From a distance, the house on the hill at the end of the road looks abandoned and silent. But up close you can hear the old house noises—the *drip drip drip* from loose pipes, the groan of sills, the hush of settling dust, old bones aching.

Jonathan presses his face and hands to the rippled glass of the upstairs window.

I climb the ivy ladder near the window. It's not hard. I cling to the thick, dry vines. I reach for the window. I can almost touch it.

A broken branch with crooked fingers is just the ticket. It scratches at the glass. Jonathan opens the window and leans out.

"I'm Gracie," I say. "Would you like to come out and play?"

His face is almost a perfect oval, his eyes dark are shining and solemn, his hair long like a girl's.

"You're not scared of the dark, are you, Jonathan?"

He shakes his head.

"Meet you by the cemetery gate," I say.

He nods.

Climbing down the ivy is even easier than climbing up. I run down the hill, floaty as the fog, floaty as the moon crisscrossing the clouds.

The cemetery lies at the foot of the hill. It's called Oak Hill Cemetery, named for the trees. Some of the stones lean. Some have fallen flat on the ground. Some have lain on the ground so long they're all grown over.

Be careful where you step.

I hear the iron gate creak. "Jonathan," I say, "is that you?"

He's shorter than I am and slight. He hesitates and turns his head to look up at the house. The watching windows glow, but otherwise the house slumbers.

I take Jonathan's hand and draw him into the cemetery. It is a damp evening and the fog is rising. It dances among the old gray stones.

I press his hand to one crumbling stone. He kneels and traces the letters with curious fingers, then looks up at me, questioning.

"I'm a ghost," I say.

He doesn't flinch. He rises from his knees and stands tippy toe. His lips seek my ear. He whispers, *"So am I."*

If you're good at accents, use them—but not to the point of caricature. If I could do a decent British accent—there's something extra spooky about a British accent— I might use it to tell "A New Friend." But I can't, so I don't.

A vivacious Scottish woman offered a story from her home place, the Isle of Skye. She told it with rolled r's and growly vowels. My attempt at a Scottish accent comes out half Irish and half Klingon. Still, I'm game to try (a little) because the story is so exotic and lovely.

Wee Wellies

Bonnie said her son was as stubborn as she was and occasionally that brought them to loggerheads. One gray morning, they had a set-to and the little boy—no more than four years old—said, "I'm running away from home." He pulled on his slicker and wee wellies and out he went. She watched through the window as he trekked across the moor in his wee wellies. *He'll turn back in a minute*, she thought. But his little legs kept pumping and he kept a-going. He disappeared in the mist.

It had been threatening rain all morning. The rain started to fall. Heavier and heavier. *He'll be back any minute*, she thought. But the minutes ticked by and there was no sign of the little boy in his wee wellies.

Finally, after what seemed like hours, here he comes in the pouring rain, trudging across the moor in his wee wellies.

He opens the door and steps into the kitchen, dripping. He says, "Mother, I've decided to give you another chance."

Which reminds me of another story of a stubborn little boy and the time a woman recalled a story she said she hadn't thought about for years. This happens. A story causes a long-lost memory to surface.

Henry's Mistake
His Big Sister, Judy Whitcomb

At our house, cursing was strictly forbidden. One day, my little brother Henry made a mistake. He'd have been just four, maybe five years old. Which would have made me six or seven.

Henry did a bad thing. He said a curse word right in front of Mother.

Mother said, "Henry, you know the rule. No cursing in this house. You're going to have to move out."

So he packed his little bag.

I stood beside him at the front door. He looked up at me with his big sad eyes. "Oh Henry," I said, "where are you going to live?"

He said, "How the hell do I know?"

I tell stories with a fairly thick New Hampshire/Maine/Massachusetts/Vermont accent. The accent for each New England state is unique. It varies region to region within the states. New Hampshire, my home, borders the other three, so the closer you get to Vermont going west, the more likely it is that some Vermont pronunciations and vernacular will slide in. Same with Maine to the east and north. Same with Massachusetts to the south.

That said, my accent must never interfere with the story. The audience must understand exactly what I'm saying. If that means lightening up on the accent, so be it. You don't want to be so authentic that the audience gets lost or irritated. Sometimes a suggestion of an accent is all you need. In my case, I don't have to drop every "r" or "g," or stretch out every "a." Drop a few, stretch out a couple, and the audience gets the idea.

Enunciation matters.

I first heard this classic story at a Farm Bureau supper from a woman named Sabrina, who assured me it happened to her uncle in Barnstead. I believed her. Still do, though I've heard it many times since about other people's uncles or granddads or brothers or buddies. Variations on a theme. It is, in fact, a yankee classic, yet each teller assures listeners: "This is a true story."

In the months following the Farm Bureau supper, I told the story a few times and got comfortable with it. The last line was sure to get a laugh. Until the night nobody laughed.

Turns out, I had failed to enunciate one word and the whole story fell apart. Here it is:

Harvey's Coat

Sabrina's uncle Mason renovated houses in Barnstead. "Yup," she said, "folks from the city would buy an old house from some family that had been living there for five generations. Then they'd hire my uncle to completely redo the house to make it livable." One family said to make the house just as it had been in the 1800s. Historically accurate. Mason said, "Where do you want the outhouse?"

Turns out indoor plumbing was just fine with them. They didn't want that much historical accuracy.

Harvey worked for Mason. One day Mason got to the site a little late. There was Harvey standing beside the dug-up septic tank. The lid was off.

Harvey was poking around the hole with a long pole. "What you doin', Harvey?" Mason said.

Harvey said, dejected, "I dropped my coat."

Mason looked down in the hole. He said, "Harvey, say goodbye to that coat. It's ova for that coat."

Harvey said, "I don't care about that old coat. My lunch is in the pocket." ⌒

Turns out the word "coat" sounds a lot like "coke." If listeners hear "coke," they think soda. Neither a can nor a bottle of soda has a pocket. So the story makes no sense.

Now when I tell the story, I say the word "coat" with an exaggerated "t." What you do with your voice must serve the story by making it clearer to listeners. That's all.

> **Ova:** Adverb. Finished. Once a coat gets dropped in a septic tank, it's ova for that coat. Can also be used as a preposition to mean above or beyond. In some contexts, ova is the opposite of undah. The coat Harvey dropped was most likely an ovacoat, worn—perversely—ova his ova-alls. Conversely, most people enjoy the security of undahwear ova their bare skin but undah their street clothes and ovacoats. Men's undahwear is sometimes referred to as undahshots or, simply, shots, as previously mentioned.

Bear in Easton

On the way to Easton for a story session, John Rule and I passed through the still-smoldering Lost River Valley. We saw and smelled the smokey remnants of a forest fire a week or more earlier. The terrain on the mountainside is so steep, rocky, and remote, some of the fires had to burn themselves out.

Maybe it was the smoldering that upset the wildlife, but as we were passing through, a bear ran across the road not 100 yards in front of us. Far enough away that we didn't worry about hitting it, but close enough to see clearly.

At the hall in Easton, I made a big deal out of seeing a bear run across the road. People were not impressed. When I think about it, there are probably more bears than people in Easton, which has one of the lowest tax rates in New Hampshire. Why? No children, therefore no schools to pay for.

What happened to the children? They didn't say.

My bear story inspired a resident to tell how one afternoon she heard scratching at her glass patio doors. Sure enough, there stood a bear stretched to his full height, trying to get in. She shooed the bear away. "Get out of here," she said. And it did. It went around the house to her back door. On its hind legs stretched to its full height, it's trying to break through that door. She shooed it away. "Get out of here," she said. And it did.

It went to the side yard. Next thing she knows the bear is at her clothesline swatting at her laundry, pulling clothes right off the line. It grabs a pair of her husband, Phil's, underwear, stuffs 'em in its mouth and shakes them side to side like a big dog with a chew toy, then runs off in the woods.

A few days later, Phil's in downtown Littleton, the nearest metropolis, having coffee with a friend, who says, "That bear you had up to your place made an appearance here in town yesterday. Went up a tree by town hall and set for an hour. The tourists all gathered around and took pictures."

"How'd you know it was my bear?" Phil said.

"Well, it was pretty tame," the friend said. "And about the right size."

Phil said: "Was it wearing my shots?"

"Priorities" is another story that fooled me into thinking it was certifiably true when, in fact, it might be apocryphal. Doug from Langdon told it with such authority and detail, I was sure it had actually happened to him. Later, I heard a very similar story from another "Doug" in another town. *What a coincidence*, I thought.

Whatever its origins, "Priorities" lends itself to lots of vocal variation—matter-of-fact narration at the beginning, rising tension as Doug comes upon a terrible scene, a pained request from the accident victim, a low-voiced struggle to remove the heavy object from the back seat, and—finally—the tentative "Hello" from the front when all is revealed and the story lives up to the promise of the title.

Priorities

Drove almost two hours through four counties—Rockingham, Merrimack, Cheshire and Sullivan—to find Langdon, a small town of fewer than 700 souls, snugged between Charlestown and Walpole in a part of the state I call the Heart of Darkness (pronounced Haht a Dahkness)—rural, heavily wooded, steeped in hills, and laced by streams and rivers. Signage is rare in the Heart of Darkness. GPS lies if it works at all. Cell phone service? Iffy to nonexistent. Driving those windy roads along those rushing brooks and rivers with those steep embankments in the dark and in the rain is harrowing.

It's one of my favorite places in the world.

The people who inhabit the Heart of Darkness seem extra hearty, welcoming, and tolerant of a storyteller who's fifteen minutes late to a gig on a dark night in the driving rain.

This is a true story, told by Doug in Langdon, who hardly ever lies. The action actually takes place one town ova in Acworth. I call this story "Priorities." Sometimes titles matter.

One evening out late—must have been 9:00, 9:30—Doug happened upon a terrible scene. A Ford Escort had gone off the road into a ditch and flipped onto its roof. The accident was so fresh the wheels were still turning and steam was rising out of the radiator.

Doug took out his cell phone and dialed 911. By some miracle, the call went through. Help was on its way.

Meanwhile, Doug made his way down the embankment to the upside-down Escort. A man was hanging upside down from his seat belt. Doug recognized the guy as a local fellow who was big in the Grange.

Doug said, "Are you okay?"

The granger said, "No! I was just in an accident."

Doug said, "Are you hurt?"

The granger said, "My shoulder hurts real bad."

Doug managed to get the upside-down door open. He cut the seat belt with his pocket knife and gently extricated the granger from the car and spread him out on the ground. In the distance, he could hear the sirens. Help was on its way!

The granger motioned Doug to come close. Doug knelt beside him. The granger whispered, "Would you do me a favor?"

"Sure," Doug said. "I will if I can."

"When the ambulance gets here, they're gonna to haul me off to the hospital. And the police are gonna tow my car away." He said, "There's a watermelon in the back seat. Would you get it out for me and keep it until I can collect it from you? It's a big watermelon. A prize winner. I grew it myself."

It wasn't easy getting the back door open, but Doug managed. Sure enough, there was a huge watermelon resting on the ceiling of the Escort. Intact. He wrapped his arms around it and was about to pull it from the car when he heard a small voice from the front passenger seat, "Hello?"

It was the granger's wife.

And that's why this story is called "Priorities."

ABOVE ALL, FIND YOUR TERRITORY
AND TRUST YOUR VOICE

We learn to tell stories by listening. We teach ourselves the ins and outs of stories by telling them. But the most important skill storytellers need to develop is how to recognize a story that's right for them.

I tell humorous stories set in New England. I don't tell Native American stories or African folk tales. I don't do fables or heart-tugging sagas of overcoming adversity. Forget Beowulf, Paul Bunyan, and talking rabbits. I know a story that I *can* tell when I hear it.

Each teller must find his or her own bailiwick and tell the stuffing out of it.

I sit back and enjoy the brilliance of other tellers, but almost never think, "Gosh, I'd like to tell that one," or "Gee, I wish I'd thought of that." Even other yankee humorists choose to tell different stories because our Voices (with a capital V) are so different. Not voices in the sense of the sounds that come out of our mouths, but Voices in the sense of who we are and how we see the world. The recordings of Mary Vittum, a.k.a. Auntie Henrietta, play on a loop in the bathrooms at Common Man restaurants. People think it's me. Mary's physical voice and mine are similar. So are our accents. But our subject matter is different. About once a month, somebody will grin and say, "I heard you in the bathroom at the Common Man." Sometimes I nod and let it pass. Usually I explain that the woman telling stories about hapless husbands and domestic discord ain't me.

When you're a storyteller, people offer you stories all the time. They call on the phone, send e-mail, and letters. Sometimes they show up at your house. I'm pleased to receive these stories, invariably entertained by them, and honored to be entrusted with them—but only a few work for retelling, because only a few match my Voice.

The minute I heard this next one I knew I'd be telling it. It is a perfect fit. At a gathering at a retirement community, Skip shared a true story from his hometown of Sunapee.

Sunapee Speeder

Frank and Walter—as frugal with words as they are with money—were driving through town in Frank's truck. Frank had a bit of a lead foot and that old pickup still had a lot of zing. Out of the corner of his eye, he glimpsed something on the side of the road. "Walter," he said, "was that a cop we just passed?"

"Yup."

"Did he pull out on the road?"

"Yup."

"Is he following us?"

"Yup."

"Does he have his blue lights on?"

"Yup ... Nope ... Yup ... Nope ..." ~

Not many words in "Sunapee Speeder." It's mostly dramatic pauses. The story pairs nicely with "Colebrook Speeder," another favorite. A quilter would say of fabric that one "walks" into the next. They share an element: color, pattern, even a theme like birds or flowers or in this case flouting the law. Stories seldom stand alone. One informs the next.

When you tell ten stories in a row, they form a story of their own. Listeners will find the commonalities. They will understand how the stories fit together. It is in our nature to seek out and impose patterns.

Once in a while I get invited to do a keynote talk. This puts the fear of god into me. Keynote means important. The only thing I know to do is tell stories. My intention is that the stories I choose for a keynote will fit together in a way that's appropriate, maybe even illuminating, for the group I'm addressing. The minute anybody uses the word keynote, my fee goes up to cover pain and suffering as I agonize over which stories will be appropriate and illuminating for caregivers, medical professionals, municipal association members, librarians and trustees, teachers, business and professional women, court reporters, volunteers, or writers.

Luckily, almost everybody likes to laugh. Luckily, most audiences listen carefully and extract meaning from the stories individually and in combination, so I don't have to explain them. If you have to explain what a story means, it's not a very good one.

Colebrook Speeder

This one works only in New Hampshire, because only New Hampshire people get it. Well, maybe a few from Maine or Vermont if they've got their thinkin' caps on and know geography.

It takes place in Colebrook. You know where Colebrook is? You been to Colebrook? If you hit Canada, you've gone too fah.

Fella drivin' through Colebrook, exceedin' the speed limit. Gets pulled over. Cop says: "License and registration." Fella rolls down his window. This was in the days when you had to turn a handle to lower your cah window.

Guy fumbles around looking for the paperwork.

Cop says, "Where you from anyhow?"

Guy says, "Pittsburgh."

Cop says, "Now I know you're a liar. You got Pennsylvania plates."

Fah: Adverb. Long way from heah. Fah is the opposite of nee-ah. Makes me think of the song from that sad movie I've never watched—*Titanic*—*Nee-ah, fah, wherevah you ah*. . . . Which makes me think of the singer in Maine—I think she was called Roberta or Alberta—who took requests. Asked if she'd sing a couple's favorite Barbra Streisand ballad for their anniversary, she said, "Which song do you mean?" The couple replied, in unison, "'The Way We Was.'"

Cah: Noun. A motorized vehicle. Not a truck.

Shared knowledge—like the existence of Pittsburg, New Hampshire—allows us to understand each other. The listener connects the dots. The more dots the teller can leave out, the better. Remember those puzzles that, even as a kid, you take one look and see the outline of a turkey? Why bother doing the puzzle if you already know it's a turkey? Think of a story as a pencil sketch, not a full-fledged oil painting. The teller provides just enough structure and detail for the listener to fill in the rest from his or her own knowledge and experience.

It's code. It's inside jokes. The more knowledge you and your audience share, the more cryptic you can be—and, in turn, the more the story accentuates the connections between you. Family sayings are the ultimate example. Every family has expressions that only people within the family understand. In our family, when we say, "You've embarrassed me, and you've embarrassed Doug," we laugh. Uproariously. Usually the saying diffuses a tense situation.

The saying references Adi Rule's first boyfriend. They dated through high school and college. Adi Rule is our daughter and only child. (She's also a writer. Look for her young adult and middle grade novels in bookstores.) She claims not to remember the exact circumstances, but she made a misstep in the presence of her boyfriend and his older, much admired brother Doug. The boyfriend admonished her: "You've embarrassed me, and you've embarrassed Doug."

She laughs about it now. We all do. Moral of the story: If you're being yourself, there's nothing to be embarrassed about.

Sally in Woodstock, Vermont

Telling stories in Woodstock to a large group of medical professionals, I asked who had one to contribute. Julie said she'd worked as a visiting nurse for many years. She often visited seniors in the outlying towns to determine whether they might be able to use some of the social services offered by various groups.

She met Sally at Sally's home. Over tea, they chatted. Sally was a lovely older woman, Julie said, with bright blue eyes and long white hair that spread across her shoulders. To assess Sally's mental capabilities, Julie—with Sally's permission—asked a series of questions. The first questions were pretty easy: What day of the week is it? What month? What year? Who's President of the United States? and so forth.

Gradually, the questions got more difficult.

"Do you ever get depressed for no reason?"

"No," Sally said, "not for no reason."

"Have you ever gone outside in the street with no clothes on?"

Sally hesitated. Her bright blue eyes grew wide. "Oh, my dear," she said, "those were the days!"

The sketch includes a visiting nurse, an older woman, tea at the older woman's house, a few questions, and two specific answers. It's simple. A pencil drawing—soft gray on white paper, with a touch of blue at the eyes.

The listener fills in the rest with cues from the teller's voice, gestures, and facial expressions. The teller leaves lots of room for the listener to create Sally's world in his or her mind. What does a chat over tea at Sally's house sound like, look like? The listener creates a table, tea cups, maybe a plate of cookies. The sun shines through the window. The curtains are lace or printed cotton. Strawberries? Sunflowers?

The detail of Sally's long white hair and bright blue eyes suggests other details. The listener pictures her face, her facial expressions, her clothes, the way she sits at the table, leaning forward to hear the questions, her head tilted a little to the right.

The scene is set, so when the final question comes—"Have you ever gone outside in the street with no clothes on?"—the listener sees Sally's beautiful eyes widen and wonders what her response will be.

Sally's surprising answer—"Oh, my dear, those were the days!"—changes everything. Those of us who remember the days of communes, hippies, free love, and peace symbols are transported to those days. We see Sally and her friends shedding their tie-dye and dancing in the sun. The fact that this happened in Woodstock is a bonus as we recall the other Woodstock and all that it stood for.

Together, the teller, the listener, and Sally create a technicolor story.

Trusting the listener to fill in the details allows the teller to keep Sally's story short. The shorter the delivery, the more intense the effect. This is especially true for humor. For maximum impact—that is, if you're going for belly laughs—don't dilute the humor with anything extraneous. Not one word.

In other words, no fahtin' around. Don't worry, listeners know what to do. When in doubt, leave it out. What you leave out, they'll put in. What you drop, they'll pick up and examine. Believe in the power of what is not said.

Some audiences are, of course, more sophisticated than others. Once a year I perform at the Corner House Inn, Sandwich, New Hampshire, where Don Brown has been hosting weekly storytelling dinners on Thursday nights, spring, winter, and fall, for thirty years. Some of the locals attend most every session—for one low price you get a three-course meal, a glass of wine, and an hour of stories.

You'd think telling would be easier with an experienced audience like that. In some ways it is. The venue is homey. The audience is eager and welcoming. They know how to listen. But they also remember the stories you told a year ago, so you better have some fresh material. Plus, they've heard eight different storytellers in the last two months, so they know what a great story sounds like. Expectations are high. *Becky*, I say to myself, *no fahtin' around. Time to step up!*

Fahtin' around: In the case of storytelling it means elaborating unnecessarily. The longer the story, the better the payoff better damn well be. With humor, the longer the story, the funnier the punch line better damn well be.

A yankee classic, "The Three-Legged Pig," can go long or short. The gist is a fella notices a pig with three legs and asks what happened. The farmer explains this pig is a hero and goes into detail about how the pig saved him from fire, drowning, tornado, robbers, etc. This explanation can go on for some time. Finally, the fella, as frustrated as the listeners, says, "But how come he has only three legs?" evoking the punch line: "Good pig like that you don't eat all at once."

When I tell this story, which is rarely because it's gross, I make it quick. That lame punch line deserves two minutes or less of build-up with apologies in advance. Still, it's a sound example of a grotesque tale—funny and horrifying at the same time.

Fahtin' around is similar to dubbin' around, the difference being that while a dubbah can dub around, a faht can't faht around, unless it's an old faht. When you creep past a hundred orange cones on I-95 and, at the end of the ordeal, spot three or four construction workers in a row giving you the hairy eyeball as you pass, you might think they're dubbahs dubbin' around, but they're probably on a break or maybe calculating their next move in the spirit of measure twice, cut once.

Pamona and the Balloon—A Yankee Classic

This story was represented as having happened in West Townsend, Massachusetts. I'd heard it before, but this teller, Herc, told it with so much confidence and in such detail it seemed like it must be true. If you don't know Herc from West Townsend, you should—he's a pistol.

Herc said Gary Stockwell and his boy Nawman were walking home from the fair. Nawman was draggin' along a pink balloon on a string. He was pretty proud of that balloon.

As they were passing Pamona Atherton's place, Nawman told his father he had to go to the bathroom real bad. Pamona had just put in a new outhouse and Gary was sure she wouldn't mind if Nawman used it in this emergency.

So Nawman did.

Unfortunately, he dropped his balloon down the hole. Gary was not inclined to fetch it out. So they went on their way, unhappy about the loss of the balloon, but *c'est la vie*. That's French for suck it up.

That evening, Pamona also had occasion to use the outhouse.

And she did.

When she shined her flashlight down the hole, she spotted that pink balloon and thought she'd passed something maybe she shouldn't have. She called Doc Churchill, who come right over. He looked down the hole. Saw the balloon. Poked it with a pitchfork and it popped.

Doc turns to Pamona. "Nothing to worry about," he says. "But amazing all the same."

"What can you mean?" Pamona says.

Doc says, "Pamona, I think you and I are the only people ever to actually *see* a faht."

Nawman: Proper noun. A boy or man's first name. Spelled Norman but pronounced with an "aw" in place of the "or." Naw-man, as if he were gnawing a bone. Which reminds me of my Dad's old friend and working buddy Nawman Perkins who called everybody Jawge, spelled George. Nawman and Jawge are two fine old yankee names. Never met a Nawman or a Jawge I didn't like. Though Normans and Georges are sometimes difficult.

The detail of "Pamona and the Balloon" makes it believable, especially the names—Gary Stockwell and his boy Nawman. They sure sound real to me. Another plus: it's set in a specific place on a specific day—Townsend, Massachusetts, on fair day. The fair makes the balloon logical. A boy doesn't usually walk down the street with a pink balloon, but he probably won it at the fair.

The fact Gary Stockwell and Nawman are walking home from the fair and a fancy lady like Pamona Atherton has an outhouse suggests a time in the past before balloons were filled with helium. If it were a helium balloon it would have floated out of the hole and the whole story would be ruined. It all makes sense.

It's easier to believe that such a momentous event happened in the fairly distant past rather than last week. Last week seems too convenient. The fact that the story is remembered all these years later gives it gravitas.

Finally, we all know people like Pamona who are gullible. We also know people like Doc Churchill who enjoy a good joke. Pamona and Doc Churchill could be people we know—or us.

Gravitas: Noun. Weight or substance. Gravity makes things heavy, so gravitas refers to something weighty or important. Years ago, some friends gathered to talk about the new Sherlock Holmes movie with Robert Downey Jr. We all loved Sherlock Holmes, from the original Conan Doyle stories to the Basil Rathbone films. During the discussion, one friend said, solemnly, she thought the new movie "lacked gravitas."

No one giggled, but I've loved the word ever since. In our house, we use it often.

"How'd the Red Sox do?"
"They lacked gravitas."
"What did you think of Clyde's new girlfriend?"
"She lacked gravitas."
"Was the turkey moist?"
"No. It was wicked dry. Not only that, it lacked gravitas."

The story of Pamona and the balloon brings to mind that other classic yankee outhouse yarn, "The Quarter Down the Hole." Here's one version.

The Quarter Down the Hole

After using the outhouse, Lippy accidentally dropped a quarter down the hole. He told his brother Zip.

Zip looked down the hole and saw that shiny quarter settin' on top of the pile. He took a dollar bill out of his wallet and dropped it in.

"What'd you do that for, Zip?" Lippy said.

"If you think I'm reaching down in that stinky hole for a quarter," Zip said, "you're crazy." ⌒

I include "The Quarter Down the Hole" because it's so well known, though it's not a story I tell, or have ever told. It's a little too earthy even for me.

The better you know yourself, the better you'll be able to recognize the stories that are just right for you. But there's no substitute for a test flight. You get an idea for a story from hearing it, reading it, or from your own experience and imagination. A story catches your ear and takes shape. The next step is to try it out.

THAT REMINDS ME OF A FUNNY STORY | 83

Trying it out might mean writing it down—in a journal, in a blog, in an essay or short story. Some stories don't want to be told. They want and need to be written. Until the words come out of your mouth and fly free into the ears of listeners, you'll never know for sure if it's a story that you can tell—one you want to tell, one that fits your Voice.

Scientists say everything we've ever experienced is imprinted on our brains. It's all there. Somewhere. Every moment of every day. Since birth. Heck, probably even from the womb. Yet we have access to only a fraction of those experiences. Does what we remember shape who we are? I think so. Do we remember certain events—and turn them into stories—because of who we are? I think that's true too. Do we value certain experiences and stories because they reflect our values? Absolutely. Can stories help us become the people we want to be? Of course.

We know who we are by the stories we remember, and tell, and love.

PART III
A Storyteller's Life

People ask: "What do you do?"

I answer: "Not a helluva lot."

People ask: "How did you become a storyteller?"

The short answer is: "I don't know."

Maybe I was born a storyteller. Maybe my first squawk out of the womb was a story. "I'm hungry, Ma. Been floating around in this umbilical fluid too long. 'Bout time you sprung me."

Maybe one experience—reading, writing, shooting my mouth off—led willy-nilly to another and here's where I ended up.

Maybe if I'd majored in something sensible like nursing instead of English, I would never have become a storyteller. Or maybe I'd be a better storyteller if I'd become a nurse too.

If that children's picture book I almost sold in 1995 had actually sold, maybe I'd be thirty books into a career as a children's book author and reading from my work to kindergarteners every week instead of telling humorous stories to grown-ups.

The long answer is: "Becoming a storyteller was the path of least resistance."

I started out as a serious writer of literary fiction. When my first collection of short stories was published, I did readings at bookstores and libraries. It was hard at first. But before long, I got to like reading to audiences. Even more than reading, I liked putting the book aside and talking to people, telling them about the writing. When I read the ten-page story, "The Widow and the Trapper," to a patient audience, I'd grow impatient myself. I'd skip a few paragraphs, summarize a scene, stop the story entirely and tell how the story was based on something that happened to my grandfather, Bill Barker. I'd tell how a nosy neighbor had given him a copy of the magazine it was published in. How I hadn't dared to show him the story, for fear it would piss him off. How it did, in fact, piss him off.

But not for the reasons I thought.

In the story I invent a love story between an aging fisherman (like Grampa Bill) and a neighbor lady who'd moved in from out of state. Grampa wasn't bothered at all by the invented love story. What bothered him, he said, was, "You almost give away some fishin' secrets. Luckily, you got it wrong."

Grampa Bill, like most (all) of my relatives, was not thrilled about having a writer in the family. Aunt Florence said it best: "When are you going to get a real job?"

Never, as it turns out. Not so far anyway. At sixty-four my prospects for landing a real job are dimming.

Over time, I did less reading and more talking. The talk turned into stories. When people started telling me stories, that was the turning point. Their stories seemed better than any I could make up. It took years, ten or more, but eventually I was telling stories, receiving stories, and retelling them. I immersed myself in the ancient tradition of preserving culture and history—plus keeping myself and others entertained—by shaping stories and passing them on. One led to another.

Willy-Nilly

At the meeting of the select board, a citizen confronts the town fathers with a complaint. His road needs repair. It's needed repair for years. It's been getting worse and worse. "Is there a plan for fixing the roads in this town," he demands, "or is it willy nilly?"

"It's willy-nilly," says the selectman. ⮞

I didn't start out to be a storyteller. I didn't choose to be one. For many years I resisted the title. But gradually, it happened. I even joined a storytellers group and discovered a community of people just like me who tell for the joy of telling. Getting paid is a bonus.

From the beginning, I loved writing. One of my earliest memories is playing with letter tiles on the kitchen table. Moving them around. Putting them in different orders. I spelled P-O-P. My dad said, "Becky, that's a word. You made a word."

I made a word?

"Yup," he said. "You made *pop*."

Amazing. Miraculous. Life-altering.

SCHOOL: IT WAS THE BEST OF TIMES AND SO FAWTH

Writing was my best subject in school. Even handwriting. How I loved handling that thick, triple-lined paper with the fragrance of dry wood. The fat pencil with an eraser on top, just in case, scraped the surface with just the right amount of resistance. We practiced our letters. The small letters skimmed the bottom line and the dotted middle line—*a, e, c*, and the perfect *o*. Small *o*'s between the bottom line and the middle line. Capital *O*'s stretched top to bottom. *O O O O*. All meticulously shaped, spaced, and ordered. The way the world should be.

To this day writing a few rows of perfectly formed letters that fit between the lines and slant a little to the right calms me.

In sixth grade, we had to write a one-page theme each week. Any topic we liked. I wrote a theme on skiing—and how much I disliked it. Drinking cocoa in the lodge was way more fun than freezing my feet on the slope. Lessons were the worst. I'd wait my turn as child after child executed excellent snowplow technique, and then, when it was my turn, fall on my can. Many people seemed to like skiing, including my brother, and Aunt Florence and Uncle Elliot who treated us to equipment, lift tickets, and day trips to Ragged Mountain. Not me. I'd rather be home reading a book.

In my theme, I misspelled skiing about twenty times. It wasn't carelessness. I really thought skiing was spelled s-k-i-n-g. Two i's in the middle of a word made no sense. Mr. Arata's red pencil corrected every *sking*. I appreciated his attention to detail. A writer's best friend is a good editor.

School, from the beginning, was a tightrope walk. I lived in terror of making mistakes. My *O*'s had to touch the lines but not cross them. If I got into trouble at school, I knew I'd get into even more trouble at home. I knew this because my parents said so. In first grade, when I tipped over my plaid thermos and the milk went all which-ways, I felt like sinking through the floor in shame. I can still smell that spilled milk and the bologna sandwich that went with it.

In first grade, in anticipation of recess, I turned in my chair and pointed my feet toward the aisle—blue oxfords scuffed at the toes, white ankle socks. The substitute teacher pointed her bony finger at me: "You may all go out to recess except for . . ." (she didn't know my name). I was mortified. I never wanted to go out to recess again. Didn't like goddamn recess anyway. After everybody else had filed out, she said I could go. And I went.

But I never turned in my seat and pointed my feet toward the aisle in anticipation of recess again, not even when our real teacher, Mrs. Dearborn—who was, in fact, very dear—came back. She told us stories and moved cutouts around on the felt board to illustrate them. She blew on a pitch pipe so we'd all be in tune for "Good morning to you / good morning to you / we are all in our places / with bright shiny faces / now this is the way / to start a new day." When Mrs. Dearborn came back, school returned to the way it should be. I was a well-behaved girl and everybody knew it.

Luckily my parents never found out about my anticipation-of-recess transgression. Far as I know.

MAKE THE MISTAKES YOU NEED TO MAKE AND MOVE ON

So you go along in life just being you, trying to do right, trying to balance on the tightrope you've invented for yourself, but some people—like that mean old substitute teacher—have it in for you anyway. They just don't like you. Don't like anything about you from your pigtails to your scuffed blue oxfords. After a while—took me about fifty years—you get used to it. You accept it. You swallow hard, tell the story, and move on.

Medora's Mother

Medora said she came out of the woods when she was seventeen years old. She'd grown up in the logging camps—a rough life for a child, you'd think. But she loved it.

"There was no indoor plumbing," she said. "At one camp we had a twelve-holer outhouse. You'd step over people's feet to get to an open seat."

"Wasn't that embarrassing?"

"Oh, no," she said. "It was just about the only time people had to sit and visit."

I asked if she ever felt scared way out in the woods among all those rough lumberjacks. "Oh, no," she said. The loggers were kind to her and her siblings. Most had families they'd left behind, so they loved seeing the kids. They carved little toys for them and treated them like little princes and princesses.

"My mother gave us a good scare once," Medora said. To cross the river, the men rigged a flat-bottomed boat—a bateau—on cables and pulleys attached to trees, one on each banking. A person could stand in the boat and pull herself from one side of the river to the other on those cables. Medora's mother had given a logger a ride across. On the return trip, one of the cables let go and catapulted her into the frigid water.

Medora's little brothers and sisters saw what had happened. They came running into the cabin crying, "Mother's in the river."

"I practically sunk into the floor when I heard that," Medora said. She knew how cold that river was. And how swift the current. "I thought for sure Mother was gone."

But Medora's mother didn't drown that day. She went down but "came right back up. Happily, she came up right at the side of the boat, so she grabbed ahold." The rescuers found her hands frozen to the gunnel. They pried them loose, brought her home, set her by the wood stove and thawed her out. ❧

For a couple of years, I told that story along with two others that ended similarly. I liked the way the stories played off each other, and how the macabre joke of getting thawed out by the wood stove grew increasingly ridiculous. Here are the other two thaw stories.

Jeannette King's Ghost

Like Medora, Jeannette King lived in the woods for many years. Her parents had a cabin deep in the forest, convenient to her father's work as a logger. The nearest children lived miles away in another remote cabin. It was Jeannette's habit, even as a very small girl, to walk through the woods to the neighbors' cabin to play, then walk home before dark.

One afternoon, she stayed too long. She was still deep in the woods when darkness fell and a terrible cold settled in. She knew the way, so she wasn't too worried. She kept walking. The night woods made rustling sounds that might have scared a child who wasn't used to them. But Jeannette wasn't much scared. She kept walking. She walked as fast as she could.

At last she spotted the light from the kitchen window through the trees. Almost home. But . . . between herself and the cabin door she spotted a ghost—pale and hovering in the darkness. A man ghost. She could tell it was a man ghost because of its long pale legs that swayed side to side. When she looked up to where the face should be, there was no face, only darkness.

Being a child of the North Country, she knew she had to get to the warmth of the cabin or she'd freeze in the woods. To get safely inside, she'd have to pass the ghost.

Bravely, she inched toward the cabin, staying as far from the ghost as she could.

As she got closer, though, she saw that it wasn't a ghost at all. It was her father's long johns, hung on the line to dry and frozen stiff.

"What did you do then, Jeannette?" I said.

"Pulled them off the line, took them in the house, set them by the wood stove, and thawed them out." ❧

The third thaw story:

Skaters on the Androscoggin

Lisette loved to skate. One day she was skating on the Androscoggin when the ice gave way and down she went.

Happily, not far downstream, Rudy and his friends were playing hockey. Rudy looked down through the ice and he saw Lisette floating by underneath.

He smashed the ice with his hockey stick, fished her from the drink, took her home, set her by the wood stove, and thawed her out.

I stopped telling the trilogy when, after one session, an earnest young man who had some difficulty speaking, managed—after a fashion—to explain he liked my stories but wished I hadn't told the one about the girl under the ice. His sister had fallen through the ice and drowned. The story made him sad.

I never told it again.

Much humor, yankee or otherwise, has a dark underpinning. The dark in contrast to the light (Lisette is rescued, Jeannette's ghost isn't a ghost after all, Medora's mother lives) gives stories much of their power and makes the humor even more humorous. Too much dark defeats the purpose of helping us laugh at our vulnerability, of helping us laugh at ourselves.

All the *O*'s must line up. They must slant perfectly to the right.

"At Cathedral Ledge" is an especially dark example of yankee humor. It takes place at a well-known New Hampshire landmark and is chillingly true. Too true as it turns out.

At Cathedral Ledge

Cathedral Ledge is almost 1,200 feet of sheer vertical rock on the town line between Bartlett and North Conway. Hikers enjoy a great view from the top. It's a favorite challenge for rock and ice climbers. Unfortunately, every once in a while, somebody falls off and dies.

The select board in Bartlett received a bill from an ambulance company. A man had fallen from the lookout and died on impact. The board chair asserted that, by rights, the ambulance bill ought to be paid by North Conway. "That man was alive when he left Bartlett!" he said. ~

The story came to me by way the wife of the board chair, so I knew it was a true story of yankee frugality, wit, and irreverence. It struck me funny. I told it at a large gathering in the mountains, where I was one of several speakers. It was quite a fancy do. We each had only a few minutes to speak, so I picked what I thought were my three funniest stories for that North Country audience. One was "At Cathedral Ledge." It got a big laugh.

Afterwards in the lobby a woman took me aside. She was a fan, she said, but warned about telling the Cathedral Ledge story. Some people might not like it. Then she explained that her husband had committed suicide by jumping from the ledge a few years earlier. She was sure the story was about him. She felt the crowd's laughter came at her expense.

I felt like two cents and never told the story again except as a cautionary tale. Be careful what stories you tell. You never know who's listening.

Humor is dangerous. A hundred people might find a story uproariously funny, but if there's one person who finds it downright hurtful, it's not worth the risk. As a humorist, I'm okay with sometimes offending listeners, but I truly do not want to hurt anybody. That's not my job. That's the opposite of my job.

To tell or write a story from someone else's perspective is to walk in that person's shoes, to begin to understand how that person sees the world. You can't be a teller or a writer without developing empathy.

Harry Prouty and I couldn't be more different. He's a retired woodsman, raised tough. I'm a writer and storyteller, raised soft. We've spent time together swapping stories, in particular, a long afternoon at his home where he talked about the logging life. The man can tell a story with the best of them. Each story brought me deeper into his world.

We can't ever *know* another person, but stories help us know *something* about them, which makes us feel less alone.

Here's a transcription—almost word for word—from my "interview" with Harry Prouty. By interview, I mean I said something like, "Tell me your story," and he did.

Harry Prouty on Working in the Woods

When you're a woodsman, that is your lifeline—the ax and the saw. I can make a chainsaw so sharp you wouldn't even see it cut. Especially back in the old days. The ax was more lifeline than the saw. The ax was like a lumberjack's woman. I'm telling you, anybody touch that ax and they'll flatten you like a bug.

When I was a kid working in the woods, my father would say, "You stay away from that ax, boy. Don't you touch it. I don't want you near it." He had that ax razor sharp, like a straight razor.

My father, he'd set there at night and hone that ax with a stone. No computers like modern society today. He had to have that ax sharp for morning. They were quite a bunch of chaps. I've seen them get in fights.

Here's a true story: I was a kid, probably, I'm going to kick it around nine years old. This old-timer that worked for my father back in the twenties, his name was Fred Gibbs. He was one of the stoutest men, my father said, he ever knew. His hand would make my father's hand look like a baby's. Fingers like gun barrels. They were huge.

My father was shoeing a horse one day there in the dooryard. He had the anvil setting there. Weighed about 150 pounds, that anvil.

Fred said, "Boy, I'm gonna tell you something. I'm gonna show you something. Only once. But you always remember it. You see that anvil. I'm gonna take that anvil by the horn and I'm gonna hold it right out straight. Then I'm gonna swing it over my head. And set it right back."

He clamped onto that sucker. He done just what he said. He held it right out straight, swung it over his head and set it right back down. Then that big gun barrel finger pointed right at me. He said, "Boy, when you are able to do that, you're gonna be a man."

I never forgot that.

When I was twenty-three, I used to take a twenty-pound sledge hammer, hold it right out straight. Then bring it back and touch my nose with it. So I was pretty stout. But I never tackled the anvil. That was a little too much for me. One of the biggest trees that I cut had 2,000 feet in it. That was a red oak. Oh, she was a huge one.

You know I worked all them years and I never got hurt.

Oh, once I almost lost my two legs. It happened because I was working with a wacky modern machine, a skidder. Stratton Mountain, Vermont. We had to go pretty near a mile from where we left our pickups in the morning up the mountain to where we were cutting. Jesus, by the time you walk a mile with your saw and your gas and chainsaw and all that, it's a long ways. You get tired. So I'd ride up on the skidder.

I sat on the hood of that skidder. My uncle would be in the cab where he could get in with my father. The blade of that skidder came right up tight to the radiator of that skidder, right up tight. My father would put it down a quarter ways so I could put my feet down on it to balance on the hood. Which was all right. He'd done it many, many, many times.

That morning, it had rained and the water was in the brooks so my father, he come along and drop the blade down and make a hole to let the water drain off. This one time, he dropped it down, he happened to look back to see where he was backing, and I was waiting for the blade to come back half way. The blade kept a-coming. The more you stepped on the throttle the faster that blade come up. Started crunching my feet. Crunching 'em. *Crrrrrrrrrrk*. Just like being in a wood splitter. Cracking 'em.

Holler. I think you could have heard me for twenty-three miles. It's a good thing that we was right in the middle of that big brook. When he let that blade up, I passed out and landed in that big brook, cold water, April. Brought me to. Kept me alive. Took me to the hospital. Didn't break a bone—just sprained 'em. ~

Harry, I can't feel your pain, but your story brings it right up tight.

STORIES ARE PUZZLES

You have to be intelligent to appreciate told stories in general and yankee humor in particular—wicked smaht—because stories are puzzles. Logic and a good imagination are musts. The best stories are not spread out before you like supper—beans to the right, ham to the left, brown bread in the middle flanked by butter and the pitcher of milk. The best stories take place mainly in the listener's head.

Fiddler, dance caller, writer and raconteur—ray-con-too-ah—Dudley Laufman tells this next story. It's short, international, and an example of how listeners connect the dots. When I tell it, there's always a little pause after the last line. A moment of silence. The words hang. And then people laugh. Usually.

A Fiddler Like Dudley

Who's heard of Dudley Laufman? He's a famous fiddler and dance caller from Canterbury, New Hampshire, and a National Treasure. He really is. The National Endowment for the Ahts says so. He tells this story and I pass it on to you.

Up in Newfoundland, Canada, there's a fiddler and dance caller like Dudley who fiddles by night, but by day is a lobster fisherman with his own boat and a mate and everything.

One day, this lobster fisherman was hauling in a trap when the rope caught around his hand and sliced off the end of his finger.

He looks at that bloody finger. He turns to his mate. He says, "Dere goes B-flat."

When I tell this story I hold up my right hand, look hard at my extended middle finger, and turn to my invisible "mate" before saying the last line.

One observant audience member pointed out that the right hand is for bowing, the left for pressing the strings to create the notes. I tried switching hands, but that only confused me. In my head, the Canadian lobster fisherman and fiddler is left-handed.

> **Ahts:** Noun, plural. Those activities in which a person known as an ahtist creates something unique from little more than imagination and raw materials—paint, stone, fabric, musical notes, words, you name it.

What's the difference between an aht and a craft? All I know is it takes a lot of craft to get anywhere near the vicinity of aht. Fiddlers fiddle. Storytellers tell. Writers write. Donald Murray—writer, teacher, mentor—when asked if he ever got writer's block, would say, "Plumbers don't get plumber's block." Plumbers plumb, writers write, tellers tell. The aht paht takes care of itself.

Smaht: Adjective. Intelligent, canny, intuitive. All the smaht people I know have good senses of humor.

Smaht people are smaht enough to know what they don't know. "Hard tellin' not knowin'," says the wise man.

Smaht people are smaht enough to recognize when they aren't being smaht. Variation: Smaht ass. A sassy pants with a quick wit who knows how to wield it.

This head scratcher from Barbara in East Kingston requires considerable dot connecting, trust in the audience, and vice versa. Typically, only one or two extra smaht listeners laugh right away. Sometimes nobody laughs except me. One fella groused: "Is that *it*?"

Auntie's Willow Ware

Barbara inherited a set of willow ware from her favorite aunt. What's willow ware? It's cups, saucers, plates, platters, and so forth. Blue and white. Collectible. Barbara didn't want to sell the china because it was precious to her, but she was curious about the value. So she took one piece to her local antiques dealer and explained about the inheritance. She didn't want to sell, she said, but "Could you tell me—just for my own curiosity—how much this soup tureen might be worth?"

The dealer said: "You ain't served any soup in it yet, have ya?"

Hilarious. But only if you know soup tureens resemble chamber pots. Question: What's the difference between a soup tureen and a chamber pot?

Answer: The soup tureen has a cutout in the lid for the ladle.

It's great if the answer—the key to understanding the joke—comes from the audience. More often than not, it does. When listeners talk back, they're engaged. When they're sassy, they're extra engaged: "Is that *it*?"

The perfect audience is stacked with smaht asses.

A mention in passing that I recently spent time at the state prison prompts the question, "How long were you in for?" Sometimes audience members earn the biggest laughs of the evening. I don't begrudge them. The success of a session is measured not by my stories, but theirs. I've heard all mine before.

Recently a teacher asked if I remembered a story she'd shared at a gathering some years ago. "Remind me," I said.

Seems a colleague had moved to Namibia (of all places) where she got engaged. When the teacher shared the news with her class, the kids wanted to send notes of congratulations. One girl wrote: "I'm so happy you got engaged, Miss Ford. My mother says a hard man is good to find."

"Now, I remember!" I said to the teacher. And I did. I remembered her rising to speak and how her story, rightfully, received the biggest laugh of the night. Teachers have magnificent senses of humor. They have to. It's a survival skill.

Note: This must be a true story. It's set in Namibia. Nobody from New England would make up a story set in Namibia.

Or would they?

At the beginning of "Auntie's Willow Ware," I ask, "Who knows what willow ware is?" Somebody will say, "It's china," or "an old pattern, blue and white." "Collectible," they'll say. "I have some," or "My grandmother had a set." The best response came from a tough old yankee. I could tell he was tough by the fold of his arms, the scar on his chin, and the glint in his left eye.

"What's willow ware?" I said.

"Dishes," he said flatly.

Nobody who hears "Auntie's Willow Ware" will ever mistake a chamber pot for a soup tureen. This is, in itself, a public service. Bonus: The subject of chamber pots, also called thunder jugs, prompts childhood memories among those of a certain age. On a good night, we'll ooze onto the subject of outhouses and from there to pranksters and practical jokes. Yankee humor can be subtle. But it can also be in-your-face slapstick. Some of the funniest stories combine the two.

George Washington and the Outhouse

The most classic of all classic outhouse stories features a couple of brothers who push an outhouse into the river. When their father demands to know what happened, Elmer, the younger one says, "Just like George

Washington, I cannot tell a lie. Me and Emery pushed the outhouse into the river."

Father gave the boys a thrashing. Or maybe it was an extended time-out.

"But Fathah," says Elmer, "George Washington told the truth about the cherry tree and he didn't get in trouble."

Father says, "That's because George Washington's fathah wa'n't in the cherry tree when he cut it down."

Fathah: Noun. Paterfamilias. Dad. In nuclear families, there's sometimes a fathah, mothuh, sistah, brothuh, and so fawth. In my family there was a fathah, mothuh, sistah (me), and two brothuhs. My fathah and mothuh are dead. One brothuh's dead and the other one doesn't speak to me. Which makes me an orphan and an only child.

WHAT DOESN'T KILL YOU MAY EVENTUALLY MAKE YOU LAUGH

It's not so bad being an orphan and an only child. They're all still with me in stories. Often I think: *Dad would have got a kick out of that*. Or, *Jeesh, that's something my mother would have said*. Or, *That guy's an elbow, just like my brothuh*. Dad used the term elbow to describe a person he didn't much like, in particular a human of the know-it-all-pompous-ass variety. I take after my dad in that particular aversion. Anything I can't stand is an elbow. I think Dad learned the term from Patrick McManus, an outdoor writer and humorist Dad enjoyed.

Pretty sure Dad read every book McManus ever wrote. He was a great reader. Always had a book going. Seems like the older Dad got, the more he read. When he became incapacitated with cancer, he read and read and read. When he was so sick he couldn't focus on the page, he listened to books on tape. He'd lie down on a blow-up bed in the spare room—so he wouldn't keep my mother awake—and listen to Sherlock Holmes all night long. When nothing else could take his mind off his illness, he turned to stories.

His last words became a story. Maybe they weren't his very last words, but pretty close.

At the hospital, he'd stopped eating and drinking. Potassium was being pumped into him at an alarming rate. One nurse said, as she hooked up the IV, "Somebody must not like him very much." I didn't ask her to elaborate. Should have. Wasn't thinking. My mind was in neutral. That was another of Dad's sayings. When somebody made a stupid mistake, he'd say they'd put their mind in neutral, like when my propane grill failed to light and I leaned over it with a lit match. Now we grill with charcoal.

The doctors wanted to move Dad from his hospital room to the hospice house, but inertia reigned. Hospital room, hospice room, as Bobby Valentine said of the pathetic 2012 Red Sox season, "What difference does it make?"

I stayed with him in the hospital nights and for the good part of every day for nearly three weeks. I didn't want him to die alone. That seemed important at the time. Toward the end, it occurred to me that Dad might like a final drink. He'd always enjoyed the sauce. I sneaked a flask of Laphroaig into his room. His eyes lit up at the sight. I dribbled some on his lip-moistening sponge and put it in his mouth. His eyes widened and he pulled a face. Though he hadn't spoken in a couple of days, he spoke then. "Needs to be cut," he said, clear as a bell.

How Are Your Dear Parents?

A man I'd known since he was a boy but hadn't seen in decades accosted me at a business event. We exchanged pleasantries. "And how are your parents doing?" he asked.

"Ma's doin' good," I said. "But Dad, not so much."

"Oh," he said. "What's the trouble?"

"He's dead."

Dad would have got a kick out of that. He enjoyed a mawbid joke.

Mawbid: Adjective. Characterized by or appealing to an interest in disturbing subjects like death, illness, or injury. Making light of disturbing subjects helps you cope. It does me, anyway.

Dad would also have enjoyed "Nolan and the Vault"—coming up—about a childish prank well executed. It has a couple of things going for it. The little guys put one over on the big guys. And it takes place on a dark and stormy night in a cemetery. It's also a bare-bones story that depends on listeners to fill in the spooky effects with their own memories of being small and in a strange place after dark when maybe they would have been better off snuggled under the covers in their own warm beds.

Reminds me of a cold and windy Halloween night, trick-or-treating. I was little and chasing after the bigger kids—probably the Huckins boys and my friend Patty. Clad in the only store-bought costume I ever recall having, I was a light-footed fairy princess in pale blue taffeta with a crown and a magic wand until I fell down and my dress got all dirty. But that wasn't the worst part. The worst part was I lost my magic wand. I've been looking for it ever since.

John Rule tells a similar story of childhood loss. He was riding with his parents and brother to go swimming. He had a new beach ball and was pretty excited about it. As they were driving along the flat stretch past the County Farm in Boscawen, windows down—it was a hot day— his ball flew out the window. He saw it bounce off the road and land in a swale. He yelled for his father to turn the car and go back for it.

Nope.

That was the last John ever saw of his beach ball. And every time we drive along that flat stretch past the County Farm and see that wetland on the left, he looks for that long-lost beach ball. I swear he does. And so do I.

Nolan and the Vault

Nolan and his friend, Pret, were walking home after a school function with a group of bigger boys. It was dark and cold. Moon clouded over. Spittin' snow. Their path would take them past a cemetery with a stone vault, also known as a receiving tomb or a crypt.

As they walked, the older boys got to daring each other:

When we get theyah, let's go in the vault.
I dare ya.
You're too chicken.
YOU'RE too chicken.
It's probably locked anyways.
What if it's not?
Nawthin' in theyah. Nobody's died lately.
You sure?

As the big boys argued, Nolan and Pret slipped from the back of the pack and took a shortcut through the woods. They beat the big boys to the cemetery by a hair and scaled the slanted back wall of the vault. At the top, they found a small vent pipe and waited.

They could hear the older boys coming down the road, still daring each other. Nolan and Pret stayed quiet. The group congregated at the gate. Whispering and jostling and giggling.

At last, one brave boy walked up to the vault, and knocked on the big heavy door.

Nelson said into the vent pipe in his deepest voice: "I'll be right with you."

A SKOSH ASKEW

Much humor is unintentional and unselfconscious. It reflects a way of looking at the world that's a little different, a skosh askew. Yankee humor is dry, earthy, and philosophical. The twist that creates the joke floats just far enough below the surface that listeners have to dip for it. Same with meaning. To get the full benefit, you have to work a little. It's like dipping for smelt in Walker Brook. Sometimes your net comes up full. Sometimes empty. You have to stand in the dark and get your feet wet to net a mess of smelt. Your timing must be impeccable. Smelt run when they run and stop when they stop. But are they ever delicious deep-fried and crispy. You eat them bones and all. But not the heads. Cut off the heads. You don't want to be eating eyeballs and brains. Not even tiny ones.

Same with yankee humor. You eat it bones and all. It ain't pretty. It ain't fancy. But it can be satisfying.

Skosh: Adjective. A little bit. More than a smidge, less than a dite, but not much.

Around the table on the screened porch at the house on Corn Hill Road (that's Cawn Hill Road) in Boscawen (that's Boscoin) eating deep-fried smelt from a paper-towel-lined mixing bowl, the whole family tucks in. The table was Formica, the floor plywood painted black, the bowl large and full of smelts no bigger than my finger. Us kids—my brother Robert and me—could eat as many as we wanted because Dad had gone out in the middle of the night and netted a bushel, seemed like. My little brother Steve was just a baby if he was born at all. I picture him in a car seat on top of the chest freezer against the porch wall. He might have been present for the big smelt feed or not. I can't remember.

I may or may not have gone smelting with Dad the night before. Sometimes he took Robert and me, sometimes not—depended on how late he expected to be out and, maybe, how much liquor he expected to drink to stay wahm.

Thanks, Dad, for catching those smelts and thanks, Ma, for frying them up. It was one of the best meals I ever ate. The circumstances—me, my brother(s), Ma and Dad, steamy summer evening, screened porch, abundant smelt—were never to be repeated, as are so many special moments in our lives. Just the once and never again. All that remains is the story.

Cawn: Noun. A yellow vegetable that grows on stalks. Makes a wonderful chowdah with milk, onions, potatoes, and a little fried salt pork for flavor. Ma said she and her sister, Lila, made a pot of cawn chowdah one noontime and served it up to much acclaim. "Delicious," said the husbands and kids of which I was one. Only later did Ma and Lila realize they'd forgotten to add the cawn.

Chowdah: A soup made with milk or cream (if you're rich). Start by frying salt pork in the bottom of a heavy kettle. Add onions and brown them. Add potatoes chopped but not too small. Add clams for clam chowdah or cawn for cawn chowdah. When the clams or cawn are cooked, add the milk or cream (if you're rich) and heat through. Add salt, pepper, or paprika (optional) to taste.

Boscoin: The correct pronunciation of the town I grew up in, Boscawen. This I know because when I was just learning to read, when I pictured the name it was B-O-S-C-O-I-N. That's how the people around me said it. That's how I said it and say it still.

I haven't lived in Boscawen for over forty years. Since my time there, the proper pronunciation has become a topic of debate. Some say Bos-cow-en. Some say Bosquine. Some say Bosquin. But I'll go to my grave saying Boscoin and remembering a happy childhood in the little house at the intersection of Cawn Hill and Knowlton Road.

The Difference Between Durham and Gorham

There are many different New Hampshires. It's a small state with distinct regions. Hanover is home to Dartmouth College, chock full of book-smaht people from away. Same with Durham, home to the University of New Hampshire. Most of the professors there are not homegrown and neither are their kids. Gorham, on the other hand, lies on the far side of the notches—a true North Country town.

Visiting a high school English class in Durham, I mentioned Thomas Williams. Among my favorites of Williams' short stories is "Horned Pout are Evil." The title seemed to puzzle the students. "Who knows what a hawnpout is?" I asked.

One young man raised his hand and ventured: "Is it a bird?"

A week later—true story—I was at the Ed Fenn school in Gorham. The third graders and I were writing a story together, trying to decide what animal might serve as our main character. "What kind of animals do you have around here?" I asked. They named them off: deer, bear, moose. "Oh," I said. "Let's write about a moose. First you have to know about your character. What's a moose like?"

A boy raised his hand.

"What's a moose like?" I repeated.

"Delicious," he said.

And that's the difference between Durham and Gorham.

Hawnpout: Noun. A fish of the catfish variety with sharp fins and thin, wiggly, black appendages poking out from its face. Handle with care—those fins cut like slimy razor blades.

UNDER THE INFLUENCE

Thomas Williams changed my life. I was maybe eleven years old when Connie Broughton, the Boscawen town librarian, suggested I read Williams' novel *Whipple's Castle*. She said, "I think you'll like this, Becky. It's about New Hampshire and it's by a New Hampshire writer." Connie didn't realize that, despite the word "castle" in the title and the gothic house on the cover, this was not a kids book.

Later (after she read it), she said, "Maybe I shouldn't have recommended it. It's really a book for grown-ups."

But I'm forever grateful she did. For one thing, I'd never read a sex scene before. More than that, *Whipple's Castle* proved that books were written about my own state, by people who lived in my own state. A New Hampshire person could be a writer. I could be a writer. That was a revelation.

Years later, I studied with Tom Williams at UNH. In our first class, he asked what book we'd read last. I said *The Shepherd of the Hills* by Harold Bell Wright, a book from my grandparents' closet. He said, "I haven't heard that name in a long time." This was in 1973. Only later did I realize *The Shepherd of the Hills* was published in 1907. He must have thought me an odd duck.

I learned so much from him. When I wrote a story about a person with a mean rooster, he said to have the character cut off the rooster's head. I didn't. But I should have. Thinking about killing a mean rooster is one thing. Chopping its head off, that's a story.

When I struggled with a description of a dirty bathroom, he crossed out all my adverbs and adjectives until all that remained was, "A hair curled in the sink."

When I overshot an ending, he pointed to a paragraph on the next-to-last page and said, "Your story ends here." He was right.

He told our class that in the final edit of his latest novel, he took out all the *that*s. Hundreds of them. I never write a *that* without wondering if it's necessary and remembering Tom Williams.

Mostly, he encouraged me. He read beginnings of stories to the class. After each lead he'd say, "Is this a story?" When he read mine and asked the question, some students said no, but he stepped in. "Yes," he said. "This is a story." It was the first paragraph of my first publication in *Yankee* magazine. The story begins:

My brother Thomas's snowshoes were bigger than mine, though he was smaller than me. Father made the snowshoes. It took a long time because the ash for the frames had to be aged and steamed into shape. The deer hide had to be soaked in the brook until the hair floated off and then tanned in our cellar. One year the neighbor's dog dragged the hide out of the brook and chewed it. Father saw the tracks. He found the ruined hide. Later, he shot the dog. I think the neighbors knew, but they never said so.

That story, "Walking the Trapline," wrote itself. It seemed to rise from the earth, pass through my body, and spill out on the page. Tommy Makem described writing folk songs that way—rising from the earth, passing through the soles of your feet and through your body, as if they always were and always would be. You just happened to be in the right place at the right time for them to find you.

A lot of revision went into getting the words just right in "Walking the Trapline." It is based on a true event from childhood, but the story itself seemed to come into being whole—a beginning, middle, and ending. It hatched. Some say it's the best story I ever wrote, which is sad, considering it was among the first. Seems like I should have made a little progress over the years.

I wished some day my dad and Tom Williams would meet. Maybe go fishing together. That seemed like a thing that ought to happen, but it never did.

I wished some day my dad and Tommy Makem would have a sit down and swap stories. Have a little sing-song. That also seemed like a thing that ought to happen, but it never did.

The best I can do is remember them and tell their stories.

Here's my best Tommy Makem story. Andi Axman, editor of *NH Home* magazine, asked me to write a holiday piece for the December issue. This was a challenge. What could be said about the holidays that hadn't been said before? Then I remembered Newgrange.

Solstice—The Sun Stands Still

This time of year, we move stoically through our days as darkness eats the light, confident that December 21st will come—it always has before—and it'll be light's turn. Some years ago, after the darkness that followed 9/11 but not long after, my family and I toured Ireland, where this time of year the nights are even longer than they are here. Our guides were famed Irish folk musician Eugene Byrne and the Bard himself, Tommy Makem, singer and songwriter. Immigrants the two of them, they called New Hampshire home and raised their families here. On the tour, we stayed in castles and haunted hotels. We learned history and folklore. We may have enjoyed sips of poteen at a farm with a panoramic view for spotting revenuers. We sang every night. We stopped on the bridge where Tommy got the idea for "Four Green Fields," his most famous ballad. Some tunes, Tommy said, rise up from the earth into your body.

We lingered at Newgrange in the Boyne Valley, an archeological site older than Stonehenge and the Egyptian pyramids. It's an acre-sized dome, grassy on top with a stone foundation carved with triple spirals, triangles, leaves, and flowers—more cathedral than tomb.

We slipped behind the monolith that guards the entrance and passed beneath a capstone so weighty that if it had fallen, a person would surely have been smushed. But that stone had held fast for 5,000 years, so we weren't too worried. We walked along a narrow passage—careful, don't hit your head. The floor rises as you move deeper into the mound. At the end of the passage, the stones open into a cruciform chamber, not large, but large enough for us to gather.

Here Tommy Makem told of his initial visit to Newgrange some years earlier. When he first set foot in the chamber, he recognized it. He knew he had seen this place before. Deja vu? No—stronger than that. He *knew* he had been inside this stone chamber before. But something was missing. A feather.

His guide at that time assured him there were no feathers carved in these stones. But he was just as sure he had seen one. In this place. A place he had never visited in this lifetime.

Then the guide stepped to one side and he saw it—the feather. Her body had blocked it from view. "It's not a feather," she said, "it's a fern."

When Tommy finished telling the story to our group, he stepped aside, so we too could see the fern that looked like a feather. Or was it a feather that looked like a fern? The power of his words and the power of that sacred place made me feel as though I, too, had been here before.

Tommy visited Newgrange many times. He was among the special few to wait within the chamber for sunrise on one December 21. It's a chancy thing, the sight of a rising sun on any given morning in Ireland—that green and misty place. But if, like Tommy Makem, you have the privilege of being inside Newgrange at dawn on the solstice, when the clouds part and the sun shines, you witness a transformation.

A small opening in the stone ceiling allows a narrow beam of sunlight to penetrate the absolute darkness of the chamber. The beam reaches ceiling to floor. As the sun rises, the beam widens—slowly, slowly—until, at the end of seventeen minutes, the entire room and everyone in it is illuminated. Winter solstice—the return of light to the Earth, and the promise of more to come.

On the darkest and longest night of 2016—the night of the lunar eclipse on December 20—I attended a select board meeting in O' Little Town of Northwood to report on it for the local online paper.

During a lull, a story came to me. I hadn't thought about it in a long time but its coming confirmed the notion that every story I've ever told (or heard) is still in my head, somewhere, just waiting to pop out. Here goes:

Most Romantic

Two brothers tried to outdo one another in most things—even their choice of wedding days. One brother bragged, "I'm the most romantic. I married my wife on June 21, the longest day of the year. I wanted our special day to last as long as possible."

The other brother said, "I married my wife on December 20, the longest night of the year."

THEY JUST KEEP COMING

Years ago, I met up with Paul Currier at Grantham Town Hall. Paul asked if I recalled a story he shared last time we met, a few years earlier. "What is it?" I asked. He reminded me. I'd call it a yankee classic, but Paul is positive it happened to his uncle—not just positive but adamant—so we'll go with that.

I have to hear a story two or three times before it sticks, so Paul's patience is appreciated. Here's his true story about his uncle and a Canadian trucker.

Paul Currier's Uncle and a Canadian Trucker Have a Go-Round

Said the trucker: "I was rolling along with a load of logs, come to a long steep downgrade and, wouldn't you know, the brakes failed. I was picking up speed, headed for disaster on the curve I knew was coming, when a tire blew. That slowed me, but the truck kept going at a good clip down that steep hill. I thought I was a goner. Knew for a fact I'd never make the curve at that speed. Knew for a fact the truck and me would sail off into the ravine and that would be the end of me. I closed my eyes and started to say my prayers. Then another tire blew. And another. And another. Six in all. Those blowouts slowed me down just enough I could pull over to the side of the road and I was saved."

Said Paul's uncle: "I was out hawnpouting in the dead of night with some buddies. We was fishing by the light of a kerosene lantern and having good luck, until somebody leaned the wrong way and the boat flipped. We swum to shore. Had to pull the upside-down boat behind us. We lost the poles, the tackle, the fish we'd caught. We even lost the lantern.

"Next morning, we went back. Rowed the boat out to where we'd been fishing, near as we could figure. Lowered a grappling hook, and sure enough, managed to locate and haul up most of what we'd lost: the poles, the tackle, the hornpout still in the bucket. We even got the kerosene lantern back. And you know what? That lantern was still lit."

Said the trucker: "You're pulling my leg. There's no way that lantern would have still been lit."

Said the uncle: "I'll blow out the lantern if you blow up five of them six tires."

An overturned boat is almost always funny, so long as nobody drowns. It's symbolic, I guess, of life being turned upside down and the struggle to right it. Here's another Paul Currier story:

A Rainy Day Tale

Eldon and Alden were out duck hunting on a drizzly day. They set out fifteen decoys, slid their eight-foot skiff up tight to the weeds, erected a camouflage tarp. The plan was that one would steady the boat while the other took the shot.

After a bit, they counted decoys and somehow now there were sixteen. One took off, they forgot the plan, and both let go with four barrels, knocking them back. The aft end of that little boat went under. The boat began to fill and kept on filling. They were in only about three feet of water, so they stood in the pond and tipped the water out.

As they held the boat aloft between them, they noticed onshore a line of kids from the Cardigan Mountain Camp. Hiking. One kid says, "Why you got that boat over your head?"

Eldon says, "Cause it's raining."

Nancy Richards of Mason tells a story of a remote pond that is also a cautionary tale. Stories teach us how to be in this world, and the moral of this story is a good one to heed.

A Foggy Day at Lonesome Lake

Up at Lonesome Lake, Nancy and a friend had finished a long hike and they were hot. The fog was thick, so they thought, "Why not?" and went for a cooling swim.

Hadn't been in long when the fog, all of a sudden, lifted, revealing two boats, closer than you'd expect and manned with fishermen who were looking their way.

"What did you do then?" I asked.

"We told them to turn around and don't look," Nancy said, adding, "Never skinny dip in the fog."

My little room at the little house on Corn Hill Road was maybe ten feet by ten feet including a doorless closet with a ladder and trapdoor to the attic. My brother Robert and I shared that room when we were small. Our twin beds pretty near filled it. Dad cut a hole through the wall, neatly framed, so he and Ma could hear us if we got into difficulty.

When we got bigger, Ma and Dad added on to the house—a whole new living room and bedroom, so Robert got the old living room for his bedroom. The piano from Grammie and Grampa Stewart's house made a partition so he could have privacy.

I liked my room better. It didn't have a door, but the curtain where the door might have been gave me all the privacy I needed. It was my haven.

But at night, it could get scary. I was prone to nightmares. Still am. Up until I got my tonsils out in second grade, I was plagued with tonsillitis, strep throat, and the fevers that went with it. Spent a lot of time in bed. Missed a lot of school. Fever dreams made me prickly all over, falling and falling. In nightmares—or maybe they were night terrors—all kinds of monsters climbed down from that attic, pushed through my hung-up clothes, slinked into my room and hovered over my bed. So real were those monsters, I'd pull my hand from under the covers and strike out at them. Never made contact. They were too quick. Or maybe they were without substance, like ghosts. Either way, they scared the hell out of me.

Over my bed Dad built a shelf, painted robins-egg blue like the walls, special for my books. I kept them in alphabetical order and even had a card system for lending them to friends. In my next life I'll be a librarian. And a musician.

My room had two windows. One faced the road, so I could see the comings and goings from my little desk. I loved being at that desk. Writing or drawing. Watching the world through the window. Come to think of it, I still sit at a window-facing desk, watching the world. As I write these words, wet snow falls on the overgrown evergreen hedge. The road is dark and slick. The cars shush by. It's a busy road. I don't pay much attention to the cars. I barely hear them. I barely see them. It's the snow I see. The bend of branches. The trees in the wetland across the way. When I look up from my work, I'm looking for wildlife. Birds, especially. From this window I've seen hawks, owls, cardinals, blue jays. I've seen squirrels galore. Woodchucks. Stray dogs. Sometimes I spot one of my own dogs escaped from the backyard. That always gives me a start.

Once, years ago, I saw a meandering moose.

Once I saw four police officers walking down the road abreast. Heavily armed. They were after a bad guy with whom other officers had had a shoot-out in the cemetery on Route 4. That sighting turned into a short story.

Writers need windows.

The chair for my childhood desk at the window of my childhood bedroom stood on a fluted metal base, intended to be bolted to the floor. It wasn't, so it was kind of tippy. When I changed a light bulb standing on that chair, over it went, and the metal base hit me square in the back. It hurt for a long time. Didn't tell my parents. If I was stupid enough to stand on that tippy chair, I deserved what I got. Besides, I knew what they'd say. Dad would say, "Must have put your mind in neutral." Ma would say, "You know better than to stand on that tippy chair." Evidently, I didn't.

The other window faced the hill. Our house was built into a hill, the woods held back by a retaining wall my dad built stone by stone. To get the boulders down to size, he'd spend hours with hammer and chisel pounding holes until the rock split. He'd come home from work, have a little supper, then spend the rest of the evening pounding until it was too dark to pound anymore. I pretended the rock dust, soft as chalk, was magic, saved it in folded bits of cloth or paper, and hid it away.

The sound of Dad pounding away at rocks is among the soundtracks of my childhood. He seemed to really enjoy it. He often told the story of the Jehovah's Witnesses who came to call. Asked if Dad had a minute to talk, Dad said, "Yes. If you can talk louder than I can pound, go right ahead." The Witnesses didn't even try.

When Bill Twombly of Wakefield described his love of splittin' rocks, my mind snapped back to my dad. That's probably why I liked Bill's story so much.

About Like Splittin' Rocks

An old-timer named Bill, a native, enjoys splitting boulders. And he's good at it. He uses the hammer and chisel method—wedges, half rounds, feathers. To split a stone with a feather, that's really something. Bill can.

Pound, pound, pound. You pound long enough, hard enough, steady enough in the right place on any rock—granite, quartz, feldspar, what have you—it'll give eventually. That's Bill's attitude.

My dad also liked to split rocks. Took pride in it. "I may not be able to out-muscle that rock," Dad said. "And I probably won't outlast it—but I'm pretty sure I can outsmart it."

When Bill has an audience for rock-splitting, which he usually does because it's so interesting, he'll *pound, pound, pound*, and the people gather around. Just as the rock is about to split, he'll tell them: "Now you're about to see something no one has ever see before."

The rock splits.

And there it is—something no one has ever seen before: the inside of the rock, all its secrets revealed. ∼

Bill's story might have slipped away except for the connection it has to growing up and my dad and the wall he built that held back the hill. The stories that stick—the ones that want to be told—are the ones that connect. I don't want to get too philosophical, but what is life except a sequence of moments recalled? When we tell stories, we revisit, reorganize, and prioritize those moments. We create something unique and true. In a way, we create ourselves.

THROUGH THE WINDOW

Between my window and the retaining wall, there were, maybe, eight feet of stubbly grass, moss, plantings, and weeds. Mayflowers grew along the top of the wall in early spring. I tried to transplant them when we sold the house—after Dad died, after Ma came to live with us in Northwood—but they didn't take. Mayflowers, like lady's slippers and blueberries, grow prolifically where they choose to grow, but don't like to be moved.

Not much sunlight penetrated the space between the wall and the house, so the vegetation was sparse, the soil tamped hard from footsteps.

As if I didn't have enough trouble with monsters climbing down from the attic in the middle of the night, one night aliens invaded that space and shone a bright light through my window—so bright it hurt my eyes even though I kept them shut. The aliens had come to abduct me in their UFO. I lay still under layers of blankets. Against all odds, the blankets protected me. I still sleep under layers of blankets, two or three at least (except when it's hot). I appreciate the weight as much as the warmth.

Either the aliens didn't see me, couldn't get the window open, or decided I wasn't worth the trouble, because they went away and never came back.

If they had come back, my plan was to run to the woods. I knew the woods behind our house better than any aliens ever could. Come to think of it, that's still my plan. I know the woods behind our house here in Northwood pretty well—miles of it stretching all the way up Old Mountain Road to Saddleback Mountain, Betty Meadows, and the state park. In the event of an alien invasion, deep woods are probably the safest place.

Nawthin' Much

My father always said, "Nawthin' to be afraid of in the woods around here, Beck." I believed him. Animals were way more scared of us than we were of them. Not smart to get between a mama bear and her cubs, he said. But that's just common sense. I spotted a mama chowing down and cubs romping on the far edge of the blueberry field. Those cubs were "awful cunnin'," as my mother would say, but I stepped back, stood quiet, and did my heavy looking-on from a distance.

Even as a child, the woods didn't scare me. Neither did bears. Nor moose.

UFOs, on the other hand, gave me pause. In 1961, Betty and Barney Hill of Portsmouth were abducted by aliens near Indian Head in Lincoln. The Hills were driving home late at night from Canada. They got grabbed and probed by some short gray fellas, then sent on their way.

I was six. The Hills' encounter didn't surprise me. My family spent more than one summer evening by the lake watching the sky for UFOs. I kept my eyeballs peeled and tried my best to stay awake.

One night on the road home, we saw one. It slid silently over the top of the car then disappeared. Don't know where it went or what it was after, but I was glad it wasn't after us.

UFOs connected in my child brain to nuclear war—probably all that glowing. In school we learned about the mushroom cloud, shock wave, radiation, how to make a splint from a broom handle and turn a sleeve into a tourniquet. By fourth grade, I knew for sure if the UFOs didn't get us, the mushroom cloud would.

Not much I could do about the radiation. "In the event of a nuclear disaster," as the man on the black and white films intoned, I'd be cooked and so would everybody I loved. We had no bunker. If we had time, I thought, maybe we could drive to Grammie and Grampa Stewart's big house on the hill in Danbury. They had a deep dirt cellar with no windows. Maybe the radiation wouldn't get us there.

I was a teenager when Walter Bower, Sr. of Webster spotted Bigfoot, nine feet tall, reaching into his apple tree. The *Concord Monitor* said Bower was upset because nobody believed him.

I believed him. Dad had seen Bigfoot tracks many times. He took pictures.

On a snowmobile expedition from Boscawen to Kearsarge Mountain and back, four out of six snowmobiles broke down. Huddled by the fire in the deep woods, awaiting rescue, we sensed Bigfoot watching from the darkness. I wasn't afraid. Bigfoots are notoriously shy. "How do you think the Bigfoots got here?" somebody whispered.

Dad said, "The UFOs brung 'em."

Now that I'm grown, I'm not so sure about UFOs or Bigfoot, and my fingers are crossed regarding nuclear war. Not much scares me these days. I hear my father's voice: "Nawthin' to be afraid of around here, Beck."

Nawthin' much.

LOSS SHAPES US

I miss my dad. Same with my mom. It's been years since they left us, but it's still hard to believe in a world without them. I try to give as much weight to their living as to their dying, but it's hard. Was Dad scared to die? I'm not sure, but he was really pissed about it. Ma, on the other hand, eased by dementia, said toward the end of her life, "I don't worry about nothin'." She'd always been a great one for worrying—suspicious and afraid for much of her adult life. But in the last two or three years—especially when she was living with us, surrounded and by family and cats and dogs—she feared nothing. Certainly not death. In the end, I think, she welcomed it. She was ready to go.

Life After Death

The son, at his mother's bedside as she lay dying, asked if she believed there was life after death.

"Lawd, I hope not," she said. "I'm tired." ~

The longer you live, the more you become acquainted with sickness and death. If you're lucky, the people you love don't die out of turn. My parents were forever changed by the death of my brother, Stephen, who died out of turn at age eighteen, two months before high school graduation. After his death, my parents were all of a sudden sadder, slower, older. Beaten down.

Steve got drunk at a party, fought with his girlfriend, took off, and drove his brand new truck into a tree on Clothespin Bridge Road in Webster. He died on the spot of massive trauma. In fantasy, I get to the truck before he dies, touch his poor smashed head and heal it. In a dream soon after he died, the world ended in massive nuclear explosions and my final thought is, "Steve was only a little ahead of us, so it's all right now."

Dad stopped drinking for a few years after Steve died. He said he liked the drink too much and wouldn't hurt my mother by becoming a drunk. When he started drinking again, I saw it as a return to normalcy. It wasn't. When someone dies out of turn—especially your child—normalcy flies out the window.

Steve was twelve years younger than me. I mothered him. Adored him. If Steve hadn't died, I wonder, how would life be different? When I think of him, I picture him six years old with dark, wide-set eyes, and hair so dark it was almost black. Like mine.

KINDRED VOICES

One of the first things David Emerson ever said to me was, "I've already died twice." He'd survived two heart attacks. He'd died during those attacks and been brought back to life. He was a walking miracle as well as an historian, storyteller, and a devilishly funny man. I met him at a writing conference where he knelt before me like a knight of the realm and declared: "You are a goddess!" I liked him right away.

Later I learned he'd mistaken me for someone else, Susan Poulin. Susan does a one-woman show called *Ida: Woman Who Runs With the Moose*. At the time David and I met, I was calling myself the Moose of Humor. *New Hampshire* magazine named me Thalia, Muse of Comedy, in its list of NH Muses. A man with a lisp introduced me as "Thalia, the moose of humor," hence the nickname. David got his mooses mixed up.

He grew up in what he called Chatham-New-Hampshire-Sister-City-to-Stow-Maine (all one word). He loved to talk about Big Marge—his diminutive mother—and a cadre of eccentric neighbors. One couple was notorious for driving real slow on back roads with no room for passing. They got a new car and, as David tells the story, it was a speedy one. "We got going fawty-five miles an hour," the missus said. "Wa'n't I scay-ed."

Scay-ed: Adjective. Frightened.

Fawty-five: Adjective. More than forty. Less than fifty.

David and I—not unlike Mickey Rooney and Judy Garland—decided to "put on a show." We called it *Full of Moxie*, his idea. Moxie is a carbonated beverage. Around here some of us call bubbly beverages "tonic," which is pretty accurate when applied to Moxie since it was originally marketed for the health benefits of one of its ingredients, gentian root. It's a sweet, fruity soda with a bitter aftertaste.

David and I decorated the stage with a pyramid of Moxie cans. He refused to take them home after the show. Being frugal, I did. It took three years to pawn them off on unsuspecting visitors.

We charged for tickets. I said, "David, I don't think people are going to pay much to see me tell stories. Don't know about you."

He said, "They'll pay. I'm playing the cancer card." He had recently been diagnosed.

They came, they paid, we told stories for a couple of hours.

Of all the storytellers with whom I've shared a stage, David's voice was the best match for mine in outlook and subject matter—small towns, small-town characters and their foibles. His story about the farting horse (fahtin' hoss) and the schoolteacher brought down the house.

David died after a long bout with multiple myeloma—same as my dad—a real stinker of a cancer. In his lengthy instructions regarding his funeral, he stipulated that I tell a story—one of just three speakers, along with his wife and his best friend. I was puzzled. David had many friends. Why me? His wife, Susan Bruce, explained: "He said you're funny and draw a good crowd."

The funeral included a parade down Main Street, Conway, during tourist season. Traffic stopped. The tourists were puzzled and annoyed. Friends marched and twirled black umbrellas per his instructions. His pets, including a turtle and chickens, also participated. At the reception, vegetarian dishes were to be turned away at the door. The funereal jar, front and center, was secured with duct tape.

One woman said David's was the second best funeral she'd ever attended. "What was the best one?" I asked.

"My husband's," she said.

What story to tell at David's funeral? I agonized over this. A funeral is a one-shot opportunity. People remember what's said forever. You want to be funny but not too funny. You want to be irreverent (maybe) but not too irreverent. You don't want to talk too long. Or too short. Poignant? Maybe. But not sappy. David despised sappy.

In the end, I chose a story he'd told at *Full of Moxie* that seemed profound, though I can't explain just how. Luckily, a good story doesn't need explaining.

Maynard Record's Beagle Dog

Maynard Record ran a gas station at the crossroads of Chatham, New Hampshire, and Stow, Maine. His beagle dog loved nothing more than to sleep in the exact geographic center of that crossroads, plumb in the middle of traffic. Luckily, in those days, there wa'n't much. Locals knew to watch out for Maynard Record's beagle dog. They'd see him asleep in the middle of the road and they'd swerve.

Maynard Record's beagle dog not only slept in the crossroads on sunny days, he was apt to be out there in the rain, fog, snow, hurricanes, what-have-you. He always slept in the same spot, so locals, even if they couldn't see him because of pea soup fog or blinding snow, knew exactly when and where to swerve.

The dog lived a good long life. So did Maynard Record. They're both gone now, but at the crossroads of Chatham, New Hampshire, and Stow, Maine—rain or shine, fog or snow, good visibility or pea soup—the locals still swerve.

On the Other Hand

Pam says to Esther, "Your cousin Gail's funeral's tomorrow, isn't it?"
Esther says, "I ain't going to Gail's funeral."
"Really?"
"Not on your life. She wouldn't come to mine."

One of my favorite teaching exercises involves an egg. I ask participants to write about it without using the word *egg*. What does it look like, feel like, remind them of? What's special about it? "Be inspired by this object," I say. "See where it leads you." After a few minutes, each of us copies one sentence from what we've brainstormed onto an index card. The cards are collected. We read them aloud one by one and guess who wrote what. We're almost always right—whether we've spent a few hours together or a semester. We can tell by word choice, sentence structure, and where each writer's imagination went: egg as architectural masterpiece, egg as sustenance, egg as fertility symbol, egg as fairy house, egg as weapon, egg as head. We recognize each other's voices.

If you asked ten storytellers to tell a story involving an egg, we'd scurry back to our ten different bailiwicks—our fertile territory, the source of our stories—and look for eggs. In mine, after a bit of thought, I find a couple.

In one, the city cousin comes to the country and, eager to help, collects a basket of eggs from the henhouse. When she shows Auntie her bounty, Auntie tells her those eggs will make a poor breakfast. They're wooden.

Then there's the egg story Dick Wakefield tells about Uncle Bub Wakefield and Wes Tewksbury of Tamworth.

Wes's Eggs

During prohibition, Wes had a bunch of buddies over on a Saturday night to play cards and sample his home brew. On the table sat a big bowl of raw eggs, must have been two or three dozen. As the evening wore on, the buddies got to breaking the raw eggs into the mugs of brew and slurping them down. Nourishment, you might say.

Eventually the bowl emptied. "Got any more eggs, Tewksbury?" one of the buddies asked.

"Nope," he said. "Only got the one hen."

The most important thing we bring to the table is ourselves. Ten people write about the same object at the same time in the same place—the egg—and come out with ten completely different stories. And by completely different, I mean *completely different*. Same egg, unique voices.

We can even tell the exact same story in the exact same words and it will still sound different. It might even *mean* different. We emphasize different words. We pause at different places and for different lengths of time. We speak faster or slower. We pronounce words differently. You say Anti; I say Awntie. You say evening, breaking, and slurping; I say evenin', breakin', and slurpin', all with the silent *g*. You say Tewks-bur-ry; I say Tewks-bree, like Bob Tewks-bree from Pennycook (Penacook), who went to my same high school a few years behind me and pitched for the Yankees.

Take this sentence, once uttered by my daughter, age five, upon returning from Disney World to find her pet duckling stiff and dead in a paper bag left on the porch by the house sitter. "Leafo is dead," Adi said.

Say it out loud. Put some emotion into it. Try sorrow. "Leafo is dead." Try amazement. "Leafo is dead." Try anger. "Leafo is dead." Try resignation. "Leafo is dead."

Adi is pithy. She kin be. On the train ride from Florida to New Hampshire after our extravagant Disney World vacation, she said: "Disney World's not all it's cracked up to be." Say it out loud. Say it with sorrow, amazement, anger, or resignation.

She said it like a true yankee—matter-of-factly. "Disney World's not all it's cracked up to be."

EMBRACE EVOLUTION

Stories will change over time and you probably don't even notice. In the fish story, the fish gets bigger. Many years ago, Heather Pike kindly sent an audiotape of stories. The tape was made by Heather's grandmother, Corrine Morse, in 1973. It's a tape of Heather's great-grandfather (Corrine's dad), Warren Angus Wilbur—in his eighties at the time. On the tape, in the background, are the voices of family members egging Warren on—"remember the time," "tell us the one about."

Heather wrote about Corrine: "A home ec teacher who loved to cook, wrote cookbooks, loved her family, and loved the outdoors, too. She was quite a lady when ladies were ladies. I remember the year my uncle towed the toboggan with his motorcycle in the snow and I fell off and hurt my hands on the crust; my grandmother was furious. She never lost her temper except that one time she spoke sharply to my uncle."

Warren Angus Wilber, known in the family as Pa and to friends as Doc, worked as a machinist at United Shoe. He loved to hunt, fish, and tell stories, many about his hometown of Seabrook, known for its unusual dialect. Heather wrote: "He used to say 'don't say *hunh* say *whatsa*' to me as a kid, and when he swore, he said 'mygolrifus' at his worst, and he used 'shan't' in speech. Always wore a hat and remembered fishing up country when all was done on horseback."

I've been telling several stories from that tape for years. Not long ago, I looked back at the transcription and compared what Warren Angus Wilbur actually said to what I say when I tell his stories. My renditions have strayed a good long way from the originals. In the story "Boston Wife," for example, I leave off the whole last line. Not on purpose—it just fell away like poor little Colin Feral's tail. Also, I got the name of Warren's friend wrong. How the heck did that happen?

Here's the story as I tell it now:

Boston Wife
My Version

Warren Angus Wilbur, walking down the street in Seabrook, meets his friend Alan.

"Alan, how you doing?"

"Good."

"How's your wife?"
"I don't know."
"What do you mean you don't know?"
"She's down to Boston visiting her sister."
"How long's she been in Boston visiting her sister?"
"About a year and a half."
"Your wife's been in Boston visiting her sister for a year and a half?"
"Ayuh. Last time I seen her, she said when it was time to come home, come get her."

Here's the transcription—the story as Warren told it on the tape.

Boston Wife
Original

He says, "Austin, how's your wife?"
"Well," Austin says, "I don't know."
"You don't know?"
"She's down to Boston visiting her sister."
"When's she coming back?"
"I don't know."
"How long's she been down there?"
"Well, she went down there a year ago last July. Last I saw of her she said, when I was ready for her to come home, to come down and get her. I ain't been down and she ain't come home."

The changes aren't huge, but they are significant. In the original, Warren tells about "he." The encounter happened to somebody else. In my version, Warren's the one who encountered his friend, whom I call Alan, not Austin. I misremembered—probably because I don't know anybody named Austin. I added the detail about Seabrook. Warren didn't need to mention that to his audience—they all knew the story took place in Seabrook. Alan/Austin's last speech is where the biggest changes come. I shortened it. Left out the detail of the wife's traveling to Boston last July and cut the final sentence altogether. These changes were unconscious and were, no doubt, made as the story adjusted to audience response. With the addition of an "ayuh" and a "seen" instead of "saw," I adjusted it to my voice and dialect. Generally, my version is tighter. "She said when I was ready for her to come home to come down and get her" gets shortened to "She said when it was time to come home, come get her." Seventeen words cut to twelve—not a change in meaning, but in rhythm and timing.

My favorite of the Warren Angus Wilbur stories concerns ice fishing, which I loved as a kid, so it's right up my alley. It takes place in Pittsburg, one of my favorite New Hampshire towns. And there's a prank involved. I've told the story a hundred times and in the telling it's changed a lot. I do not remember changing even one word intentionally, and yet Warren Angus Wilbur's original and the story I now tell are remarkably different. Here's the unadulterated transcript from the tape:

Warren Angus Wilbur and Razor True Go Pickerel Fishing
Original

Voice: Tell about Razor True. They were smelting.

Warren Angus Wilbur: No, not smelting, they were pickerel fishing. There's a little pond over there up near camp. They'd logged it off and then it'd been damned up afterwards. They chopped the trees down in the wintertime and the snow was deep. And the stumps, oh, they'd stand high as that or more. Come off cold and froze over. Then they opened the dam and drew off the water and of course those stumps held the ice up. We went over to go pickerel fishing. Chopped down through the ice and there weren't any water under it. So Ray True got under it. A couple fellas come down a ways, they saw us chopping through the ice so they chopped a hole. Ray done heard 'em. He went along and popped his head up through the hole. "Where'd you come from?"

"Oh," he said, "I was swimming in here last summer. I couldn't get out and I drownded. It froze over and this was the first chance I had."

Young voice: Was that part true?

Warren Angus Wilbur: Well, the part about the pond was. ~

Here's the story that Warren's two hundred or so words has become.

Warren Angus Wilbur and Razor True Go Pickerel Fishing
My Version

A few years ago, a woman named Heather Pike sent an audio tape her great-grandfather Warren Angus Wilbur made in 1973 when he was in his eighties. You can hear on the tape they're probably in the kitchen—the clink of silverware and so forth. You can hear family members egging him on: "Warren tell us the one about . . . ," "Warren, remember the time . . ."

Warren Angus Wilbur and his best friend, Razor True, loved nothing more than to go to Pittsburg, New Hampshire, in February, ice fishing. They had a cabin up there where they stayed. They'd go up for a couple of weeks and enjoy themselves.

One time they were driving on a back road and they spotted a pond they'd never fished before. Looked perfect for pickerel fishing—not too big, not too deep. Pickerel like little ponds that are shallow. They like to slide around in the weeds.

They took their equipment out of the back of the pickup truck. They didn't have anything fancy like an auger. They had an ax and a chisel. Went out on the ice and commenced to make a hole for fishing.

Unbeknownst to them, this pond had a history. A few years earlier, in the dead of winter when the snow was about four-and-a-half feet deep, the loggers come through this little valley and clear-cut it. Course when you're logging, you don't dig to the base of the tree to cut it down. You cut it as it lies. So when the snow melted come spring, what you had was a valley full of four-and-a-half-foot stumps.

Which was okay because the beaver moved in, dammed up the brook that ran through the valley. The water rose and covered the stumps and made this nice beaver pond.

The only thing was, unbeknownst to Warren Angus Wilbur and Razor True, this fall after the ice had set, the beaver moved out and the water drained away. So what you had was a foot of ice setting on those four and a half foot stumps.

When Warren Angus Wilbur and Razor True finished making their hole and looked down through, there was no water.

This was a great disappointment to them. However, they noticed a couple fellas at the other end of the pond making a hole of their own. Musta seen Warren and Razor making their hole and thought this was a good pond for pickerel.

That's when Razor got an idea.

He slid down through the hole. He crawled the length of the pond.

And just as those other fellas finished making their hole and stepped back, up he popped.

"What are you doing down there?" they said.

"Well," Razor said, "I drownded last fall and this is the first chance I've had to get out."

But that's not the best part of the story. The best part of the story is a voice on that audio tape that says, "Grampa, is that a true story?"

Warren Angus Wilbur says, "Yuh. Well, most of it."

My version is more than double the length of the original. The biggest change was creating a beaver pond instead of a logging pond. Woodsmen dammed up brooks to create these small ponds to float the logs and make them easier to collect and transport. I am more familiar with beaver ponds. The deliberate removal of the logging pond dam is more likely and believable, but when I picture the scene, it's a beaver pond. I saw a lot of them on the trapline with my dad.

At the end, instead of Warren's "Well, the part about the pond was [true]," I say, "Yuh. Well, most of it." This feeds my theory that stories have a lot of truth to them, and some deviation from the truth is perfectly fine. I can hear him say that. Even if he didn't.

If you compare the two versions, you'll see how Warren's voice and mine differ. "Come off cold," he says. I love that line, but have lost it somewhere along the way. Maybe next time I tell the story, I'll try to squeeze it in. Thing about stories, you can change them and then you can change them back. Of all the materials in the world for creating art (or craft)—clay, paint, marble, papier-mâché, fabric, wood—words are the most forgiving and malleable. Words and music.

"There weren't any water under it," Warren says. "So Ray True got under it."

Gosh, I love that line too, the repetition of "under it" in particular. Maybe next time.

"Drownded" is Razor's word and it's a keeper—colloquial and authentic. "Drownded" is exactly what Razor would have said in that moment. If a person "drowns" it's tragic. To say "I drownded" makes a joke of the situation.

Out of respect for the story and Warren Angus Wilbur's voice, I stick as close to his version as I can. Still, my voice, my dialect, are a little different from his and, again over time, the wording shifts: the clink of silverware; loved nothing more; not too big, not too deep; slide around in the weeds; an ax and a chisel; unbeknownst; cut it as it lies; a great disappointment; that's when Razor got an idea.

The more I tell the story the more it sounds like me. It's like those sci-fi movies when the alien takes over the body of the human, and the resulting creature combines the sensibilities of the two. Not sure which of us—me or Warren—is the alien.

CHOICES

Storytellers face an abundance of choices with every word and every line. It's like playing Scrabble—no game is ever the same. No told story is ever the same. John Rule explained chaos theory to me on the dock at the lake while drinking a margarita. I don't understand chaos theory but am pretty sure it applies. Here goes: A penguin flaps its wings in Antarctica and changes everything. One tiny movement creates a domino effect and before you know it, there's a tsunami in the waters off Hawaii.

You say a line a hundred times but it's never the same. For one thing, you never feel exactly the same when delivering it. You're telling a happy-ending-love-story, and the auditorium is hot, your throat's scratchy, you think you might be coming down with a cold—whatever you feel in that moment will color the words you speak. A penguin flaps and you're off on a tangent. Sometimes it's all you can do to pull yourself and your audience back to the original story line.

I've developed the ability to find the way back. Tangents are just fine, if you remember the way back. In fact, sometimes the tangents are the best part. They're fresh. Surprising. Of the moment.

I begin to tell the story about Joel Sherburne, childbirth, and fancy Barbados molasses from Calef's Country Store, when someone says, "We used to visit Calef's Country Store on our way to camp when I was a kid." People describe their favorite country stores. This leads to penny candies and favorite treats. I'm reminded of Hod Hastings' store I used to walk to from my grandparents' house on High Street in Danbury. Next thing you know we're talking about going down-street, up-street, and cross-street. Next thing you know somebody's from Melrose, Massachusetts, and I'm saying that my favorite Massachusetts town name is Athol, pronounced Ath-hole. We laugh together. Other people have favorite town names and share them. "The PTA in Effingham put out a cookbook," I say. "Effin Ham and Beans." We're on to eating beans on Saturday night. Bean sandwiches. Beans for breakfast. In a family story, I say, my mother and father and grandfather drove from Danbury to Cape Cod to visit my aunt and uncle. They left early in the morning and by the time they got to Massachusetts they were wicked hungry. Upon seeing a sign on the highway announcing upcoming towns, my Grampa Stewart famously said, "I Needham breakfast. If I don't get breakfast, I'll be Dedham." Isn't that a funny thing to remember all these years? To be passed down through the generations?

Eventually, I pull the conversation back to where we turned off the main road and took a wander. The key is remembering just where you turned off. But, guess what, if you don't, an attentive audience member will remind you: "So what happened with the fancy Barbados molasses?"

Oh, the molasses.

Here's Joel Sherburne's word-for-word version of "Two ccs of Fancy Barbados Molasses."

Two CCs of Fancy Barbados Molasses
Joel Sherburne

I taught for the Red Cross for about thirty-five years. Oh, I don't know how many students I've had, a mess of students. And it was very rewarding.

I used to do emergency childbirth classes for the Red Cross. I had police, state police, nurses. I said, "Now we're gonna have a practical at the end of this class and you're really gonna have to do childbirth on a mannequin." And I said to 'em, "Now this is required. You have got to do this. You've got to have string in your pocket to tie the umbilical cord off. And you've got have about 2 ccs of Calef's Fancy Barbados Molasses."

They said, "2 ccs of molasses?"

And I said, "Yes, this is mandatory. You've got to have this when I show you how to do a delivery."

They said, "All right."

The trooper, he went to a doctor at Portsmouth Hospital who done deliveries all the time. And he says to him, "You know, I'm in a Red Cross class for emergency childbirth and he said for our practical exam, he told us we got to bring about 2 ccs of Calef's Fancy Barbados Molasses." And he says, "What's it for?"

Doctor says, "Beats the hell out of me. Find out." He says, "I've never heard of it."

So, the night of the exam, oh it's about fifteen or sixteen of 'em. They all come in. And I said to 'em, "Now do you have your string?" And they all said yes. I said, "Do you have your molasses?" And they all took out their little bottle of molasses. I said, "That's great."

"Now," I said, "I suppose you want to know what the molasses is for?"

And they all said, "Yes."

And I said, "When the patient starts crowning, you take a little bit of that molasses on your finger and you rub it right around the opening. And when you do that, the little fella will smell that molasses and he'll want to come out and lick it."

You should have seen the trooper when I said it. They didn't expect that was coming but it come. Just to see the expression on their faces. I loved it. A lot of them, they swore a little bit. The trooper went back and told the doctor. Doctor laughed like the devil.

You've got to keep 'em interested.

At times I was a little witty. But at times you've got to be serious. You're not working with machinery. You're working with people.

I done it about every class I done. It went over good. ∽

2 CCs of Fancy Barbados Molasses
My Version

My friend Joel Sherburne has worked at Calef's Country Store in Barrington, New Hampshire, for more than sixty years. I write about him in my book *Sixty Years of Cuttin' the Cheese*. He wears many hats in Barrington—head of the Historical Society, founder of the ambulance service, designer of the town seal, for starters. To say he is beloved in town is an understatement.

For many years, he taught emergency response and first aid courses for the Red Cross. Included in the training was how to deliver a baby. Each student had to pass a practicum involving a mannequin and a rubber baby. "Next week," he'd tell the group, "you're going to have to deliver a baby. It'll be hands-on experience." He instructed them to bring two items to the delivery class: a couple feet of string and 2 ccs of fine Barbados molasses from Calef's Country Store. When asked what the string and molasses were for, he'd say: "You'll find out. Just bring 'em."

Among the students was a state trooper who happened to have a doctor's appointment that week. He asked the doctor about Joel's instructions. The doctor said the string was for tying off the umbilical cord. But he had no idea what the 2 ccs of fine Barbados molasses from Calef's Country Store was for. "If you find out, let me know," the doc told the trooper.

So class time arrives. All the students have brought their string and molasses. The trooper steps up to deliver the mannequin's baby. "I know the string is for tying off the umbilical cord," the trooper says. "But what's the 2 ccs of fine Barbados molasses for?"

Joel says, "When the patient starts crowning and you can see the top of the baby's head, you take a little bit of that molasses on your finger, and you rub it right around the opening. The little fella will sniff that molasses and he's gonna want to come out and lick it."

Same story. Same surprise ending. The more times 2 ccs of fine Barbados molasses gets repeated, the more it turns into a chant. The phrase holds the story together. Joel meanders more in his version—and he can get away with it because he's Joel telling his own story and reflecting on reactions to his antics. My version is shorter and more linear. Joel's version is more about the students' reactions over time to him and his instructions, what it means to be a good teacher. My version is more tightly focused on the moment of revelation—the prank itself. The elements are all in place, but I get to the punch line a little quicker. Instead of the little fella smelling the molasses, he sniffs it. I sniff when the little fella does. Audiences have taught me that the story ends with the words "lick it," enunciated clearly. That's when the laugh comes.

HONORING WAYS OF LIFE

Robert Theriault and I spent several hours together in 2007. One afternoon of stories was not enough. Come back another day. So I did. He told about his life working in the Berlin paper mills. We sat together in the home he shared with his wife, Eveline. Some doorways, like the one to the cellar, had ribbons draped across them so she knew not to go that way. The stairs were dangerous. In the living room a big screen TV occasionally caught her eye and she paused in front of it. She carried her bright red purse tight against her stomach. Robert told the story of how he and Eveline met and some highlights of their life together.

A Rare Majorette

"She was a rare majorette," Robert Theriault says of the woman who would become his wife. "When she lifted her leg and swung her baton, I fell in a trap."

Eveline Fleurquin was a majorette for a snowshoe club from Montreal. Robert Theriault played in the drum and bugle corps for Berlin's snowshoe club. They met halfway, in Sherbrooke, at a snowshoe club convention. Because of a mix-up with room reservations, Robert ended up sleeping on a couch in the hotel mezzanine. On the train, there had been much partying, so he was tired. "I go up the stairway," he says, "throw my satchel underneath there. And bang—go to sleep after that big party."

He slept well until about 4 AM when, *balang, balang, balang,* a great ruckus in the lobby woke him. The train had arrived from Montreal, and the bands marched from the train to the hotel. "I had a hard time to open both my eyes at once," he says. Once open, his bleary eyes saw the lobby was full. He scanned the crowd and spied a beautiful majorette. "I couldn't believe it. I had never seen such a tall majorette like that." Eveline was five foot nine. She was standing on a step with high boots and a tall hat. It was love at first sight.

"So I go over," Robert says. Excuse me, excuse me. "I took out my best French and asked if she was going to dance with me tonight at the ball. She said, 'Okay, as long as you don't drink.' Unbeknown to her," Robert says, "if I hadn't been half lit, I would never have gone so brazenly over to her."

"Our relationship was a destiny," Robert says. Sherbrooke was a hundred miles from Montreal and a hundred miles from Berlin, but they found each other. They married in 1952. "We were too much in love. We had six kids in six years."

Robert and Eveline raised their children in Berlin. Both worked in the mills. He worked thirty-seven years as a millwright and foreman and served one term as union president. He took the millwright job in 1950 at age twenty, the youngest ever hired. That caused hard feelings among the older millwrights. "I was as dumb as they come, then," he says. "The handle of a hammer is this long. I'd grab it here (close to the head), so I wouldn't miss the nail. You've got to use the whole hammer!"

Robert and Eveline were in the front line of the movement in the early eighties to make the mills equal-opportunity employers. "I was familiar with the national law," Robert says. "I went to the union. I said, 'Women are tired of working in the towel room. They should be able to work in other parts of the mill for equal pay.'" The women were among the lowest paid workers. Eveline, along with other brave woman, signed the complaint to the government. The fight was not just between the women and management, it was between the women and the union. A friend of Robert's said about Eveline: "Why don't she stay home and wash her dishes like everybody else?"

But the law was on the women's side. Eveline earned a job in paper testing. Some of her colleagues tried to make her quit. When she went to the cellar to work on a mixed starch that would feed up to the paper machine, the man who was teaching her the job told her there were rats all over the cellar. "It was a true statement," Robert says, "but the rats were rarely seen."

Eveline's reply to the threat of rats: "As a rule, small animals can't eat big animals."

Told she had to lift a hundred-pound barrel onto a platform to feed the paper machine, she said, "You show me how." The man said, "Oh, you got to take the truck there and lift it to the platform." But, he added, "You don't have a license so you can't go on that truck." So she said, "You get me a license then."

In the end, Robert says proudly, "Eveline Theriault became foreman."

Robert and Eveline celebrated their fifty-fifth anniversary in 2007. At that time, Eveline had suffered with Alzheimer's for seven years. She still lived at home, where Robert took care of her with the help of two experienced aides. "Us people," he told me, "we take care of each other from way back." ❧

Robert Theriault was not only generous with his time, but he had a natural storytelling ability and a strong will to get his stories out into the world. "A Rare Majorette" is one story among many. It spans decades. It is a story of love, perseverance, hardship, and courage. The teller, in the moment, decides which of those stories to tell by deciding which parts to leave in, which to take out, which to emphasize, which to skim over. The line, "Us people, we take care of each other from way back" seemed to me the natural ending. It states a dearly held value expressed by Robert and by many of the Berliners I interviewed:

We look after each other.

It was a hard life and a fulfilling one.

We are all one family.

We take care of each other from way back.

In another story, Robert tells of a mill worker who got his arm caught in the gears. It was a job to extricate it—"You could see the bones and the nerves and everything."

"Gosh," Robert said, "I hope they can save his arm." They took the worker off to the hospital. As soon as he was gone, the foreman says, "Okay, get back to work."

"It was a rough way," Robert recalled, "but that was how things were done in those days."

Never say never and never say always, but I *almost* always begin this story with Eveline lifting her leg and swinging her baton. It's such a powerful image. From the moment they met, Robert saw Eveline as the strongest and most beautiful woman in the room. That never changed.

I *almost* always include the part about being too much in love, six children in six years. People chuckle at that. They identify. In those days, a child a year was not so unusual.

The hammer, the union, the rats, the license, the proud husband bragging that "Eveline Theriault became a foreman," those pieces come and go. Another teller might emphasize Eveline's struggles at work and the way she moved up through the ranks. Another teller might frame the story as a fight for women's rights with the line, "Why don't she just stay home and wash her dishes like everybody else?" It's a provocative line, but more often than not, I leave it out. Not sure why. Maybe because it's my nature to reveal rather than provoke. That line—"Why don't she just stay home and wash her dishes like everybody else?"—makes the speaker seem not just old-fashioned, but narrow-minded and mean. It makes him seem like a bad guy. For a long time, I believed there are no good people or bad people, just people. With experience, I've—sadly—come to understand that there are indeed bad people in the world—greedy, cruel, and selfish—but in the stories I tell, each character is, at heart, a good person. This is how, despite some bitter disappointments, I choose to see the world.

"A Rare Majorette" became a different story for me when my mother's dementia changed my life. Before that, I didn't truly understand how hard it is to watch a loved one decline. I didn't fully grasp the physical and emotional toll of caring for a loved one with a debilitating and progressive disease.

Robert died before his beloved Eveline. I never mention Robert's death when I tell this story, but I'm positive listeners hear it in my voice.

The more clearly you picture a scene, the more clearly your listeners will see it. Eveline's red pocketbook brings me right back to that living room in Berlin. I see the big screen TV, the ribbons across the doorways, Robert standing straight and tall, gesturing broadly as he speaks—a proud Acadian.

When I tell the story of Robert and Eveline's meeting, I hear the band as it marches from the railroad station. I see the crowd in the lobby. I am ready to tell a love story.

It was a privilege to spend forty days and forty nights in Berlin in deep winter 2007 collecting stories for a group called the Androscoggin Valley Community Partners (AVCP). The Robert and Eveline Theriault story came out of this project. The sponsors included arts and charitable organizations, churches, businesses, and town government. At first, I resisted the challenge. I'm a humorist, I said, not a trained researcher. But the powers that be—especially my friend Frumie Selchen, one of the committee leaders—were convinced I was the right person for the job. At that time, the paper mills—the heart of this community for more than a hundred years—were being torn down brick by brick. It was the end of an era. The community was in mourning. The stories needed to be collected and told.

Over the years, the mills had their ups and downs, but they always made a comeback. This time, people realized, the mills weren't coming back. Gina Belanger said she was driving through Berlin one night when she noticed lights on the east side of the river. She couldn't figure out what they were at first. Then it dawned on her. They were street lights. "I'd never seen them before," she said. "There was a mill in the way."

The AVCP decided it was important to save as many stories about paper-making, logging, and life in the Androscoggin Valley as possible before those stories were forgotten. The plan was to collect the stories and give them back to the community in some form or another. We would see where the stories led us. My job was to interview people, write their stories up, and find a meaningful way to preserve them and pass them on.

The local newspaper published an interview each week with a photo of the person interviewed. Some months later, I wove the interviews together for a staged reading by a community theater group at the St. Kieran Art Center, previously a Catholic church. Ten years later the stories live on in a traveling program called *Crosscut*, available to libraries, town halls, and nonprofit groups. A teacher in a Massachusetts mill town even adapted the program for kids studying the industrial revolution: *Crosscut Junior*.

Berlin was once the paper-making capital of the world. And it still is—in stories.

This one from Helen Burns shows how a single line can add a level of meaning. Helen's voice is so strong and her manner of speaking so unique, when I present her story I read it out loud. These are her exact words (lightly edited) in her voice.

Helen Burns, Lady Logger

"Must have been great working in the woods," I said.

"I didn't see anything so great about it," she said. "It was damned hard work. No wonder I got no back. Started out helping my father in the woods. He was my stepfather, really, but I called him my father."

"What did you do?" I asked her.

"Run the other end of the crosscut."

A crosscut is one of those big two-man saws or, in this case, a man and a teenage girl; one pulls one way, the other pulls the other way, and the tree comes down eventually.

"Take your shoes off if you're gonna ride!" That was an old saying. "You'd get tired and relax a little and if your end went down, it would bind. I heard that saying a good many times. It was hard work. Some dangerous."

Then she said, "Would you like to hear about the time I saved a man's life?"

I said I would.

"We was up in Jefferson cutting on government land. Mr. Tyler, he had a pair of hosses. We done the cutting and he done the hauling out with the hosses on a scoot. They built a big skidway with a road underneath, so they could drive the big truck right under and roll the logs onto it.

"Mr. Tyler was taking the logs ofen the skidway and climbed on to free a log that was hung up. All of a sudden the logs behind him started to let go. Well, I grabbed a cant dog and grabbed the log he was holding onto, held the logs back 'til he could pull himself out of the way. Nicest old man you'd ever want to meet. Just as gentle as he could be. Boy, when I let them logs go, that whole skidway come down through there. Would have squashed him to death."

"Helen," I said, "What did he say?"

"He thanked me and told everybody he knew about how I saved his life." She said, "You didn't think anything of it at the time, but I did think of it in years later. I was scared to death. When I jumped in there by side of him to hold them logs, I had no idea whether I could or not. We could have both been killed right there. I'll tell you when he got out of there and I let go and them logs come together, there was quite a bang."

She said, "It's strange how things will happen. At the time you don't realize what you've done. You see it and you have to do it. He could jump like a rabbit for a man his age. He was very limber on his feet. He was an elderly man so we always called him Mr. Tyler. If he would have said to call him Clarence I would have, but he never did." ⁓

Helen speaks for many who faced the dangers of working in the woods without worrying too much about it. She speaks for those who worked so long and hard their backs and knees and shoulders and elbows and hips gave out, crippling them in not-so-old age. She instinctively saved a man's life, but, looking back, she's not sure where she found the courage.

It's a harrowing tale. At the end, she does something special. With one line—"If he would have said to call him Clarence I would have ..."—she reveals how people treated one another in those days in that culture. Yes, she saved Clarence Tyler's life, but young Helen would never have called an elder by his first name without permission. It was a matter of respect.

I didn't realize how often I imitated characters—like Helen Burns—until a listener complimented me on it.

"I don't do voices," I said.

"Yes," she said, "you do."

In telling a story as I hear it in my head, evidently, distinct voices—not my own—come through. If I hear myself talking like somebody else in a story (it's an out-of-body experience), I think: *That sounded natural. Next time you tell the story, do it again.* Or, *That sounded forced. Stop it!*

Mostly, when I'm telling, I don't hear myself at all. I'm just the conduit for the story. My focus is on the audience and the effect the story has on them, not on my delivery. If I become self-conscious, the telling becomes stiff and stilted or uncertain and shaky. The story suffers.

LET STORIES TELL THEMSELVES

"If you are in the moment, you are in the infinite." —Swami Pragnanpad

Saw it on a mug. Actually, I saw it on the internet in an advertisement for a mug.

When the stories flow—easily, naturally, and without self-consciousness—time seems suspended. Some sessions are like that. All of us in a room together telling, listening, and, best of all, laughing.

During some sessions, the scenes in my head are closer and crisper. Other times, the audience may not be able to tell I'm distracted, uncomfortable, or troubled by the events of the day, but I'm aware of the disconnect. And it sucks. Still, I press on. It's not about me.

When I come home after a gig and my husband asks, "How did it go?" I say okay or good or great. Great means connected. Not perfect, but connected teller to story to audience to story to teller. Sometimes—on those evenings when all the troubles of life recede and it's just the stories and the audience, when an hour passes in a moment—I say: "John, it was magic."

A KIND OF IMMORTALITY

In Potter Place, a woman named Gracia Snyder told about Woofy George. Gracia has since passed away. Woofy died years before I heard the story. He lived a long life and the story goes back to when he was three years old. His is the only line of dialogue, the last line of the story. I've yet to say it right. He's three. He's speaking for the first time in his life. In writing, the process of revision stops when the book is published. In storytelling, revision doesn't stop until you do.

Woofy George's First Words

When Woofy George was one year old, two years old, three years old, he never spoke. He never uttered a syllable. Some people thought maybe there was something wrong with young Woof. But others said, No. He had four older brothers and sisters. They talked all the time. Woofy didn't need to say anything. I call him the littlest yankee.

One day Woofy was home alone with his mother. The older children were in school and Mother was baking beans in the big old Glenwood cook stove.

She'd started a fire in the firebox with some newspaper and kindling. Then she went to the wood pile for a chunk of wood or, as they say in Berlin, a junk-a-wood.

When she went to put that junk-a-wood into the fire box, she discovered—to her dismay—that it was a dite too large.

However, on those Glenwoods, you can access the fire box from the top by removing the cast iron lids and the piece of metal in between. This she did. She shoved that junk-a-wood into the fire box from above.

It went in about half way and stuck.

She couldn't push it in. She couldn't pull it out.

That's when the smoke began to fill the kitchen and the flames began to lick. That's when Woofy George, three years old, spoke his first words. "T'won't go, Ma. Too goddamn big."

Gracia delivered the story with gusto and the roomful of locals erupted in laughter. Most of them knew the story already. You could tell by the way they nodded as Gracia spoke. It was a community story that had been passed from person to person through generations. When a story is told and retold within a community—a town, a family, a school, a church group, coworkers, long-time friends—it unites and, in a way, defines that community. To be the subject of a community story is a kind of immortality.

Gracia's telling included the names Woofy and Potter Place. It referenced the older brothers and sisters. It ended with these exact words, "T'won't go, Ma. Too goddam big." That's the line that makes the story. The rest of the language, pretty sure, comes from me: dite, junk-a-wood, couldn't push it in, couldn't pull it out, access, dismay, lick. The kernel comes from Gracia who heard it from somebody who heard it from Woofy's mother. Gracia told it in her voice. I can only tell it in mine.

Recently, an old friend of Gracia's heard "Woofy George's First Words" and was moved by it. He was in touch with Gracia's son in California, he said, and would let him know his mom's story lives on. I was moved by that. Didn't cry—but felt a prickle behind my eyes.

When telling the story, I usually ask who in the audience knows what a Glenwood stove is. Some do. Do they know you can get to the firebox from above by taking off the cast iron lids and the piece of metal in between? They do. They've done it. They've had a chunk of wood stuck in a stove, can't push it in, can't pull it out. This, I say, is called an "oh-shit," a technical term. Sometimes listeners describe other "oh-shit" moments. At an event for a construction company, I invited "oh-shit" stories. A man stood, surveyed the crowd, and held up his three-fingered left hand for all to see. That's dry humor.

Sometimes, if the audience is open to it, I talk about Grampa Bill Barker and how he bought my grandmother a Glenwood in 1919 secondhand. The stove now sits in my kitchen and works perfectly. No rust at all, in large part because my grandfather, who lived alone for the last thirty years of his life, was not much of a housekeeper. He cooked on that stove every day, but never cleaned it. It came to me caked in grease, which preserved the metal. It took a lot of scraping and Goo-Be-Gone, but the cast iron, once revealed, was pristine.

I fire that stove up once every couple of years, during a cold snap, to bake beans in Grammie's pot. This exercise in nostalgia warms the kitchen.

The rest of the year, I feed the cats on the stove top. I have to feed them up high on account of the dogs. I tell the cats it's not a good idea to jump up on the stove when it's in use, but every year at least one of them finds that out the hard way.

Gosh, I wish I could remember for sure who told me this next story. I thought it was Dudley Laufman, but he says, no, t'wan't him, so I guess the source will remain a mystery. It's a cat story.

Three Holes

Setting down for coffee at Mac's house, Dudley (we'll call him Dudley) notices, down along the mop board, three holes through the wall clear to the outside. You can see daylight through them. "Mac," he says. "What are those holes down along the mop boards?"

Mac says, "Them's cat doors."

"Why are there three of them?"

Mac says, "I got three cats."

"Couldn't the three cats take turns using the same door?"

Mac says, "When I say scat, I mean scat."

As in "Helen Burns, Lady Logger" and "Woofy George's First Words," one line can make all the difference. One line can turn an anecdote (this stuff happened) into a story (this stuff happened and it meant something). Even the simplest stories have layers. Sometimes the simplest stories resonate loudest: "When I say scat, I mean scat." Mean what you say and say it like you mean it.

HOW DO YOU GET TO CARNEGIE HALL?

I've never been to Carnegie Hall, but Adi Rule sang there as a member of the Tanglewood Festival Chorus. No doubt she wore the required floor length black, stood at the back with the other tall ones, and hit some very high notes. Wish I could've seen it. I was busy telling stories that day.

We learn from other writers and tellers. We respect their craft. We even imitate them, but at some point we come into our own. Maybe it's the 10,000 hours of practice supposedly needed for mastering a skill—though that seems arbitrary and excessive. As a writer, teller, learner, and teacher, I know each of us has a unique voice that is present from the beginning. Helen Burns is Helen Burns and always was. Through practice and by trusting our intuitions and audiences, our voices flourish.

Open a favorite book and read a paragraph aloud. How does this author use language or phrase ideas differently than anybody else would? Listen to comedian Paula Poundstone on the radio show *Wait Wait Don't Tell Me* or watch her on tour. Her ad-libs, jokes, self-deprecation, the way she interacts with audiences, even the brightly striped suits she wears, it's all pure Paula. Her presence, her take on life, her voice as well as her *voice* are unmistakable.

One of my college professors said, ruefully, that writers who taught in graduate writing programs were creating their own competition. Really? If that's the case, why would the professor teach aspiring writers anything worth knowing?

His comment never left me, but I've since decided he was wrong. He probably didn't even believe it himself. It was a notion that he tried out to see how it flew. In fact, he was a wonderful writer and teacher, generous with criticism and encouragement. I don't compete with other writers. Can't do it. My voice takes me in certain directions and leads me to certain kinds of success as do theirs. I've known, from the beginning, that my work fits best with small, regional presses. My short stories appear in *Yankee*, not the *New Yorker*. My essays run in *New Hampshire* magazine, not *The Atlantic*. The first run of my first book was 600 copies. The publisher traded the first copy, fittingly, for a truckload of manure.

In a college workshop, we took turns reading our stories aloud. They sounded so good! The professor said, "You can't go around reading your stories to people one at a time. They have to stand on their own on the page." I thought, *Wanna bet?* Even then, as a ridiculously shy twenty-something college student, I knew that I would, in fact, bring my stories to listeners one-by-one if necessary. On some level, I knew I would be a storyteller.

To me, writing and storytelling are so tied to our distinctive voices that competition is beside the point. Does a cactus compete with a Maserati? I don't think so. Paula Poundstone has no competition as a comedian because there's nobody like her. Stephen King writes horror stories. Does he compete with Shirley Jackson? Nope. They're just different. Picasso painted Picassos. End of story. Who sings like Willie Nelson? Nobody. Strong voices earn strong loyalties. The more distinctive your voice, the more apt it is to be loved. And hated. Somebody says, "That movie was brilliant." Somebody else says of the same movie, "It was terrible." Better to be loved and hated than to be just okay.

When you say scat, say it like you mean it.

Whatever you do, make it a pissuh.

Pissuh: Noun. Related to urination. As the story goes, "That fella's hat better be waterproof because it's a pissuh." More broadly, pissuh can mean remarkable in a good or bad way. A word can mean the opposite of itself. The good news that Frannie earned a scholarship to Hahvid might prompt a supportive, "Ain't that a pissuh." On the other hand, Chickie explains that the snowmobile trails were so rough his Ski-Doo bounced from mogul to mogul. "Hit one bump so hahd," he says, "Mothuh bounced right off the back of the machine and landed in the trail."

"Pissuh," says his friend, with feeling.

"I guess!" Chickie says. "She makes awful good biscuits."

Hahvid: Harvard, an Ivy League school in Cambridge, Massachusetts. Once at a fund-raiser, featuring readings by two or three writers (including me), I met a couple who owned a summer home on the shores of a nearby lake. "Where do you winter?" I asked.

"We live in Cambridge," they said. "We teach at Harvard."

"I heard that's a good school."

It is much easier for me to talk to a thousand people in an auditorium than one-on-one at a social gathering. Small talk is not my strength.

AS POPEYE SAID, I YAM WHAT I YAM

Snowmobiling was my family's sport of choice. The only brand-new anything we ever bought (besides socks and underwear) was a 1968 Polaris, blue and white. When we first got it, Ma and Dad went trail riding out behind the house with my brother Steve, just a baby, in a car seat on the back. He bounced off. They didn't notice until they were a mile or two farther along. Turned around. There he was. Just setting there, still strapped in the car seat, upright in the middle of the trail.

Dad called the Polaris a business expense because he used it to check his trapline. He trapped for extra money—fisher, fox, muskrats, otter, beaver, mink. He learned how from his father. I thought it was a family thing, secrets passed down through the generations all the way back to, I don't know, Lewis and Clark—until I found Grampa's trapping books. He was a trapper and a reader.

Reading was my favorite activity as a child. Trapping was not. Didn't care to learn how. Didn't care to be around it. Skinned beaver carcasses—pale, fatty and pocked from the action of the knife—repelled and saddened me. The smell of beaver cooking in a pot made me sick. We didn't eat beaver. We fed it to the dog—thank god. There were always dead animals on the premises: the whole animal, the skinned carcasses, the skins stretched on boards and hung on the walls. Dad wore gloves when he skinned so he wouldn't get rabies.

He never did, but he got terrible blood poisoning once from an infected needle. He'd popped a blister on his hand, wrapped the needle in a tissue, then picked up the tissue and the needle went deep into the flesh.

By the time he got to the doctor, a couple of days later, the red lines of infection were all up and down his arm. I thought he was going to die. Pretty sure he and my mother and the doctor thought he might. He didn't. I wrote a story about it called "Sometimes in August" about a kid, like me, acting out because her father was sick. Getting in trouble for it. Trying to figure out a world in which a parent she depended on was in mortal jeopardy.

The story never made it into a book but it did find the light of day in a literary magazine, more of a broadsheet than a magazine. To save space, the editors took out all the white spaces I'd left to show transitions from one point of view character to another. As printed, the story made no sense.

These things happen. The only feedback I got on that story was from an acquaintance who said when she read it she thought I must be a crazy person. Pretty sure she meant to add, "But now that I've met you I see you are not."

My first commercially published short story, "Walking the Trapline," was loosely based on a trip Dad and I took on the Polaris to check his trapline one winter evening. By law, you have to check your trapline every day or maybe every other day. It was forty below. A true forty below, not *feels-like* forty below. I wore a neck-to-toe aviator coat donated by Uncle Elliot, who flew the hump during World War II—that is, he piloted a plane over the Himalayas. The coat was heavy and musty. I sat on the back of the snowmobile behind my dad. Oversized deerskin mittens over knit ones kept my hands warm. Dad made those deerskin mittens. He killed the deer, skinned it, soaked the hide in a brook, tanned it, drew the pattern, cut it out, and sewed the pieces together. He was Davy Crockett. For much of my life I believed he could do anything—he could make anything, he could fix anything, and he was, pretty much, invincible. As we rode the trail on that clear, freezing night, his body blocked most of the wind.

Sure enough, we found a dead fisher cat hanging from a tree in a conibear, a wire trap that snaps on the neck. Dad handed me the fisher cat. I climbed onto the back of the snowmobile and hugged it all the way home. The fisher cat wasn't even stiff yet. It was soft and pliable in my arms.

When the story came out in *Yankee*, years later, my family didn't know what to think. Or maybe they did. It was—as much fiction is—a mix of experience and imagination. Instead of checking the traplines on a snowmobile, in the published story, the father, the daughter and a son go out into the woods on snowshoes. Instead of bitter cold, the weather is snowy. But the dead fisher cat is a central image. The child's mixed reactions to the dead animal and to her father create the emotional tension.

It was my story to tell, so I told it. Had to. Some people say they don't give a hoot what other people think about them. Writers and storytellers can't afford to give a hoot. What people think about us can't matter. The story is all that matters.

It's a risky business. When you write and tell in your authentic voice, you reveal who you are. You have to be willing to accept the consequences of that kind of exposure. It's no picnic. Dad said, of the story in *Yankee*, "Is that what you really think of me?" He looked pained.

I said, "Dad, it's fiction." Pretty sure he didn't understand what that meant. I'm not even sure I did. Having a storyteller in the family is a pissuh.

NanDavis and the Moose

Steve in Greenville spoke of his great aunt NanDavis. Nan had some age to her. She was a strong, stubborn, independent yankee woman. She lived alone away out in the wilds of Greenville. She cooked for herself, kept her house in order, heated with wood, split and carried wood for the stove.

Because of Nan's advanced age, every evening, Steve's mom would give her a call to make sure she'd survived the day. NanDavis often let the phone ring many times before picking up. It was her phone. She'd answer in her own time. Upon answering the phone, she'd give the traditional warm yankee greeting: "What do you want?" Then the family would know she was okay.

One evening the phone rang and rang. It rang longer than it had ever rung before. Mother says, "Get your coats on. We're going to have to drive out there. Something's happened to NanDavis."

Just as they were about to head out the door, Nan finally picked up, all out of breath. She said, "What (gasp) do you want (gasp)?"

Mother said, "NanDavis, what is going on?"

"You won't believe it," NanDavis said. "I looked out my kitchen window and there was a moose on my po-utch. It had a big rack all covered in velvet. That moose was rubbing its antlers against the uprights that hold up my po-utch roof. So I grabbed my broom and went out the door to try to persuade it to leave. It didn't want to leave. Took a lot of persuadin', but finally off he went down the road. And then I heard the phone ringing, so I come in to answer it."

Mother said, "NanDavis, are you all right?"

"No," NanDavis says, "Not by a long shot. Broke my best broom."

I tell this story with yankee inflections and phrasings, *po-utch* instead of porch, *persuadin'* instead of persuading, *come in* instead of came in. NanDavis answers the phone, "What do you want?" When said aloud it comes across with a touch of hostility. She would be irritated by a ringing phone. She's like me—irritated or alarmed—whenever the phone rings. I absorb the story (thank you, Steve), filter it through my own sensibilities, and tell it in my own way. NanDavis becomes my eccentric relative—she's Aunt Harriet, Grampa Bill, John's Grammie Lena, my mother-in-law Lillian Rule, and my mother re-envisioned.

Some scribbled notes from the Greenville session read: "Steve, Nan Davis, moose on porch, broke broom."

The first interpretation, posted as a blog, reads:

NanDavis and the Moose

First interpretation

Steve in Greenville spoke fondly of his great aunt called NanDavis (all one word). NanDavis was in her late eighties, a strong, stubborn, independent yankee woman, living alone in her own house set back from the road and the rest of civilization. Every evening, Steve's mom would give NanDavis a call to make sure she'd survived the day. NanDavis often let the phone ring many times before picking up, but this one evening it rang and rang and rang. Steve's mom said, "Oh my god, I think something's happened to NanDavis." It rang a few more times and NanDavis finally picked up. Out of breath.

Mom said, "What's going on?"

NanDavis said a moose had come right up on her porch and was rubbing the velvet off its antlers on her uprights. She grabbed a broom and went out to dissuade him. He was almost as stubborn as she was, but eventually she drove him off. Damn moose.

Mom said, "NanDavis, are you all right?"

NanDavis said, "No! Not by a long shot. Broke my best broom."

NanDavis's character develops over time. Same with the character of Mom, who becomes "Mother," in keeping with the family I imagine. Steve wasn't specific about how Nan manifested her independence, but in my mind, she cooks, cleans, and heats with wood. She's coming alive. Both NanDavis and Mother become a little more yankee-fied, because that's my territory. The kernel remains, but the story evolves.

NanDavis reminds me of a story my dad used to tell about his buddy Marcel. In a way, it's the same story.

Marcel and the Broom

In the basement of the Wilson's Meats building, a conveyer belt moved the slabs of meat along for cutting and processing. A backup occurred and the slabs started piling up on themselves, so—thinking quick—Marcel stuck a broom handle into the gears to stop the belt.

Dad watched from across the room. He described the action: "The broom broke and went flying. Half of it struck Marcel between the eyes. Down he went. I hollered for help. Went over and tried to bring him to. Down come the boss, John Babcock. By then Marcel was awake and sitting up, holding onto his head."

"Jesus, Marcel!" John Babcock says. "What the hell were you thinkin'? You broke our best broom!"

Poor Marcel. Whatever became of him?

Dad worked as a meat cutter at Wilson's. He became a salesman for Jordan Meats after they bought Wilson's out. In essence, he worked for the same company his whole adult life. Dad hated being a salesman, but he was good at it. He inherited the gift-a-gab from his Irish mother, pretty sure, though I never really knew her. He and his cousins, the Barker boys, all had the gift-a-gab. They were double cousins. Two Irish immigrants—Elizabeth (Lizzie) and Julia Moynihan—married two brothers, Bill and Frank Barker. They all lived in Danbury. Not sure what Frank did for work or how well off that family was (not too, was my impression), but Grampa Bill had not been scrupulous about supporting his family, so Dad valued a steady job more than anything.

Grampa Bill trapped, fished, hunted, and logged. He liked to work in the woods. The man did what he damn well pleased his whole life except for a stint in the Marines. Enlisted. Got sent to Haiti. Didn't like it. Tried to get sent home by placing his hand on a train rail and waiting for the train to pass. Chickened out. When he got back to New Hampshire, he swore he'd never leave home again. And he never did. Occasionally, he'd drive to Bristol for supplies or to Concord to visit a lady friend. He had a lot of lady friends, including one who lived, for years, a couple miles up the road in a camp he built for her. Yup, my grandfather kept a mistress within spitting distance of the little house where he lived with his wife and raised his two children. He also had a whole other family from a first marriage. His marriage to my grandmother was his second. I didn't know it until I was maybe forty years old. My father had a half-sister he never met.

The Old Man (Dad called his father that) worked for a while in a local mica mine. I know this because Dad said a neighbor bet Grampa Bill that he could not, in three days, cut and split an enormous elm that had been knocked over in a big wind. Elm is notoriously hard to split, all crookedy in the grain. Bill won the bet. He used dynamite from the mica mine to blow the tree to bits.

After both Grampa Bill and my dad died (twenty years apart), I found a letter from father to son. In the letter Bill expressed regret over a fight they'd had and hoped they could let bygones be bygones. He wrote, "I never knew you kids went hungry."

I never knew, until reading that letter, that my dad and his sister had gone hungry. They lived in a one-room shack and went hungry. This explains a lot. To them, security was paramount. Florence married a man with a good job. They rented an apartment in the city. Never had kids; her choice. She worked her way up through the secretarial ranks until she was secretary to the president of a big utility company.

Dad made sure his kids—me and my two brothers—never went hungry. People will say, "Yes, we were poor, but as I kid I never knew it." I knew it. Didn't bother me much, but I was aware that others lived in houses with second floors, basements you could walk around in, and clapboards instead of asphalt shingles for siding. Some kids got new clothes for school. I did, too. Once. Going into 8th grade. There was a sale at Britt's Department Store. Three dresses for ten dollars. Ma bought me a blue plaid polyester, red plaid polyester, and green plaid polyester, all with white Peter Pan collars. My aunt Lila bought my cousin Deb the same. Twinsies. Once I got a new coat—fluorescent orange corduroy. It was ugly but on sale. My mother insisted and I really liked the idea of a new coat, even a fluorescent orange one, so I wore it until the cuffs were up to my elbows (almost). In high school I wore hand-me-downs from Aunt Florence. She had to dress shahp for work in an office in the tallest building in the state's biggest city, Manchester. At fifteen, I was wearing suits to school—matching wool skirts and jackets over pastel polyester blouses, like every late-sixties businesswoman. No wonder I never got asked out on a date. Well, just one. My senior year. It did not go well. Someday I'll write a short story about it. I'll call it: "Don't Take a Seventeen-Year-Old Girl to a John Wayne Movie on a First Date."

> **Shahp:** Adjective. Fashionable. Aunt Florence made most of her own clothes in the latest fashion. She dressed shahp. Also, not dull. The knife was shahp. Also, accomplished. Dad was a shahp salesman.

Other families went on vacations. We never did, but once. Who needs to go on vacation when you live in New Hampshire? Unless you're going to Maine. We once drove to Moosehead Lake to stay at a cabin owned by Dad's boss. Lasted two nights. Too cold and no heat. This was the end of August. Used to be Maine could be freezing cold at the end of August. The highlight of that trip was a visit to the Greenville dump to watch the bears rummage for food. That was thrillin'. No sarcasm intended—it really was thrillin'. Reminds me of other dump trips. Dad liked to go at dusk and shoot rats. Us kids stayed real quiet in the cab of the truck. Dad sticks the .22 out the window. Something skitters. Hands over ears. *Ka-pow!*

> **Thrillin':** Adjective. Exciting. You could say thrilling, but thrillin' implies a little more excitement. Yankees in general and Mainers in particular are known for keeping their emotions in check. As in:
> "What do you do for excitement around here?"
> "Couldn't say. Never been excited."

We had an old power boat at camp that John was sick of hauling in and out of the water spring and fall, so we put a notice up at the Trading Post offering it for free. A young clam digger came by to look at it. He was impressed. The boat had all its parts. No holes. He said most free boats were in pretty bad shape. We said we'd gladly give it to him if he was willing to haul it away.

When he showed up with a couple of friends to collect the boat, he let us know how pleased he was. He looked me straight in the eye and said, flatly, "I'm jumpin' for joy."

Later he dropped off some clams and some fresh fish as a thank you.

Mainers, some of them, take the yankee habit of being frugal with words and emotional expression to the limit. Mary Bray hailed from Phippsburg, where many in her family made their living from the sea.

She moved to the lakes region of New Hampshire, but invited family down for holidays. At one gathering, she raised a sensitive subject. She'd heard through the grapevine that something bad had befallen one of the fishing boats. She asked about it. Her cousin Greg, the most taciturn of all her relatives, explained. The conversation went something like this:

Mary: So what went wrong, Greg?

Greg: Boat sunk.

Mary: Whose boat?

Greg: Moyn.

Mary: How'd that come about?

Greg: Filled with water.

Mary: What are you going to do?

Greg: Pump it out.

Moyn: Possessive. Belonging to me. In certain families in certain parts of Maine, New Hampshire, and much of Vermont, the vowel sound "oy" creeps in, possibly a carryover from upstate New York. Some in my family three generations back were farmers in upstate New York and when my grandfather Stewart and Uncle Junior spoke, you could hear the "oy." Greg has the "oy." It's a beautiful sound.

"How you doin' today, Greg?"

"Foyn."

Mary Bray said Greg was frugal with words even as a child. "What'd you have for snack, Greg?"

"Snaps."

"Snaps?"

"Yup. Ginja."

I WANT TO SEE THE OCEAN

Once my family started off for the ocean in one of a series of Ford Fairlanes an uncle sold to us for cheap after he got through with them. I must have been very little, because—as I recall—Grammie and Grampa Stewart were with us. So it would have been my mother, my father, Grammie and Grampa, me and my brother squished in. (Steve wasn't born yet.) Dad must have gotten up really early, driven a half hour from Boscawen to Danbury to pick up Grammie and Grampa (they never owned a car), then back to Boscawen, and we all headed out for the ocean, a couple hours away.

We were almost there—in my child's mind we were *almost* there—when we got a flat tire and had to turn around because we had no spare. This was one of the greatest disappointments of my life. I really wanted to see the ocean. I had never seen it before or, if I had, I'd been too young to remember. I wanted to put my feet in the ocean. I wanted to swim in the ocean.

I couldn't understand the logic. We got a flat tire, so we put on the spare and now, just a few miles from our destination, we have to turn around and drive all the way home, in case we get another flat. But, I reasoned, if we didn't turn around and we did get another flat, at least we'd be at the ocean. *Take a chance,* I thought. *Couldn't we just the one time take a chance, and continue spareless to the ocean.*

Nope.

If there was a chance to be taken, my parents (and by parents I mean my mother) were determined not to take it. She was the cautious one. Had to be; I came to realize this as an adult with a child of my own. Sometimes Dad showed no commonsense at all. I'm not sure he ever really grew up. Aunt Florence said it was because he married so young (just eighteen), and my mother was three years older, so she bossed him around.

Florence was highly opinionated and didn't hesitate to share her views. "Most of the women in our family," she said when I was a teenager, "are short and dumpy." Not her—through sheer will and self-control she was thin until the day she died. Oh, Florence.

"When you laugh after you say something," she told me, "it makes people take you less seriously." Little did she know those were nervous giggles. She made me nervous. I felt as though she was always judging me. Because she was! I felt as though I always came up short in her estimation. Because I did! "You look just like your Aunt Florence," people said. And it's true. We bore a striking resemblance.

Florence, I learned later in life, was my mother's best friend growing up and right through high school. Ma said she always thought of Dad as "Florence's little brother." Until she married him.

Whatever the reason for the family dynamic, it became Ma's job to protect her children from Dad's excesses—drinking being the main one, but hunting, trapping, and even pounding boulders until they cracked also counted. His temper, too. He was quick to flare, quick to lash out. Us kids knew to get out of the way. Once, just once, I was too slow. He gave me a little shove and I fell against the washing machine, broke my glasses, got a black eye. He was very, very, very sorry—especially when he had to pay for new glasses.

Has this affected the way I choose and tell stories? Absolutely. Everything that has ever happened in my life affects the way I choose and tell stories. And it's the same for you. The same for all of us.

Uncle Junior Goes in Search of Lobster

One summer, according to legend, Uncle Junior drove all the way from Danbury to Portsmouth to buy fresh fish and lobsters and clams for a family feast. It's hard to imagine what the occasion could have been—generally, the family didn't do occasions—but it must have been pretty special. Maybe Junior's safe return from World War II. In those days, a trip to Portsmouth from Danbury was a major undertaking.

Junior made it to the docks. He spotted a sign: Daggett and McGregor, Fresh Fish Market. Out in front of the shop he saw a fellow in a yellow slicker shucking oysters. "Are you Daggett or McGregor?" Junior says.

The shucker says, "Don't much matter. One of us is dead."

That was before my time. Another time, the whole clan gathered at the big house on High Street. As a kid, I thought Grammie and Grampa Stewart must be rich because their house was so big compared to ours. They had stairs with a bannister wide enough for sliding down. They had an upstairs with four spacious bedrooms. They had a third-floor attic big enough to walk around in. Not to mention the barn, the barn attic, and the barn down-below where the pigs lived. If you snorted at the window, the pigs would come running.

We had just a downstairs—tiny kitchen and pantry, tiny living room, with two tiny bedrooms and a closet-sized bathroom, more like a rabbit warren than a house. Later we added on. Twice. It was still a rabbit warren but with more rooms—just right for us.

The clan had gathered at Grammie and Grampa's big house for a family picnic on the island at Highland Lake. The whole gang was going—Uncle Junior and Aunt Leona and their kids, Aunt Lila and Uncle Fred and their kids, Aunt Barbara and Uncle Herb (they didn't have any kids), Grammie and Grampa. All of us. Fred had bought a wooden boat named the Pelican because it was so wide in the bow. We planned to motor out to the island in the boat. Such an adventure. I was beside myself with excitement.

Then, in the packing up, somebody locked somebody's keys in the trunk of one of the cars. It took a long time to get the trunk open and retrieve the keys. By then the sky had clouded over and the mood had changed. "Looks like rain," the grown-ups said, "We'll go to the island for a picnic another day."

We never did.

MONEY IS A CONCEPT

Among the ways I understood that our family was not so rich as others, we didn't own a camera. All the photos from my childhood are copies of pictures relatives took. My cousins had a camera that took home movies—the epitome of wealth. The scene in National Lampoon's Christmas Vacation where Chevy Chase gets stuck in the attic and puts on an old Super 8 reel-to-reel is a reminder that only rich people made home movies, and that wa'n't us.

Truth is, we probably weren't any poorer than the families around us—working class, single income, lots of kids. My parents lived by the Depression-era adage: Use it up, make do, wear it out, do without. If it's broke, fix it. Never go into debt except for a mortgage. Do not borrow money for a car. Do not borrow money for college. Why would anybody want to go to college anyway? And if you did get a scholarship for college, why would you be an English major? And why, oh why, would anybody in their right mind choose to be a writer? Writing is not a job. Neither is storytelling. And yet here I am, more like my grandfather Bill Barker than I maybe care to admit, doing what I damn well please.

When an Archway truck overturned on I-93, pastries spilled over the highway. Our neighbor, Bert Vorron, worked for the state on the roads. He was rich. He and Jinx, his wife, gave out full size candy bars at Halloween. Bert and his coworkers scooped those pastries up. They were wrapped and perfectly good to eat. He gave us a shopping bag full. The taste of a soft oatmeal-raisin Archway cookie fresh from its cellophane packaging and hardly squished at all made me think: *This is what rich people taste every day.*

I never wanted to be rich. Still don't. Rich is not a good fit. After my mother left me money in 2015—money she and Dad had saved over a lifetime of extreme frugality—my bank account said I was pretty well off. But my brother sued for half. And won. Most of the money went to lawyers. So that was the end of that.

A framed print hung in Ma's kitchen—dated 1907. It's a little girl with Mary Jane shoes and Kewpie doll hair holding four pennies in her hand. She's standing by a sign that says, "Soda 5 cents." The caption reads: "Ain't It Hell To Be Poor?" I take that sentiment to heart. If you've got a nickel for a soda, you're doing okay.

Some families in our part of town did not have what we had growing up—plenty to eat, decent clothes, and a warm house. On cold days, I could sit on the register over the hot-air furnace and be toasty. On the coldest days, Ma let the kids from the shack up the road wait in our front room for the school bus. When we heard the bus coming, we'd run together to the stop across the road. The kids who lived in the shack did not have warm coats or boots.

In one of my earliest memories, someone knocks on the door after dark. It was the front door, seldom used, so it was a job to get it open. Two strangers stood on the steps with presents in a bag. All wrapped. My parents turned the strangers and the presents away. Here we were living in our own house and some do-gooders thought we were so poor they had to bring presents for the kids at Christmas. We did not accept charity. No, we did not. I'd never seen my parents so angry, except at each other.

I am not complaining. My childhood was idyllic. No sarcasm intended. It was just right for me. When my mother's dementia allowed her to say things she would not have said otherwise, she told me she wished she'd been a better mother. I told her, in perfect honesty, she was the best mother I could imagine.

"You did your best," I said.

"I did," she said.

Dad and I never had that conversation. But if we had, pretty sure it would have gone the same way.

Maybe that's why there are no villains in the stories I tell. Just folks who mean well and do their best. I know there are people in the world who do not mean well and do not do their best, but I don't care to tell their stories.

The White-Faced Heifer

Bob Ramsay of Alexandria stood when he spoke. He used his cane for balance. "Bob," I said, "you can sit down and tell your story. Be comfortable."

He said, "I lie bettah standin' up."

Pretty sure the story he told was a true one, because it's so specific.

Seems Joel Gray lent his neighbor Augustus "Gus" Cheney ten dollars against Gus's white-faced heifer. He wrote the transaction down—a mortgage—and they both signed and dated it.

A good deal of time passed. Joel ran into Gus on the street and reminded him: "Gus, you owe me ten dollars for that mortgage on that white-faced heifer."

Gus cackled. "Ha," he said. "I done fooled you. I et that heifer."

Joel reaches into the front pocket of his overalls with his monstrous dairy-farmer hand, and pulls out a slip of paper pinched between two monstrous fingers. "Ha!" he says, "but you didn't et the mortgage." ⁓

> **Et:** Verb. Consumed. I et. You et. He et. She et. They et. We all et. Yesterday we et. Tomorrow we will et. If you et too much you're apt to get a stomach ache.

Tudor Richards and the Blue-Winged Teal

Jay said it had been his privilege to go on a bird watch along the shores of Turkey Pond with Tudor Richards, a well-known naturalist, so big in the Audubon they named an award after him.

As they walked along, Tudor would identify the bird songs. He'd point. The bird watchers would train their binoculars on a particular branch on a particular tree. Tudor would explain what they were looking at.

They'd been on their quest for a couple of hours when Tudor stopped short, directed attention to the weeds across the pond and a bird floating among them. He whispered: "Blue-winged teal." The bird watchers were thrilled at the sighting.

When Jay got home, he happened to see his neighbor, a native named Randall, out in front of his house. Knowing that Randall was quite the woodsman himself, Jay explained (not really bragging) how he'd been down to Turkey Pond with Tudor Richards and they'd spotted a blue-winged teal. "Have you ever seen a blue-winged teal, Randall?"

Randall says, "Ayup. Et it." ⁓

Dad didn't love working at Jordan Meats. He didn't like being indoors, talking on the phone, paperwork. He didn't like selling. But he was good at it. The key, he said, was to make the ones you were selling to think they were just a little bit smarter than you. He'd much rather have been hunting or fishing, but he put up with it. Financial security mattered, so he put up with it —as Jenny Parent said—"for the money." The minute he qualified for retirement, he did.

In one story he loses his temper and sasses a guy new on the job. Dad could be awful sassy when he felt like it. The guy says, "You can't talk to me that way! I'm your boss."

Dad says, "Who ain't?"

His stories about his early work experience at Wilson's—before it was bought out by Jordan's—show how much he liked the hands-on heavy lifting—loading and unloading trucks, hanging carcasses from hooks, keeping his knives sharp. I still use kitchen knives he sharpened. Once those dull, I don't know what I'll do. As much as I try, I can't get a blade to take an edge the way he could, though I watched him scrape them across the whetstone a thousand times, though I can still hear the sound of steel on steel when he polished them off on the honing rod.

Dad liked cutting meat. He also liked being able to buy meat at wholesale prices for the family. We ate good. I've always loved meat. Still do. I'd choose a lamb chop over chocolate cake any day. My mother said my first words were "Mo' meat," spoken as I pounded my fists on the high chair tray: "Mo' meat! Mo' meat! Mo' meat!" Pretty sure my first words were Mama and Dada like any normal baby, but that's what she said.

BITS AND PIECES

Meredith Hall, best-selling author of the memoir *Without a Map*, described her memories as a movie. One memory led to another and another and they'd keep on coming, all connected and full of detail. She was a witness to the totality of her own life. This amazes me. I remember so little—just bits and pieces. Flashes. Small disconnected stories. Maybe that's why forging connections within and between stories seems so important.

In one flash, I'm hiding under my grandmother's bed. Willie Wentworth leans down, lifts the bedspread, and peeks in at me. I'm little and scared and angry. "I hate all mens," I yell at Willie. Each time our paths have crossed over the years, we remind each other of this incident and laugh about it.

In another flash, I'm bundled in a puffy snowsuit, standing on the round oak table at my grandparents' house, surrounded by grown-ups wearing coats. My parents want to take me home, but I don't want to go. I want to stay overnight with my Grammie. And she wants me to stay, too. I can tell. I'm having a tantrum. I'm little and angry and helpless. "When I grow up I'm gonna knock the hell out of all of you," I yell.

These are the stories I think I remember, stories my parents told me about myself. Here's what I should have said bundled in my puffy snowsuit, standing on the round oak table at my grandparents' house, defiant: "When I grow up I'm going to be storyteller."

Our camp in Maine is rustic like me—one room with attached bathroom complete with composting toilet, an upgrade from the outhouse that came with the place. It was at this lake, maybe ten years ago, a family story fell into my lap. I've told it many times—shaped it, shortened it, added a detail here or there. At this point, I couldn't say which parts of the story are absolute fact and which are tweaked. My daughter could—she's a stickler—but nobody's asking her. And, besides, I don't care. As *Yankee* editor and raconteur Judson Hale says: "Never let the truth stand in the way of a good story." As my father said, "Why tell the truth when a lie do just as well and be a lot more interesting?"

Nimrod

To understand this story, you must be familiar with a technical term. Nimrod. It's a Biblical name relating to the tower of Babel. It can also mean mighty hunter or mighty fisherman. There's a fighter plane called a Nimrod that was used in World War II. But in my family, when we use the term Nimrod, we mean someone who means well but doesn't have the training or skill or knowledge to do something the way it ought to be done. When a nephew nailed his hand to a beam with a power nailer, that was a Nimrod move.

One summer weekend at camp, we had the family for a visit and thought we'd go for a picnic on the island. We piled into the power boat. My husband, my mother-in-law, my brother-in-law, my daughter, and her boyfriend, who happens to be named Nimrod (by me). A couple of their friends. Two or three dogs.

We motored out to the island. Had a nice picnic. Piled back in the power boat, but the motor wouldn't start. What are we going to do? We're from New Hampshire. We're in Maine. Nobody's going to give us a tow.

One of the young people had paddled to the island in a one-seater kayak. We had an idea. If somebody paddles the kayak back to camp, they can get the aluminum fishing boat, row it out to the island, and take people and dogs home in shifts.

Nimrod volunteered.

Off he paddled, down the lake and around the point.

About forty-five minutes later, we see him in the distance. He's got the aluminum fishing boat. And he's paddling real hard, but he's not making much progress.

Then I see my daughter down by the water's edge. She's yelling something across the water. She's yelling, "Nimrod, Nimrod, pointy end first."

Told as is, Nimrod lasts five minutes or fewer. Sometimes I add background like the fact that my husband and his brother are engineers. They like to work on motors. Which might explain why the motor conks out. Or I say in Maine every person who owns a place on the water is required by law to own at least three boats. Not really—but it's fun to see people's reactions. The ones who have camps on the water and own lots of boats laugh extra hard. Boats accumulate. Yankees are collectors by nature. It goes hand in hand with being frugal. As my friend Jane said, "My husband collects dump trucks. But it could be worse. His friend collects culverts."

I might mention that Nimrod works as a personal trainer. He has well developed muscles. He's in the business of "lifting things up and putting them down." Sometimes at the end of the story I say my daughter and her boyfriend, luckily, decided not to have children. Lately, I've added the news that they eloped. The theme for the reception, held a week later, was dinosaurs. John Rule and I wore T-rex costumes and danced to Lady Gaga's "Bad Romance." I might mention that the newlyweds have a studio apartment over our garage, where they've resided for fourteen years with a variety of special needs cats. They're waiting for John Rule and me to die so they can move into the big house.

Pretty sure nobody used the word Nimrod during the actual event, nor do I actually call my son-in-law Nimrod. I call him K, which is short for Kris. I latched onto Nimrod as a way to pull the story together. At one time I considered writing a book (still might) called *The Chronicles of Nimrod*—stupid stuff people do, including me. At first I used the term numbnuts, but that seemed too personal.

Only after telling the story for a while did I learn Nimrod was a character in the Bible, and, still later, that the term meant mighty hunter or fisherman and was also a kind of fighter plane. Audience members contributed all that information.

Also, I don't have a nephew, but I do know a Nimrod who nailed his hand to a beam with a power nailer. So the nephew is a lie, but it's a lie that doesn't matter. I could have a nephew. Nobody will check. Nobody cares.

It's true a bunch of us were stuck on an island with a broken motor and a kayak. It's true that K paddled the kayak to camp and returned rowing the fishing boat backwards. It's true that when Adi spotted him, she yelled, "Pointy end first."

"He's Native American," she explained. "Canoes are pointy at both ends. He didn't know."

The more I told the Nimrod story, the more it resonated. We are all Nimrod. And no matter what the endeavor, it is always easier to move forward pointy end first. To departing audiences I say, "As you go through the rest of this day, the rest of this week, as you go through life, always go pointy end first."

Getting to know a story is like getting to know a person. You start with the obvious: he's tall, wears cowboy boots, and has a lazy eye. Move on to the less obvious: he's one of six children, loves Springsteen, and keeps chickens. Then you move on to deeper understandings of what motivates the person, delights him, scares him, and what he likes on his pizza. These discoveries take time and trust.

Same with stories. What strikes you first is the obvious: what happened to whom and who done it. Family gets stuck on an island. Nimrod doesn't know how to row a boat.

Then comes the less obvious. Nimrod and Adi are in love. He wants to help. She takes care of him by giving him advice. Engineers do not always make the best mechanics.

Finally, the deeper meanings emerge. We are all Nimrod. Life is easier pointy end first.

And that's just content.

Delivery, too, gets refined with each incarnation.

Luckily, you don't have to think about any of this stuff. Much. It just happens. In fact, it may be best not to think too much about a story, especially the deeper meanings part. If you try to squeeze meaning, it may seem contrived rather than revealed. Open your mouth. Let the story in your head spill out as accurately and completely as you can. See what develops.

I was thirty when my little brother Steve died. A few years later I wrote an essay about my daughter standing at the foul line on a middle school basketball court, about to shoot for the basket. Will the ball go in or won't it? The essay ends with the ball suspended in mid-arc.

Donald Murray was at a reading where I shared the essay. He knew our family history. He said: "That was about your brother." Until that moment, I had not realized the essay about my daughter was also about my brother. His life had ended mid-arc. Meaning *will* push through whether or not the writer or storyteller intends it to.

STORIES THAT STICK

Like the bits and pieces of experience that flit in and out of memory until pinned down on the page or in stories told and retold, the stories others tell me sometimes stay and sometimes go. I don't know why some stick and some slide away. They just do. Ollie Fifield's town meeting story stuck. It struck and stuck. It ticked off a lot of personal boxes—small-town politics, nuclear weapons, dry humor, and baked beans. Plus, Ollie, himself, was such a sweet, funny, wonderful man. He was small and twinkly. The kind of guy you meet once but feel you've known for always. He was known and beloved by many as a farmer and administrator at Blue Cross Blue Shield. When I mention his name at sessions people nod in fond recognition. They knew Ollie. And his brother Hughie. And his brother Stuart, too.

Nukes in Canterbury

At a session devoted to the history of town meeting, I asked who had a good town meeting story. Ollie Fifield, sitting in the front row, said, "The town meeting of 1957 was a pretty good one."

"What happened at the town meeting of 1957?" I asked.

"That was the year," Ollie said, "there was a petitioned warrant article to ban nuclear weapons in Canterbury, New Hampshire."

Word spread and the news got picked up by newspapers all over the country. It went international—AP and so forth. Japan sent a contingent of media to cover the Canterbury town meeting.

The Japanese media came early. Ollie and his wife had them to supper the evening before town meeting. They served baked beans and brown bread. "You know," Ollie says, "those Japanese reporters had never had bread from a can before." It was a cultural exchange.

At town meeting the next day the legislative body had to work its way through all the regular articles before getting to the petitioned ones. Finally the article in question came up.

At this point in his telling the story, Ollie turns to his brother sitting in the back row. Ollie says, "Hughie, what did you do?"

Hughie says, "I don't remember. That was a long time ago."

Ollie says, "I think you do remember."

"Well," Hughie says, "I believe I proposed an amendment. I believe what I said was, 'I'm not a fan of nuclear weapons, but there's one thing I hate even more than nuclear weapons and that's black flies. I would like to amend this article to ban nuclear weapons and black flies in Canterbury, New Hampshire.'"

And it passed.

And that's why, to this day, there are no nuclear weapons or black flies in Canterbury, New Hampshire. ⌣

This story has changed over the years I've been telling it—ten years at least. The changes were not calculated. They just happened. Gradually.

Early on, I talked a bit about Ollie Fifield himself, but his background in farming and insurance didn't add a lot to the story. People either knew him or they didn't. So I cut it.

I talked some about World War II being fresh in people's memories in 1957 and the ongoing Cold War. Nobody cared.

For a while, I told an introductory story about Ollie as Canterbury Town Moderator that I'd heard from one of Ollie's neighbors. It goes like this:

What the Moderator Did

Ollie Fifield served as town moderator for many years. This was back when town meeting was held at the Old Town Hall. As with most other old town halls, a steep set of granite steps led up to the heavy oak double doors.

There must have been an item of particular interest on the warrant that year—like a new fire truck—because when Joe Carbonneau arrived late, the hall was full. He couldn't find a seat. Couldn't even find a space to lean against the wall with his arms folded like the men do.

Instead he stood at the back, leaning against the double doors.

Someone arrived even later than Joe, opened the doors quick, and Joe tumbled backwards down the steps.

At the lectern, Ollie Fifield banged his gavel. He said, "I will entertain a motion to recess for five minutes to see if Joe is still alive." ⌣

Besides the excitement of a guy falling down the steps and wondering if he's dead or alive, this story shows how we care for our neighbors. Yankees get stereotyped as cool, even cold, but at heart we're just as compassionate as the next guy. The moderator and the voters were worried about Joe. Of course, they voted in favor of the recess. It's not necessary to say so. And, as it turns out, Joe was okay. If he hadn't been, it would be an entirely different story. One I would not tell.

Sometimes another little story worked its way into the middle of the falling-down-the-steps story. "Joe Carbonneau arrived late. The hall was crowded. A fella was at the mic talking. Joe's buddy tells Joe he hasn't missed much. This one fella's been talking nonstop for the last ten minutes. 'What's he talking about?' Joe asks. His buddy replies, "Ain't said yet.'"

I'd been telling the falling-down-the-steps story for some time when one of Ollie's neighbors set me straight. She said, "That story you tell about Joe Carboneau falling down the steps at town hall."

"Yuh," I said.

"I had dinner with Ollie last week and I asked him about it. He said, 'Never happened.'"

I replied in the tradition of Judd Hale and my dad: "I don't care."

But I was curious. Next time I saw Ollie I told the story and asked if it were true. He smiled coyly. "I guess it coulda happened," he said.

Good enough for me!

The nukes story stands on its own, so I no longer use Joe Carbonneau as a warm up. Not often anyway.

Some details in the original story smoothed out and disappeared over time. Hughie was sitting in the fifth or sixth row of the hall, but I changed it to back row. Easier to say and picture. Ollie described a communication problem between the locals and the Japanese media. "We didn't speak Japanese and the Japanese didn't speak English," he said. "A Jewish lady come up from New York City to translate, but nobody understood her." Which was funny but seemed to open a whole other can of worms.

A local historian and stickler checked the town reports for 1957 and 1958. He found no documentation of the nuclear weapons article or the amendment. Sometimes I mention this mystery when telling the story. Most of the time I don't. Documented or not, it's a good story. I choose to believe Ollie. It coulda happened. Maybe he got the year wrong. Or I did.

Another local insists that it wasn't Hughie at all who made the amendment, but the other Fifield brother, Stuart. Once or twice I tried to explain this to audiences. They didn't seem fascinated, so I let it go.

Both Ollie and Stuart have since died. Hughie, far as I know, is still among us. At one point, though, I thought it was Hughie who'd died, said so to a gathering, and was swiftly corrected by a retired teacher, adamant that Hughie lived. Turned out she was correct. Fox pox. (That's yankee-speak for faux pas.)

I see Rebecca Courser, historian and all-around cool person, once or twice a year at sessions, usually at the Rosewood Inn in Bradford for the annual holiday dinner. Rebecca and her family fill a table. They are a lively bunch, full of stories and good cheer. Rebecca asked if I remembered the story about Harry who worked at the dump. It had slipped my mind. She told it again, or maybe for the third time, but this time it stuck.

Harry Lives

Harry worked at the dump, so everybody knew him. And liked him. He was a good guy. Seems Harry got sick and had to go to the hospital. The gossip mill went into action and pretty soon word spread that Harry had died.

The townspeople were sad. *Poor old Harry. He's going to be missed. He certainly is. The Saturday morning trip to the dump just won't be the same without Harry.*

Only Harry hadn't died

Once a bit of gossip catches fire, especially in a small town, it's darned hard to put it out. So that Saturday morning when the customers arrived at the dump one by one, they were met with a large handwritten sign on a chalkboard: HARRY LIVES.

And so does his story. ⌒

Lynn Baker told about her grandmother who grew up on a farm in Gorham, Maine. The boy who was to become Lynn's grandfather worked as a hired hand there. So the two knew each other as teenagers. It's a family story that spans generations. It's also a Christmas story. Whenever I find a Christmas story that's not sappy, I snap it right up. Yankees enjoy sap direct from the maple tree, but we don't like sap in stories. Well, maybe a little.

Nawthin' But Brush

Lynn Baker's grandparents met at the family farm in Gorham, Maine. Her grandmother grew up there. Her grandfather worked off and on as a hired hand. They met as teenagers.

One of the hired hands—a man named Bert—was likable but a little slow. At Christmastime, Bert refused to hang up his stocking with the others because he said, "Ain't no such thing as Santa Claus."

The teenagers insisted there was indeed such a thing and if Bert hung a stocking he'd be rewarded. Bert was adamant: "Ain't no such thing as Santa Claus. No such thing."

Finally, they persuaded him that there wouldn't be any harm in hanging a stocking just in case. So he did.

During the night, the teenagers filled Bert's stocking with the usual: candies, fruit, trinkets, and so forth, with some sprigs of holly stuffed in the top for good measure. They hung it back up over the fireplace. It looked real pretty.

The teenagers rose early, hid behind a sofa, and waited for Bert to come down the stairs from his room. All the way down he was mumbling, "Ain't no such thing as Santa Claus. Ain't nothin' gonna be in it. No sir, I don't think so. No such thing."

He stopped short when he spotted the fat stocking and realized, *Oh my gosh, there's something in there.* He runs his hands all over that stocking toe to top, front to back. Finally, he pulls the stocking from its peg and looks in: "Aw hell, he says. Nawthin' but brush!"

But that's not the end of the story. Lynn's grandfather served in World War II. He was a conscientious objector assigned to the Red Cross—an ambulance driver and litter carrier.

At the time of his first wedding anniversary, he was stationed in Europe. For a surprise he filled a cigar box with holly and mailed it to his bride.

She wrote back: "Aw hell. Nawthin' but brush!"

Lynn said this was a beloved family story that she wanted to pass on. "Now," she said, "it belongs to you."

When I tell Lynn's story, it passes from her to me to listeners. It belongs to all of us. That's the magic of storytelling. Stories are spellbinding; they bind us together.

ALWAYS SOMETHING NEW

With each telling, I try out fresh language. The idea is to convey the most vivid images with the fewest words. I don't memorize. Can't. People say, "You have an amazing memory." Nope. Can't remember what I had for supper night before last. I have the same thing for breakfast every day, pretty much, so I can usually remember that. Can't remember my one child's birthday. Pretty sure it's the 30th of July. But it could be the 31st. Or maybe that's my dad's birthday—the 31st of August. John Rule remembers all dates—when people were born, when they died. Same with pets. He gets sad on those death anniversaries. Me, not so much. Dates don't matter to me so I don't retain them.

In stories I can keep track of the short sequences involved—this happened (Harry went to hospital), then that (people thought Harry was dead), and finally... (Harry lives)—but in life, I'm on unstable ground when it comes to knowing the order of events—who was born before whom, who died first, was the baby born before or after the wedding, when did the Joneses move to Arizona? What we remember reflects what we value.

I have tens of stories in my head, maybe hundreds if you count the little ones. Telling a story is like singing a song. It's associative. Once you get started, once you get the key words and say the first few lines out loud, the rest follows.

If You Count the Little Ones

Farmer and town meeting aficionado Chuck Cox said the drought a few summers back did his potatoes no good at all. Fella says, "Your potato crop turn out?"

"No," Chuck says. "Had to dig 'em."

He elaborates: "Some were the size of golf balls. Some the size of marbles. And then there were the little ones."

At Hannaford they call the small potatoes "gourmet." Used to call 'em pig feed. ✌

By associative I mean the phenomenon of "Can you hum a few bars?" If somebody can hum the first few bars, the rest of the song comes right along. If I can recall a few key words to a story, it returns—one line flowing into the next. There's science behind this phenomenon I'm sure. Maybe we memorize in one part of the brain but associate in another—right brain, left brain, back brain, front brain, that sort of thing. Gloria, who has dementia, can't remember the names of all her children or even how many children she has. But get her started on a song—"Kiss me once, and kiss me twice, then kiss me once again"—and she can sing all the verses. A friend, Neil English, memorizes and recites his poems. Occasionally he'll pause and search the files in his mind for the next line. He stretches out his arms, opens and closes his hands, sometimes closes his eyes. Within a few seconds, he remembers the line and continues. That's different from what storytellers do. We don't string together words in a preset series. We describe the pictures in our heads. And those pictures are ever changing. The more you look at them, the more you see. The story evolves accordingly.

If you're *remembering*, you can't make a mistake. You remember what you remember and that is all. If you *memorize*, forgetting is a dreaded possibility. High school students learn poems for a national competition called Poetry Out Loud. They rehearse for months, but sometimes on stage the line just doesn't come. Painful to watch. Painful, I'm sure, to experience. During my career in community theater, I experienced the horror of forgetting lines during a performance. The eyeballs of my stricken fellow actors willed me to say my words so they could say theirs. The audience waited. We all waited. It was awful. My career in community theater was blessedly brief.

For storytellers there is no memorization, only remembering. Think of it this way. You start telling a friend about a bear you encountered beside the road when you were walking home after your last visit. You haven't memorized the story of how the bear looked straight at you with his baleful eyes. You knew you shouldn't run, especially in your strappy red sandals, but you ran anyway. You remember the *slap slap slap* of the sandals on the gravel as you raced down the steep hill. When you got back to the camp you were sweaty and out of breath and your husband didn't seem to notice, until you said: "Do I look different? Has my hair turned white?"

When you tell the story again, you'll include newly recalled details but leave out some from the first telling. You never stop and search for the next line, because there are no lines. There's only the story as it lives in the pictures in your head. After a few tellings, you point to the white streak in your hair and blame it on the bear.

Yup, I saw a bear up close and I did, counter to recommendations from wildlife experts, run away in my strappy red sandals. Also, I have a white streak in my hair that has come into its own in the years since the bear encounter. Was it caused by that encounter? As Ollie Fifield said, "Coulda happened."

It was a big bear—sleek and muscular. He looked straight at me. He was not in the least afraid. I stood behind a boulder that didn't seem nearly big enough. Clearly, I was in the bear's way. I figured he'd turn and run at the sight of a human being. He didn't. He kept a-coming. That bear had somewhere to go. And so did I.

Ginger, in her nineties, attended a one-room school house in Lakeport. Every day, she said, the children would line up to receive a dose of cod liver oil. "The only thing was," she said, "we had just the one spoon." Once or twice a day the teacher needed to leave the children alone for a visit to the outhouse. She'd say, "You children behave while I'm gone." Then she'd take out her glass eye and place it on the desk. "I'm watching you." To this day, Ginger says, she's sure the teacher could see them through that glass eyes.

When I tell this story, I am Ginger. I may have changed Ginger's castor oil to cod liver oil and back—trying to decide which of those medicines disgusted audiences more—but it remains Ginger's story and I remain grateful that she told me the story so I can pass it on. The words "Ginger" and "glass eye" bring it all back.

One listener had a special connection to Ginger's story. She said, "I wish my brother were here." He too attended the one-room school in Lakeport around the same time as Ginger. He told the family he was afraid to go to school because of the teacher's glass eye. "He didn't think we believed him."

The words "Ollie Fifield" and "nukes" trigger the Canterbury town meeting story. Once I have those words, hum those bars, the story is there. The words change with each telling, however when a particular phrase gets a good response, I'm inclined to repeat it. The phrases "bread from a can," "cultural exchange," "I believe what I said was," and "it passed" found their way into Ollie's story. Ollie probably didn't say "Canterbury, New Hampshire." Didn't need to since we were in Canterbury at the time. But there's something chant-like in repeating "Canterbury, New Hampshire," so I do.

I'd probably told the story fifty times before the right ending emerged. For a long time, the story ended with "black flies in Canterbury, New Hampshire." Then I added the line "It passed," sensing this was something listeners needed to know. Later I added "and"—"And it passed." The three beats of the phrase felt right. One night, from the ethers, came the outrageous lie, "And that's why, to this day, there are no nuclear weapons or black flies in Canterbury, New Hampshire."

Eureka!

While we're on the subject of endings, this is another story that developed over many tellings. It started as an anecdote from a man who got his digging equipment stuck while drilling a well. It snowballed. The details built up, becoming more and more preposterous. The ending came during a telling. It just asserted itself.

I've come to believe that endings are embedded in the details of a story. If you listen carefully, the ending will naturally appear. If you're having trouble finding a satisfactory ending, go back into the story, check the details, beef them up. Try to envision the scene as clearly as possible. There you'll find "the end."

The Well

Vernon says, "There's all kinds of stuff in the ground around my place. Mica, feldspar, quartz, beryl. You better go careful when you're digging. Don't know what you're going to find. In 1962, Mother got it into her head she wanted a well. She was sick of the dug well drying up in hot weather. She wanted an artesian well."

Royal says, "Was she adamant?"

Vernon says, "I don't know about that, but her sister had an artesian well, so she had to have one, too. Got it into her head, she just had to have an artesian well and an indoor bathroom with a tub. Had to have it.

"Hired the job out and the fellas come in with their big truck and that big old thumpa-thumpa drill. They commenced to drilling. Course you had to pay by the foot, so the deeper they went, the more it cost ya. You could practically see the dollar bills floating up from that hole and out of sight.

"They drilled down about two-hundred feet, just a-grinning, 'til they drilled into a mess of mica.

"Course it was soft and they didn't realize until the whole thing caved in on itself. The thumpa-thumpa got buried. They couldn't extract it, couldn't afford to leave it. Had to bring in the derricks and pulleys and earth movers and so forth to dig out what they lost on the first pass. By god, if they didn't drill right into that pocket of mica again and lose that bunch, too.

"It was some mess I'll tell you. There was no way Mother and I were going to shell out for that debacle."

Royal says, "Did your mother ever get her artesian, Vernon?"

Vernon says, "They just kept bringing in more equipment and losing it down the hole—tractors, backhoes, bulldozers, cranes, bigger cranes. You ever see that big ship-moving crane up to Bath Ironworks—well it wa'n't that big but pretty close. The hole got bigger and bigger. Pretty soon the barn slid in. Pretty soon the house slid in. Mother and I had to sell off the land and move. They used to call that part of town West Woodford."

Royal says, "I heard of North, South, and East Woodford. But no West Woodford. There is no West Woodford, Vernon."

Vernon says, "Not any more there isn't. It's all down in the hole."

TRUST YOUR MATERIAL, YOUR AUDIENCE, AND YOURSELF

The order in which the details of a story are presented can make or break it—pattern of revelation. The critical stuff comes at the beginning and the end. The beginning tells us what to pay attention to. The ending tells us what the story amounts to. Have you ever read a magazine article, turned the page, and realized—*Oh wait, that was the end*. What do you do? My impulse is to go back and read the last few paragraphs again. Read them the way an ending deserves to be read, with extra intensity. Early in my telling career, an audience member observed that my voice tended to soften at the end. He was hard of hearing and this really bugged him. He was missing out on the punch lines. I'm not sure where that bad habit came from. Probably lack of confidence. But I learned to speak up especially at the end.

Pie

Digger insisted that apple pie be made without spices of any kind. But for the community supper, Persis, his wife, decided to make pie as it should be made (in her mind)—with cinnamon and nutmeg.

She watched in horror as the lady at the pie table handed Digger a slice from Persis' own pie and braced herself for his reaction.

"Persis," he said, "this pie is wonderful. Find out who made it and get the recipe."

Even in the simplest story, the first sentence sets the stage: Digger likes his pie just so. In the middle, Persis takes a chance and makes a pie the way she thinks it ought to be done. She asserts her personhood. Go, Persis! Wouldn't you know, Digger gets some of that spicy pie. Then comes the surprise ending! It's a turnabout story—the ending is the opposite of the beginning.

Sometimes the beginning of a story sounds like an introduction or a warm-up, but it is actually integral. More than one fan (a person who has attended more than one session is a fan—I takes what I can gets) has said "Wilmot Casserole" is their favorite. A little surprising, but on second thought, for a small story it has a lot to say about how we are with each other—especially in villages. Ultimately, it's a story about community pride, neighborliness, and yankee idiosyncrasies.

Wilmot Casserole

If you ask a yankee a question, make sure you're prepared to hear an honest answer. Libby, new to Wilmot, heard that her neighbor up the road was ailing. She decided to do the neighborly thing and bring him a casserole. He met her at the door. "I'm your new neighbor down the road," she said. "I heard you weren't feeling so well, so I brought you this macaroni and cheese. Hope you feel better."

He thanked her.

A week later she walked back up the hill, knocked on the door. When he opened it up, she asked if he was done with the casserole, could she have her dish back, and how was he feeling. He fetched the dish and told her he was feeling better. Then she asked a question maybe she shouldn't have.

"How'd you like the casserole?"

"It wa'n't up to Wilmot standards," he said. ∾

The delivery of the final line in "Wilmot Casserole" is tricky. I've been corrected a couple of times by those who knew the parties involved. In keeping with my resolution of long ago, I enunciate the heck out the last line and deliver it with ample volume. The question is what to emphasize. "It wa'n't UP to Wilmot standards" or "It wa'n't up to WILMOT standards" or "It wa'n't UP to WILMOT standards" or "It wa'n't up to Wilmot STANDARDS." Still working on it.

Inflection—the modulation of intonation or pitch—doesn't sound like such a big deal, but it can be.

Bruce in Lyndeborough (pronounced *Line-boro*)

Heard this story from Bruce Geiger's neighbor and later from Bruce's wife, Cynthia. She had a slightly different take on it. And so do I, probably, but here goes. It is a true story.

Bruce liked to work in the woods. It had been raining for days when, during a lull in the storm, he decided to drive his tricycle tractor out to the back forty to get some work done. He told Cindy he'd be back for lunch.

He didn't show up for lunch. After a time, Cindy got worried. She went to a neighbor, a fellow who knew the land and was handy in the woods, Tinker Johnson. She said, "Tinkah, Bruce didn't come home for lunch and here it is almost supper time. I'm worried."

Tinker knew where Bruce was likely to be working so he set off to see what was up. Deep in the woods he came upon a terrible sight—the tractor overturned on a hillock and, underneath, a body stretched out in the mud. He approached with trepidation.

Sure enough. Bruce was pinned under that heavy machine. *Oh no!* Tinker bent close to see if his friend was still breathing. He had a feeling he wasn't.

Just then, Bruce's eyes fluttered open. "What took ya?" he said. ∽

The intonation of the line "What took ya?"—meaning, "What took you so long to get here?"—must convey that Bruce is okay, while at the same time conveying the fact that he might not be in the greatest shape of his life.

Cindy added to the story. She said Bruce was pretty well stove up. She had, in fact, accompanied Tinker to the scene and saw at once that her husband was hurt. She took Tinker aside and said, "Go back to the house and call the ambulance." This was before cellphones. "If I call them he'll be mad at me."

The ambulance came, the EMTs extricated Bruce from beneath the tractor and, despite his protests that he was just fine, took him to the hospital. Not sure just what his injuries were, but the hospital was where he needed to be—for about three weeks. Stubborn old coot.

This exact same line comes at the end of another story—intonation similar, meaning somewhat different.

The Reunion

Lois was the youngest child of her father's second family. She had half-brothers and sisters who were much older, another generation really. After retirement, she decided to do some catching up. She and her husband drove from Maine to Florida to visit a sister she hadn't seen in decades.

They drove and drove.

At last—after two thousand miles and twenty-five years—they pulled into her sister's driveway. Rang the doorbell.

The sister opened the inner door and peered out through the screen, and said, "What took ya?"

This story of separation and reunion is so poignant that almost anything the Florida sister says would be inadequate and therefore funny. She could say, "Can I help you?" or "We been expectin' ya," or "You made good time," or "You're early," or "I see ya made it," or "Would you move your cah ova by the orange tree? You're in Barney's spot."

Whatever she says will fall under the category of warm yankee greeting. Yankees are not known for being outwardly warm. We don't emote. After a rare rift with my parents that lasted a couple of long, miserable months, Dad called. Said "Come on up," as well as a few choice words about how stubborn I was and how stubborn my mother was, and how somebody had to back down and that somebody was him.

John, Adi and I appeared on their doorstep that afternoon. Ma said, "Long time, no see."

To demonstrate the yankee hug, I ask two audience members to stand side by side facing forward, cross their arms, turn their heads to look one another in the eye, and nod.

On the camp road, I meet a big-ass SUV and pull over into the bushes so it can pass. The driver stares straight ahead, but as he passes, he lifts his right index finger from the steering wheel— just a flick up and down—to express his heartfelt appreciation for my courtesy.

On the subject of traditional yankee greetings: If a yankee doesn't know you're coming to visit but you show up, the traditional doahyahd greeting is "What the hell are you doin' heah?" If a yankee knows you're coming, it's "Where the hell ya been?" ᔕ

Doahyahd: Noun. The part of your property nearest the door you use most often, typically a side door. In New England we prefer side doors to front doors, probably so the winter chill doesn't blow into the front room. The side door is more likely to open to a porch or breezeway and from there to the kitchen. Some people unfamiliar with the term doahyahd think it's a space to store unused doors. This is not the case.

A doahyahd visit occurs when somebody pulls onto the driveway to chat but doesn't get out of the vehicle. The intent is not to stay too long, though such visits can be quite lengthy. A doahyahd visit is less of a commitment than, say, stepping into the kitchen and refusing to sit down or have a cup of coffee. Kitchen visits can also go long and are hard on the back. Yankees have a mawbid fear of being trapped in social situations. If you're sitting in your cah and the conversation lags or takes an unwanted turn, you can start 'er up, back out of the driveway, and be on the road to home in no time. If you're standing by the kitchen door with your hand on the knob, you can exit gracefully at a moment's notice. It's the ones inside the kitchen, blocked from the door by your presence, who feel trapped.

Same thing at town meetings and other public gatherings. If you sit in one of the metal folding chairs, especially in the middle of the pack, you are there for the duration. If you're in the bleachers, forget it. On the other hand if, like Joe Carbonneau, you're leaning against the doah at the back, you're free to go.

This fear of commitment extends to getting too friendly too soon with the neighbors. You never know when they might sell the house, pack up, and leave. If you've gotten too friendly with them and they move out, you're apt to miss them. Such vulnerability is to be avoided if possible.

Mrs. Brown's Party

Neighbors Ruth and Esther chat over the fence about Mrs. Brown. Mrs. Brown has lived in town for thirty years. She raised her children here. But now—following the death of her husband—she has decided to move south to be closer to family. Ruth says: "Esther, I expect I'll see you at church Saturday afternoon for Mrs. Brown's going-away party."

Esther says, "You won't see me there."

"A-course you'll be there. You've lived next door to each other for thirty years. You'll want to go and say goodbye to Mrs. Brown."

Esther says, "I never said hello." ↝

For Esther to say hello to Mrs. Brown when she first moved in would have meant making a commitment and an assumption (that Mrs. Brown was going to stick around)—neither of which Esther was prepared to make. What if Esther put herself out to be friendly and ended up liking Mrs. Brown and being liked by her? What if she got attached to Mrs. Brown? What if Mrs. Brown, instead of settling down, moved away? Sure enough, that's exactly what she's doing. What if Esther got attached and, god forbid, Mrs. Brown died? There's a certain logic to avoiding attachment so when a friend or family member leaves you, you won't feel so bad. It's the logic behind, "I can't have a dog. I get too attached."

When Bobo died, I happened to stop in at my parents' house just as my dad was coming out of the woods having shot and buried the ailing dog. He looked ragged. Bereft. I had arrived at the exact wrong time. I was sorry for that. Sorry to see my dad so vulnerable. He wasn't real pleased to see me either.

In Dad's world, death, for the most part, was everyday, run-of-the-mill, nothing to get excited about. To him, shooting a fox that was looking you defiantly in the eye was no different than swatting a mosquito. A fox pelt was money in the bank. Killing wild animals was something he did. It was something he was really good at. He was proud of his prowess as a hunter. He didn't get his deer every season, but most. Every kill turned into a story. Every near miss turned into a story.

The running joke was, "Woulda got that deer, but it was too small, too far away." Along with "I'm going huntin' with Cousin Kyle on Saturday. Don't know why. Probably shouldn't. He's already shot me twice."

Yankees like to seem cool and detached. We like to seem tough. Nothing much phases us, including death. "Leafo is dead." Move on. It's a perverse way of being, worthy of psychoanalysis, but 99.9% of us wouldn't be caught dead in a psychiatrist's office.

Mrs. Brown's perverse neighbor Esther is not one to wear her heart on her sleeve. If she's sad about Mrs. Brown leaving, she'll never admit it. Maybe she's too sad and doesn't want her sadness to spill out in public, so she avoids the situation altogether. Some of my relatives refused to go to funerals. Or weddings for the most part. Or memorials, remembrances, ceremonies, or celebrations of any kind. Just wouldn't do it. All that making-nice nonsense. All that crying nonsense. All that exposure.

I *know* yankees feel deeply. I know our aversion to acknowledging our feelings might make the sadness or the anger or the bitterness hang on longer than it might for those who wear their hearts on their sleeves, longer and deeper than it might for those who sob their eyes out at funerals. I envy the sobbers, the ones who can let it all out at an appropriate time, rather than holding it in until it bursts like an old boil.

Our family tradition for funerals is not to have them. Somebody dies. Somebody from the Chadwick funeral home (they know us well) prepares the body for burial. A time and date are set. Some of us show up. Somebody says the Lord's Prayer, usually a Chadwick. We mumble it, too. Then we go our separate ways. That's it. More often than not, the name of the deceased is not mentioned again for, oh, twenty years.

Lately we've adopted cremation. Dad was cremated at his request. So was Ma. This eliminated the need for even a graveside prayer.

I've lived on antidepressants for thirty-five years. Not saying the way my family handles loss caused my chronic depression, but it didn't do me any good.

Eddie's Wreck

"Eddie got in a wreck on Sunday."
"Was he hurt?"
"Didn't do him any good."

A depressed humorist? From what I read, it's common. Fifteen years after my grandfather Bill Barker died, just after my dad had been diagnosed with terminal cancer, Dad brought a wooden box into the living room. "Father's box," he said. It contained letters, photographs, trapping pamphlets, memorabilia. "I haven't been able to look at it until now," he said.

Fifteen years!

It was at least that, maybe longer, before my parents touched anything in my brother Steve's room after he drove his truck into that tree. The day my brother died, I made his bed. Left alone in the house for a few minutes during the day, I couldn't resist smoothing his sheets and quilt back into place. Far as I know, that was the only thing touched in that room for a very long time. A few days after his death we went to the cemetery and mumbled the Lord's Prayer. And that was the end of that. Except it wasn't.

Toward the end of her life my mother said, "I talk to Steve and your father every night before I go to bed."

I said, "That's fine, Ma. So long as they don't talk back."

Might be that my life course has been an attempt to rebel against all the death I witnessed as a child. I have never killed an animal. Though I do eat meat, so I'm a hypocrite.

Instead of going dark, I've gone light. Nothing is lighter than laughter. Is it a contradiction that I also sought training as a hospice volunteer? That I sat for three weeks in a hospital as my dad lay dying so he wouldn't be alone? That I became my mother's full-time caregiver as she declined? I don't exactly laugh at death—it's so frickin' permanent—but I don't look away from it either. Birth and death, two sides of the same thin coin just like laughter and tears. Shortly before Dad died, we talked about what was coming. "What do you think happens after you die?" he asked. Or maybe I did. We agreed that after death we went to where we were before we were born. Not such a bad thing. Probably dark there. And quiet. Restful.

Every year for the last decade plus, I've emceed an annual caregivers conference. A couple hundred of us, mostly home caregivers, gather for workshops. We learn from speakers and each other. We gather for a catered breakfast and roast turkey lunch. Massage and Reiki are offered—some well-earned pampering. We gather, most of all, to share stories. Caregiving for a loved one is one of the hardest and most rewarding jobs in the world. It can wear you down. Statistically, 30–40 percent of caregivers die before the person they're caring for. If you're over the age of seventy, the percentage goes up. Take care of yourself first, the experts say. Most caregivers don't. It is, however, revitalizing to spend even a day with people who understand what it's like to care for someone around the clock, someone who's not going to get better, someone you love.

Keeping a sense of humor is essential. One caregiver described her husband's progressive illness and how, toward the end, he couldn't move or speak but was able to type with one finger. One day he wrote: "We should go on a vacation."

She said, "Honey, where would you like to go?"

He typed, "Egypt."

"But how would we get there?"

He typed, "First class."

They didn't make it to Egypt, but she's still smiling and telling his story.

It has become a tradition at that conference for Helen Robinson to tell this story to the group. She doesn't volunteer to tell it. She gets coerced. Sometimes she protests a little, but we are persuasive. It never fails to make us laugh.

Problem Solved

Helen's family had a farm on Block Island off the coast of Rhode Island. The island is famous for dramatic sea cliffs where the earth falls away to a beach below. Helen's family farm bordered some of these sea cliffs.

Sadly, one of the horses died near the edge of one of those cliffs where the ground was rocky. Hard digging. So they had the idea of digging a grave for the horse at the base of the cliff in the soft sand.

Once the hole was dug they rolled the corpse to the edge of the cliff and down over. The horse landed in the hole on its back. The hole wasn't big enough so when they filled in around it with sand, the four stiff legs were sticking out.

No problem. They went to the barn, grabbed an old door, set it on those four sticking-up legs, and made a picnic table.

The short stories of Flannery O'Connor are called grotesque, a term for a particular type of literature and the response it evokes. In "Good Country People" when Hulga gets stuck in the hayloft after the seductive Bible salesman absconds with her wooden leg, the reader is not sure whether to laugh or cry. It's horrible. And funny. That's grotesque—a situation that makes you feel two things at once. You're not sure what to make of it. This creates tension. Laughter releases tension. When a scene is both horrible and funny—like Hulga in the hayloft (how the heck is she going to get down that ladder?) or a picnic table made from the stiff legs of a dead horse—that's morbid. That's life.

A PARTICULAR SENSE OF HUMOR

My book *Sixty Years of Cuttin' the Cheese: Joel Sherburne and Calef's Country Store* chronicles the adventures of a man with a highly developed yankee sensibility. Joel Sherburne started working at Calef's Country Store in Barrington when he was seventeen. Sixty years later, he's still at it.

He wears many hats. For one thing, he's an EMT who founded the ambulance service in his town. Before Barrington got its own ambulance, the town used the hearse from a local funeral home to transport patients to the hospital in Rochester. "They put a red light on the top and it was an ambulance," Joel said. "Take the red light off and it was a hearse again. They'd just put 'em in the hearse, put the red light on, and go as fast as they could to the hospital." If the patient died en route, they took the light off the roof.

At one storytelling session, we got to talking about how this was a common practice in many towns, and an older woman piped up, "Yup. That happened to my husband."

I laughed. Loudly. And I wasn't the only one. Then I was stricken. Oh my god, I'm laughing at this poor woman's story of how her husband got taken away in an ambulance/hearse and died. I was sorry. So sorry. Until I realized the woman was laughing, too—in her subtle yankee way. Her lips were turned up at the corners. "That was fawty years ago," she said. "I'm over it."

Maybe my particular sense of humor developed in response to the contradictions in my childhood. Nobody loved animals more than my dad and he killed a lot of them. What's a child to make of that? After he died, it fell to me to clean out his car and garage. In the trunk of the car, I found a fox skin in a plastic grocery bag. In his garage I found a gallon jug full of what looked like pickled prunes. Didn't taste them. Luckily. Turns out they were beaver gonads. I decided against selling them at the yard sale. Didn't know whether they should be priced individually or by the pound.

Bruce Geiger could have died under that overturned tractor, but he didn't. Albert Fogg, in this next story, could've died on his way to town meeting, but he didn't. We defy death by telling stories of survival.

Albert Fogg's Trek

Albert Fogg showed up at town meeting much to the surprise of town folk. He lived on the other side of the lake, had no near neighbors, didn't drive. Even if he did drive, it was mud season and his road was impassable. "How'd you get here?" folks asked Albert.

"Come across the ice," he said.

"Albert," the town folk said, shocked, "that ice is awful thin and punky. How'd you dare cross it?"

"Well," he said, "I made myself as light as I could and walked right along fast."

I embrace Albert's solution to the problem of getting where he needs to go. I make a conscious effort to make myself as light as I can and walk right along fast.

In this next story, Edith 'bout killed her neighbor, Joanie, with her bad driving. But she didn't. Far as we know.

Edith's Yield

Joanie accepted a ride to town from her neighbor Edith, even though she was aware of Edith's reputation as a bad driver. Some called her hell-on-wheels. As they approached the V intersection where Routes 3 and 4 merge, Joanie spotted a car heading toward the merge in the same direction as them, but on the parallel road. It was moving at about the same speed as Edith.

"Car on your left," Joanie said.

"I see it," Edith said.

Didn't slow down. Didn't speed up.

The car on the left kept a-coming. The gap began to close. Edith kept going, too. Looked like they were going to hit the merge at exactly the same time. Joanie panicked. "Yield, Edith. For God's sake, yield."

Edith said, "I yielded last time."

Edith is stubborn. Many of us are. She'd rather crash at the merge than yield—again.

Stories, even the short ones, must have tension. In a yankee classic, the farmer takes his wife of sixty years for her last ride—in a coffin in the back of a wagon to the cemetery. He and his friend sit up front as the horse clops along. The farmer says, "She was a wonderful cook and housekeeper. Yup. Strong woman. She could carry two fifty-pound bags of feed, one on each shoulder, uphill to the barn. Hard worker. Good Christian. Never missed a Sunday service. Did a lot of good works out in the community. Smaht, too. She had a solution to every problem, and she let you know it. She was a wonderful mother to our children. Kept 'em in line. Brought 'em up right."

The friend murmurs words of condolence.

"You know," says the farmer, "I never really liked her."

Harry Prouty and the Old Hoss Buggy

Harry Prouty of Ashuelot grew up on a farm. As kids, they had to make their own fun. One hot summer day, he and some of his buddies dragged the old hoss buggy out of the barn and hauled it to the top of the high field. They piled in, all but one.

Harry, since it was his farm, got to steer with the shaves pulled upright. The one yet-to-pile-in gave the wagon a shove and hopped on the back.

Down the hill they went. It was a big field, steep in the middle, with a drop-off at the end—about twelve feet—to a farm road. "You know with them big buggy wheels," Harry said, "we got goin' pretty fast."

They didn't think they'd get as far as that drop-off, but once that buggy got going, it picked up speed, bouncing from one hummock to another, one rock to another.

"We're gonna die, Harry," one of the boys shouted.

"We might!" Harry shouted back. He couldn't steer for beans.

They didn't dare jump off for fear of being run over by the hind wheels. They clung to that buggy for dear life.

As they bore down on the drop-off, the boys were screaming, Harry was screaming. They knew they were about to meet their maker.

Harry said, "We sailed off the edge like Santy Claus in his sleigh. Landed in the top of an apple tree. We felt ourselves all over to make sure we weren't hurt or anything. Had to climb down out of that apple tree. Took the rest of the afternoon to get the tractor and pull that hoss buggy out of the tree and get it back in the barn."

Simple delivery techniques can build tension in any story. If the teller's voice quiets, audiences settle. Slow the delivery and an audience that has seemed disengaged will reengage. Slow translates into important. This is especially effective with children—the toughest audience of all. With antsy children I speak slower and more softly. This *usually* pulls them in. Not always. Kids are humbling.

Children's books are my ticket to elementary schools. Kids do not care how many adult books I've written, but they are impressed by books written especially for them. I often read *The Iciest Diciest Scariest Sled Ride Ever!* to kindergarteners. Everybody loves stories, but kindergarteners, enthralled by the magic of learning to read, love them especially. In *The Iciest Diciest Scariest Sled Ride Ever!*, seven kids climb a hill and slide down—that's the action. Seven kids climb a big hill and slide down even though they're scared, like Harry Prouty and his friends in the hoss buggy—that's the plot.

"There are three stories in every picture book," I say. "The one the words tell. The one the pictures tell. And the one the words and pictures tell together." Kindergarteners already know this, but teachers seems to appreciate the insight.

Then we come to Q&A. "Who has a question?" Many hands go up. I ask the teacher to call on the children because (1) the teacher knows their names and (2) the teacher just knows.

The first question goes like this: "I was riding on a sled down in my Grampa's field and I hit a bump and fell off and my brother landed on top of me and..." The teacher interrupts: "That's a nice story, Cheryl, but who has a question for Mrs. Rule?"

The second question goes like this: "My sister fell off her bike and broke her elbow." The teacher says: "That's a good story, Brandon. But who has a question?"

The third question is: "I broke my arm."

"We know that, Zach," the teacher says. "Who has a question?"

Many hands go up. The teacher calls on Betty. "Is this a question, Betty?" Betty nods. "It's a question, not a story, right?" Betty nods. "Okay," the teacher says, "ask your question."

Betty says, "Can somebody please tie my shoe?"

NATURAL INCLINATIONS

My daughter says I have the attention span of a gnat on heroin. That's an exaggeration, but my short attention span may be why I work in miniatures rather than murals. A folklorist suggested that instead of telling lots of quick stories, I turn my attention to longer ones. People tell stories that last fifteen minutes, a half hour, an hour, for goodness sake. Odds Bodkin has recorded five hours of *The Odyssey*.

I was taken aback by the folklorist's suggestion. After a stunned pause to turn the idea over and walk around it, I said, with furrowed brow, I didn't believe I was capable of telling long stories. The folklorist assured me I was. Anybody could if they set their minds to it.

I pondered that. Still ponder it from time to time. Rather than admit to a personal shortcoming, I've decided telling a long story is not in my nature. Stay true to your nature—this is a lesson I've been learning all my life.

When I was writing short stories and agents asked for a novel, I tried to write one. Tried my darnedest. Wrote a few bad drafts. The work was hard, frustrating, slow-going. I knew what novels looked like. I'd read plenty. I knew all the parts—characters, scenes, setting plot, details. I knew the shape—rising action, climax, falling action, denouement. And yet . . .

Eventually, I had an epiphany. "I can no more write a novel than build a bahn," I told friends.

"Why not?"

"Because bahns are so frickin' big and novels are so frickin' long."

(Full disclosure: I am currently working on a mystery novel. Why not?)

Same with telling. I can no more tell a thirty-minute story than I could build a bahn or sculpt a nude. It's not in me. Each of us must tell according to our nature—long, short, or middling; dark or light; absurd or realistic; personal or not-so-much. People say, "You should tell stories for that NPR program *The Moth*." Nope. Stories told on *The Moth* are true, longish, and about impactful life experiences—like getting shot or being dumped by your lover or climbing the Green Monster at Fenway. I could no more tell a *Moth* story than I could sing the lead in *Madame Butterfly*.

The muralist paints big pictures of breaching whales on the sides of buildings. Lots of paint, splashy, big strokes made with big brushes, maybe even brooms. Ladders may be involved. Miniatures are created with dabs of paint delicately applied, not a drop to spare, tiny strokes with tiny brushes, maybe even hairs. Magnifying glasses may be involved. I don't paint at all, except my house. And the shed. But only up as far as I can reach standing on the ground because ladders wobble. John Rule said he'd paint the high parts. And he will. Eventually.

The choice to work small has its own challenges, especially what comes next.

If you're going to tell one or two or even three stories in an hour, it's easy to remember the order. If you're going to tell twenty it's hard to keep the order straight in your head. It is for me, anyway. I need a set list. I have no trouble remembering the stories themselves (so far), but I need that list. Some people have nightmares about being on stage naked. Me, too. But the worst one is being on stage without a set list, unable to think of a single story to tell. Naked and mute.

SHAPING A SESSION

This is the set list for a program for the Warner Telephone Museum. I start with some telephone stories, then some local stories about a character named Jules Pellerin of nearby New London. Next a few about the tradition of yankee humor followed by stories of community and connection including town meeting. I save some favorites for the end.

As usual, when the time came to tell stories at the Warner Telephone Museum, I didn't tell all the stories on my list. Probably got to half of them. I chose according to audience reaction. I added stories on the spot when that seemed like the right thing to do. Of the favorites listed at the end, I likely picked just one—a short one if time was running short, a longer one if the audience seemed up for it. Or I might have picked one from the middle that I'd skipped but that now felt like an ending.

The set list is as fluid as the stories themselves. Has to be. I never know how much the listeners will laugh, how often they'll pipe up with stories or comments, how hot or cold or stuffy the hall will be, how hard the chairs. At a sit-down dinner, an awards ceremony, or some other lengthy, structured event, when asked how long I need for my talk, I say I'm flexible like Gumby. If people have been sitting a long time—sitting, eating, drinking, and listening to a number of speakers—shorter is inestimably better. Wise organizers hold the raffle at the end, so people will stay for the whole thing. I'm not the only one with a short attention span.

Set List for the Warner Telephone Museum

Telephone stories:
- Virgil at Town Hall
- 1 Room School—Kiss my ass
- Ginger in Lakeport—Castor oil, glass eye
- Fodd Boody's Tall Mother —Don't act like Fodd Boody

Connections
- Jules Pellerin—New London—Aluminum canoe—Does it leak?
- Yankee Humor
- Dudley Laufman—B flat
- Deep Humor—Barbara in East Kingston—WillowWare tureen
- Uncle Jr.—Daggett and McGregor

Community
- Joel Sherburne—Lime pickled
- School Teacher in Need of Sausage
- 2 ccs of Fancy Barbados Molasses
- Hurricane of '38 Vea Jenks
- Richard O'Day

Town Meeting
- Sadie Perkins, Holderness—Some holding tank
- Nukes in Canterbury

Favorites
- 4-D-L
- Warren Angus Wilbur and Razor True—Boston wife, ice fishing
- Roland Aube Trophy/Ring

Like each of the stories themselves, a story session needs shape—a planned beginning, middle, and end with ample wiggle room in between. Just as the beginning of a story needs to grab listeners' attention, so does the first offering in a session. Just as the ending of a story needs to leave listeners satisfied and with a sense of closure, so does the end of a session. I call it the grand finale, and let listeners know it's coming so they'll be prepared to clap and proceed to the back of the hall for cookies and lemonade.

"Does anybody have a story to tell before the grand finale?" I say.

If audience contributions run long, the grand finale shrinks. It's just as important for them to tell their tales as for me to tell mine. Maybe more so. "I measure the success of an evening by the stories you tell," I say. "I've heard all of mine before." And I mean it. This is our session. We make it together.

What I don't say, but what is true: Without your stories my career as a storyteller would have fizzled out year one. As much as I love the old stories, it's the new ones that keep me inspired. One story leads to another and another.

I commit to the end of a session by promising to tell just one or three or five more stories. Rule of thumb: never go longer than an hour if you can help it. The mind can absorb only as much as the butt can stand. I choose those final stories carefully. It's their job to pull the session together. If we've been telling a lot of family stories, a family story might be called for. If we've been telling small-town stories, maybe we'll end up at the dump. If we've been talking about yankees and their character, a story about yankee compassion might make for a tidy finish. Almost any story can work depending on the stories that have come before.

Jim O'Donnell tells a town meeting story from Lincoln. Seems the warrant article to purchase a new snowplow proved controversial. A new snowplow constitutes a big investment for a small town. After much discussion, a voter proposed a solution. He'd heard that the neighboring town of Woodstock also had a snowplow on the warrant. "Why can't Lincoln and Woodstock split the cost and share the plow?" he suggested.

The road agent rose to speak. "Far as I know, when it's snowing in Lincoln, it's snowing in Woodstock."

FLEXIBILITY IS KEY

Set lists change. Stories change. Audiences change a lot. The difference between telling stories in Lincoln or Woodstock is negligible, but—make no mistake about it—there is a difference. There's a difference between telling stories at a synagogue in Bethlehem, a Baptist church in Caanan, and a DAR meeting in Concord. Tread carefully, Becky Rule, especially at that DAR meeting. The contrast between speaking to major donors at the Fells Historical Estate and residents in the dementia wing at a county home is considerable. The difference between telling stories at a town hall I've visited every year for the past decade and to a group of medical professionals—none of whom know me from a hole in the ground—is cavernous. The prospect of failure looms. Always. And by failure I mean failure to connect. That's where being flexible like Gumby comes in.

For those who don't remember Gumby, he is a claymation figure from the 1950s. Two paddle-shaped arms, two paddle-shaped legs, rectangular torso—think SpongeBob SquarePants but primitive. Gumby could bend every which way. Children enjoyed his stop-action TV adventures with his sidekick, Pokey the Pony. At my house we received only two channels via the rabbit ears on our black and white Motorola. We watched *Gumby*, candlepin bowling, Marty Engstrom with the weather from the top of Mount Washington (he had a *great* yankee accent), *Uncle Gus*, wrestling, *The Wide World of Sports*, and old movies on *The Early Show*. This was entertainment. This was what I knew of the world beyond Boscawen. TV and books. I read a lot. Mysteries, romances, westerns, biographies. My parents read a lot. Grammie and Grampa Stewart had a closet in their bedroom with floor-to-ceiling books—mostly popular fiction of another era like Grace Livingston Hill, Harold Bell Wright, Zane Grey. I was free to choose any I liked. And I liked them all.

All I ever wanted for Christmas and birthdays were animal stories by Rutherford Montgomery. My favorite was *Odyssey of an Otter*. One year for Christmas I asked for a Jon Gnagy Learn to Draw kit. Got it. Drew a pumpkin. That was the beginning and end of my career as an artist. In an odd conversation with painter James Aponovich, we discovered we'd each received a Jon Gnagy Learn to Draw kit at about the same impressionable age. That and the fact that we both lived in New Hampshire was about all we had in common. The passion to become a painter was in James Aponovich from the beginning just as the passion to tell stories was in me.

Frugal yankees, we didn't buy anything new in my family—not cars, not furniture, not clothes, certainly not books. Except for those Rutherford Montgomerys. And toilet paper. (And the previously mentioned snowmobile.) How I loved those books. *Odyssey of an Otter* sits on my desk still, along with its friends *Cougar, El Blanco,* and *Weecha the Raccoon*—adventures from the point of view of the animals.

I loved rereading. Still do. If you read a book over and over, you learn how it works. You see how it's structured and how the characters develop. You notice the details that bring scenes to life. You see how point of view defines the story.

Rereading teaches the importance of word choice. As Mark Twain said, the difference between the *almost right* word and the *right* word is "the difference between the lightning bug and the lightning."

I learned to spell and punctuate by rereading. About the fifth time through you begin to notice the little things. Nobody needed to tell me commas and periods go inside quotation marks. I knew it. I'd seen it ten thousand times.

Reading is rereading, said some scholar. Telling is, of course, retelling. Nobody tells a story just once. Not if it's a good one. About the fifth time through, you begin to notice the little things—where to speak soft, where to speak loud, when to speak fast or slow, when to pause, what to put in, what to leave out. You discover the difference between the *almost right* word and the *right* word. You try them out—one word, then another, and another. That's what creativity is—being open to one word, then another, and another. It's being flexible within your discipline, whether it's writing, painting, gymnastics, conducting the Boston Symphony Orchestra, or telling stories.

Flexibility is critical when all does not go as planned: The mic doesn't work or, even worse, works intermittently. Only two people show up. There's a fire drill. The speaker ahead of you talks too long, so your time is cut by half. When you announce, "I've got just one more story," and a drunk person yells, "Good!"

All these things happen. All of them have happened to me.

What can you do except smile and carry on? Save the tears and expletives for the ride home.

I once shared the stage with a teller who pitched a hissy fit during rehearsal. He was upset about the lighting and sound. It might have been a fund-raiser for a historical society or club or school. I believe a high school student pushed the lighting and sound buttons. Nobody knew what to say when the teller yelled, "All I ask is that the audience can see me and hear me!" and stormed off.

The angry teller did, to his credit, reappear for the performance. Later, he confided he'd had a bad day. I felt a twinge of sympathy, but not much. He was not Gumby. He was the anti-Gumby. The sound and lights were not that bad. I'd seen worse. The audience didn't know the difference. The audience doesn't care about your bad day. Heck, one of the joys of telling stories is that for that one hour you can forget about your bad day.

WHEN YOUR INNER CHILD CHANNELS YOUR INNER GROWN-UP

A friend makes it a rule to perform only with people who behave like grown-ups. This is a good idea. A person can be ten years old and a grown-up. A person can be fifty-two and not a grown-up. Being grown-up means respecting others—their talent, their time, their efforts. All the storytellers I know are playful, in touch with their inner children, and also grown-ups. Except that one angry guy, and he's moved on to other pursuits. You tell other people's stories long enough, you begin to truly understand them. No wonder storytellers are so empathetic and practical. We are students of human nature.

I know this next story is true because when telling it to residents at a nursing home, a nurse stuck her head through the doorway and said, "Linwood Rogers was my uncle." I said, "Does this story sound like him?" She said it did. When nurses stop their work to stick their heads in and listen, that's a testament to the power of story.

The Sixteen Dollar Picnic Table

Linwood Rogers sold picnic tables by the side the road. This was some years ago. He sold them for sixteen dollars each. Cost you a lot more than that to get a picnic table these days.

One day a man in a pickup truck sees Linwood's sign, "Picnic Tables, $16.00." He stops. He says to Linwood, "Sixteen dollars, huh? How long does it take you to make one of these picnic tables?"

Linwood says, "About four hours."

The fella does some quick calculations. "Four hours, sixteen dollars, that's about four dollars an hour ain't it?" He'd obviously been to college. Probably Dartmouth.

Linwood says, "Yuh."

Fella says, "Can you make me a picnic table for three dollars an hour?"

Linwood says, "Sure. But it'll take me a little longer."

The tourist asks the farmer at the sap house how successful the maple season had been compared to other years. Farmer says, "Didn't go as well as expected. But, then again, we didn't think it would."

That's philosophy. Storytellers aren't born philosophers, but we become philosophical as we age.

"I can't write," the student says.

"Writing is thinking," says the teacher.

"I have no stories to tell," the student says.

"Huh?" says the storyteller.

DIDN'T GO AS WELL AS EXPECTED

Organizers of a run to raise money for cancer research asked if I'd tell an hour's worth of stories for no pay. Which was fine. It was a good cause. The run was on a Sunday and I was to be the next-to-last act. It rained hard and the wind blew all day. I drove through that wind and rain more than an hour to the venue, an athletic field at a college. There weren't too many other cars in the lot when I arrived, but I pushed through the wind and rain to a row of canopies set up along a track. One or two volunteers sheltered under each canopy behind folding tables. Some had brochures. Some had popcorn in plastic bags. Some had beverages, I guess. Didn't look too closely. Couldn't see much. The volunteers hunched over, hands in pockets, their faces obscured by the hoods of their rain gear.

"Are you sure you want me to speak for an hour?" I asked the woman in charge.

She admitted most everybody had gone home, but a band was scheduled to play after me so she couldn't shut down shop yet. She led me to a riser under one of the canopies. A tall sandwich board sported my name and likeness. There was no audience. Water pooled in the metal folding chairs. She said, "Just talk into the mic and pretend you're on the radio."

I did. For forty-five minutes. Until the sandwich board blew over and hit me in the head. I said into the mic, "Is the band here yet?"

The woman in charge slogged over. She said, "They decided not to play on account of the weather. It's bad for the instruments." Seems I was the last act after all. When I stopped yapping, everybody could go home. I stopped yapping. We all went home.

When my first couple of books came out—back then I was writing serious literary fiction—I did readings. You can't stop reading a story in the middle. Even if you feel like it. You press on. You've marked ten pages to read, you've practiced them, timed it, by god, you're gonna read those pages.

During my transition from reading to telling, I figured out that it was okay to read the first few pages, describe briefly what happens in the middle, then skip to the boffo ending. This might have been a clue I was destined to be a teller of humorous yankee stories rather than a writer of serious literary fiction. After one bookstore reading, when I had deviated into telling a funny story about writing serious stories, the owner whispered: "Stick with the funny stuff."

Professor Tom Newkirk—teacher, mentor, friend—sat front and center during one of those early readings at UNH. The audience was teachers and teachers of teachers. I read a line about somebody dropping dead. It struck Tom funny. He laughed loud and hard. Tom has a wonderful laugh—rippling, joyous, contagious. I stopped short and said, "Tom, that's not the funny part." Which made him laugh even more. And made me laugh. The whole crowd laughed. This, too, might have been a clue I was destined to be a teller. When I looked up from the page at all those hopeful faces, I felt connected and comfortable. The laughter inspired me to try and make everyone in the auditorium laugh some more.

Storytellers embrace the unexpected. The first story on the set list for Warner Telephone Museum, "Virgil at Town Hall," can be told many different ways. In this version, I embed another story—just a quick one—called "Hattie in Hebron"—for an audience of older folks who remember party lines.

Virgil at Town Hall

When I was a kid we had a party line. You'd have to wait for your special ring—two long one short or one long two short. If you picked up on somebody else's ring you could listen in on their conversation. Not that I ever did. Not that any of you ever did.

Hattie in Hebron was known for listening in on other people's conversations. A couple of her neighbors were talking on the phone. During the sensitive part of the conversation, they happened to think maybe Hattie was listening in. One neighbor yelled: "Hattie, hang up the phone!" Hattie yelled back, "I ain't listening. I'm clear over by the sink."

There was a time when you couldn't even dial somebody direct on the phone. You had to dial the operator, tell her the number, and she'd connect you to your party. Virgil was the road agent in town. He placed a call from town hall and somehow got into an argument with the operator. Ended up telling her to go to hell and slammed down the phone.

One of the selectmen overheard. He said, "Virgil, you can't be using the town phone in town hall for town business and be representing the town and tell somebody to go to hell. You call that operator right back and apologize!"

Virgil dialed up the operator. "Are you the operator I talked to five minutes ago and told to go to hell?"

"Yes," she said.

"Well," he said, "you don't have to." ⌒

Sometimes Virgil's story leads to a childhood memory from Lester. Lester had a speech impediment as a child. At recess, he tried to flirt with a girl in his class, a twin. She couldn't seem to understand what he was saying. He got embarrassed. In his frustration, he blurted, "Kiss my ass!"

The twin brother overheard the exchange and had some harsh words for Lester. Something like, "Take that back, Lester, or I'm gonna thrash ya." Next recess, Lester approached the offended girl. He said, "I'm sorry for saying, 'Kiss my ass.' You don't have to. Me and your brother have made other arrangements."

More often than not, stories of childhood draw out the audience. Everybody has a story from when they were little or when their kids were little. My one superpower is drawing stories out of people. Maybe it's not a superpower. Maybe it's a mutation. I'm a story vampire.

Proud grandparents are easy marks. They're full of anecdotes. Teachers, too, have a wealth of stories in the genre of funny things kids say and do.

Hygiene Matters

After recess, the children had a bathroom break. Joyce, a teacher, stood at the door of the boys' room. When each boy emerged, she asked if he'd remembered to wash his hands. All the boys said yes, until Scotty.

"Did you wash your hands, Scotty?" she asked.

"No, Teacher," he said. "I didn't have to. I kept my mittens on." ⌒

THE PRIME DIRECTIVE

In *Star Trek*, the Prime Directive is for the travelers on the starship *Enterprise* to refrain from interfering in the cultures they encounter. In storytelling—or any public speaking—the Prime Directive, besides making sure your fly's zipped, is to respect other people's time.

One of my dad's favorite expressions was "Life's too short," usually in the context of don't stay mad, don't hold a grudge. I think a lot about time—time passed, time wasted, time remaining. When I stand before an audience and the telling begins, time seems to stand still. I feel as though I'm in a place that is out of time, separate from its passage. An hour disappears in a flash. Riding the chairlift to the top of the mountain takes a while, but once you're at the top and the slope stretches before you and the skis start to move, the glorious ride seems over in an instant. Unless, of course, you wipe out halfway down.

That's what storytelling is like for me. The planning, the drive to the venue, the chitchat before the program—all those things take time and energy. But the telling itself seems to take no time, no energy, no thought, even. It begins and then it's over. I hope connections were made. I hope people recognized themselves in the stories. I hope we laughed together. But all that seems beyond my control. The stories take over.

Time may not mean nothin' to a pig—the teller who's absorbed in the stories and the moment—but it means a lot to other people. I've been guilty of talking too long, not once but many times. When you're in the moment, it's hard to keep track of time, but it's also critical. Since I can't always depend on my inner clock, I depend on the big clock at the back of the hall, or a friend in the audience to give me the "five more minutes" signal, or my cell phone on the lectern. When the hour is up, it's up.

It takes discipline to stop, because you have so much to say and, in your head, the audience needs to hear everything you planned and maybe some other stuff that pops up on the spot—the dreaded and acclaimed ad lib.

Ad-libs, those little time eaters, are sometimes very, very good—fresh, surprising, fun, insightful. But sometimes they are horrid—clunky, silly, embarrassing, inappropriate. Until they fly out of your mouth and into the ears of your listeners, you just don't know.

Usually the plusses of the ad lib outweigh the minuses.

Who am I kidding? I ad lib. I take my chances. The words come out like sneezes. They are flying through the air before I even think them, before I even feel the tickle in my nose.

When they fail, it's painful. But when they work, it's exhilarating and unifying. If I talk off the cuff to listeners, they are free to talk back. Let the wild rumpus begin!

Do not try this with little kids. A teacher warned, "Don't get these kindergarteners going. Once they get going, they act just like five-year-olds." When I suggested to a first grade teacher that I might invite the class to tell a few stories of their own, she shook her head, "Don't do it. They'll never stop."

If you use ad libs, you owe it to your audience to count them in the timekeeping. If you're doing an hour of stories and you ad lib for ten minutes, you have to cut ten minutes from the stories you planned to tell. Math.

Took a while, but I learned. Set a time limit and do not exceed it. Respect your audience. Respect their time.

A Mild Summer Evening in the Basement of the Presbyterian Church

It was one of those summer evenings that seem to last forever. The air is mild. The light lasts until 8:30 or 9:00 PM A mellow evening. We gathered in the basement of the church and shared stories. I remember the two Maries. The younger had given the older a ride to the hall. They were ninety-two and ninety-six respectively. They contributed to the session. Many people did. Back and forth.

The small windows in the cement block wall revealed the light was fading. Night drawing near. But we were having such a good time.

"I've got just a couple more stories to tell," I said.

One of the Maries piped up, "You said that six stories ago."

Which is why, when I near the end of a story session, I always say how many stories I will tell in the remaining time—whether it's a couple or three or five. I pick a number and commit to it. Never again do I want to hear an irritated nonagenarian say, "You said that six stories ago." Afterwards I realized Marie probably didn't like driving in the dark. She, too, saw the light fading in the windows. She wanted me to shut up so she could go home. ~

Sometimes I see the clock on the wall says 8:30, time to stop, but maybe, just maybe, I can squeeze in one last story. A brief one that fits perfectly into the trajectory of the evening. Not the ending I intended, but the ending that is called for by the back and forth with the listeners. No one is squirming or checking watches. The dad has taken the crying baby to the parking lot. A few people have sneaked out for a bathroom break but returned. One guy has nodded off and is snoring a little; he needs his rest. The cookies and punch are being set out by the Friends of the Library. I might get away with stretching my time just a dite.

Sometimes I succumb to temptation. But only if I feel the audience is truly with me and the pews aren't too hard, the hall not too cold or hot. Just one more story. Just one more laugh, in the sentiment of the Irish folk song by Seamus Moore, "A Little Bit More." When it's time for sleep, Moore sings, the children "cry and roar." They beg to stay up "just a little bit more." Morning comes, same thing, they want to stay in bed "just a little bit more." Until you're at death's door and you want to tarry amongst the living "just a little bit more."

Everybody wants a little bit more. One more beer, one more kiss, one more story before our time together comes to a close.

If all goes well, listeners will wish the session had gone on longer.

If a listener says afterwards, "I could have listened to you all night," you know she couldn't have. But you also know you timed the session right.

If you're on a panel of five and the organizer says, "You each get five minutes," it's important to speak for no more than five minutes. If the first speaker gets carried away and goes, say, twenty minutes, what then? Everybody's screwed—the organizer, the other speakers, and especially the listeners. To speak for twenty minutes instead of five with four speakers still to come, that's egregious. Beware: If you're an inexperienced speaker, wear a watch and check it. It is possible—I've seen this happen (it happened to me)—to become hypnotized by the sound of your own voice, to lose all sense of time, space, and your place in the universe.

SECRETS

Donald Graves, one of the most influential educators and gifted speakers I've ever known, said the key to connecting with audiences is to get people as close together as possible and have nothing between you and them—not a lectern, not a table, not even a piece of paper or a book. He spoke, often, without notes. His lectures were rich with stories.

In the beginning there were butterflies—in my stomach, in my throat, fluttering like mad behind my eyeballs. But the more I told, the better I got at the craft, the quieter the butterflies grew. When I stopped worrying what anybody thought of me, that was a turning point. I'm a conduit. My job is to deliver stories as they deserve to be delivered—clearly and enthusiastically.

Every time I tell a story I learn something about it. I can tell from listener reaction what went right and wrong, which arrow hit the bull's-eye and which sailed off into the woods. If there are butterflies, they have to do with a new place, a faulty microphone, or allergies. I'm allergic to the dust in old buildings. My throat constricts, my eyes water, my nose runs. Allergy meds and cold water help. The butterflies worry about whether my water bottle is full and my voice will hold out. But no longer do they bother about the stories themselves or audience reaction.

After a recent session, a woman offered a backhanded compliment. She said, "I heard you talk years ago and didn't think you were that great. You were really funny tonight. You got better."

I said, "I should hope so."

Twenty-five years of practice has to amount to something. You play piano for twenty-five years, you get better at playing piano.

If a line or even a whole story flops, there's a pause, a moment of awkwardness. Then: "Don't worry, Story. I'll do you justice next time." And, "Don't worry audience, there are more stories to come. We'll be okay."

Listeners are inclined to be patient and forgiving. They want to hear good stories. They want to absorb them and pass them on. They want to see themselves in them. They want to say: Ayuh, that's true. That's how it could happen. That's how it *did* happen.

What's the secret to good storytelling?

Practice.

The secret to good storytelling is practicing in front of people (who are not your mother, your husband, or your son-in-law) so you can gauge how the story comes across. I warn people: "I'm telling this for the first time, so it might not be that great." Sometimes I lie and say it's the first time, even though it's the fifth. We all know a story told for the first time (or the fifth or even the tenth) is a work in progress. Like life. The trick is to surround the new stories—the toddlers—with the tried and true ones. Support the little ones until they are ready to stand strong on their own. Let the audience help. "This is a new one," I say. "I don't know if it's funny or not. I don't even know if it's a story." And launch into it. Whether I'm telling stories or maneuvering through life, I'm thinking: *What's the worst that could happen?*

Sometimes the overall reaction is puzzlement. Nobody laughs. Somebody says, "Is that it?" It's not that bad. In fact, the puzzlement, uncomfortable silences, and stunned "Is that it?" are funny in themselves. When a story fails spectacularly, it's like I slipped on a banana and fell on my ass. If I can laugh at myself, the audience is free to laugh too. We laugh together. We move on.

Storytelling is call and response. I start every session with, "Hello." The audience says, "Hello." And off we go.

"If one of my stories reminds you of a story," I say, "feel free to tell it." I announce, "In the storytelling tradition, feel free to pass these stories on. If you tell a story, I'll write it down in my little notebook and tell it in the next town." That always gets a laugh. People notice when I write their stories down. They seem pleased. And I'm completely serious about telling their stories. Stories stay alive as they move teller to teller. To pass them on is to honor them.

Being comfortable in front of an audience is the natural result of practice. If I'm comfortable and confident, the audience relaxes. A relaxed audience is a receptive one. My goal is to deliver good stories intact—without screwing up the language, the order of events, the rhythm, or the timing.

The longer the story, the more satisfying the payoff had better damn-well be. I count on listeners' ability to fill in the blanks, make the leaps, know that soup tureens and chamber pots look alike.

The Grumpy Old Guy with the Cane in the Fourth Row

He looked at me. I looked at him. *Make me laugh*, the grumpy old guy said with his hooded eyes. *I haven't laughed out loud since 1985. Make me laugh. I dare yuh!*

Game on.

"That's a nice cane you got there," I say.

"Ain't a cane," he says. "It's a stick."

"I bet it's handmade from some local wood," I say. "Ash? Ironwood?"

"Nossuh," he says. "Maple suckah."

If stories are not passed on, they shrivel and die. When I remember what that grumpy old guy said, I remember him and his stick. When I tell you about our interaction, the moment rekindles.

Often an audience member will say, "I wanted to see if you are still telling the story I told you last year." I say, "Remind me." If I remember it, I'll tell it. *Yes, I remember you and I remember your story. Here it is come back to you!* If I can't remember the story or recall only parts, I ask them to tell it again. Sometimes I have to hear a story several times before understanding why it matters so much to the teller, before understanding why it's worth sharing.

At a supper, Lauren mentioned a recent encounter at Walmart. She saw two tall, good-looking gentlemen dressed head to toe in camouflage, wearing boots and hats. She was moved to approach them. "I remembered Vietnam," she said, "and how badly those young soldiers were treated when they came home. I always felt sorry about that."

So she thanked the two tall, good-looking gentlemen in camouflage for their service. They appreciated the gesture but quickly corrected her. "We're not military," they said. "We're duck hunters."

A story is an ethereal thing—delicate, short-lived, precious. Lauren's encounter with the duck hunters fluttered into her life just as she and her story fluttered into mine. The storyteller notices and remembers.

Lauren, I learned later, suffered from dementia. It had slowed her down. She no longer drove. She depended on friends to help her get where she needed to go. But her ability to make fun of herself remained intact. There may come a time when she can no longer remember her encounter at Walmart with the duck hunters, but all those sitting at the table that evening will. So will I. And, now, so will you.

Peter's Ponds

Peter Brown of Exeter mentioned the rectangular ponds visible from Route 101. He passed those ponds almost every day. One day he noticed a vehicle parked on the side of the highway and facing the wrong direction. He slowed down and did some heavy lookin' on. He spotted a yellow inflatable raft next to one of the ponds and, beside the raft, two fellas with shotguns, dressed head to toe in camouflage. You guessed it—duck hunters.

Peter said, "I felt awful sorry for that retriever."

Those ponds weren't ponds, they were sewage treatment lagoons.

I told Peter's lagoon story. A man said, "Are you talking about those square ponds you pass on 101 headed for the beach?"

"Yes."

He said, "When the kids were little and we passed those ponds, they asked what they were. I told them they were cranberry bogs."

Uh oh.

On May 3, 2003, a bad thing happened in Franconia Notch. New Hampshire's state symbol, the Old Man of the Mountain, fell off the side of the mountain and was gone forever. The Great Stone Face turned to rubble. In the Live Free or Die state, we were bereft. Novelist Ernest Hebert wrote that a few days later he made a pilgrimage to the viewing area for the Old Man—the one where the Old Man could no longer be viewed. He said it was the only time in his life he'd ever seen that parking lot filled with cars with New Hampshire license plates. Locals paying homage. He was our Old Man and we missed him already. We'll always miss him.

About a week later, I was speaking in New Boston when a butterfly of a story flew past. I wrote it down. If I hadn't been there, pretty sure, it might have flown away and been forgotten. I won't let that happen.

A Bad Thing Happened in Franconia

Ethel called her sister Gert. "Something awful happened, Gert," she said.

"What?" Gert said.

"The Old Man fell down."

"Well, pick him up and call 911."

But the Old Man couldn't be picked up, could he? He was the Old Man of the Mountain, the rock formation that had graced the cliffs of Cannon Mountain for centuries.

About a week later in New Boston, some of us lamented his demise. But out of our sadness sprang an idea. Now that the Old Man is gone, someone said, maybe New Hampshire will need a new state symbol, maybe even New Boston's very own glacial erratic, Frog Rock.

A glacial erratic is a big rock. Frog Rock is a big rock that looks like a frog about to jump.

Someone else said: "If Frog Rock becomes the new state symbol, maybe we'll get a new state motto: Live Free or Croak."

WHATEVER YOU DO, MAKE IT A GOOD STORY

This advice came from a stranger. He said he used to worry about his kids. Where they'd go to school. What they'd study. Who they'd hang out with. What kind of work they'd do. Whether they'd be successful. If they'd marry. Who they'd marry.

But as he and they grew older, he realized he couldn't control his kids' lives any more than they could. Nor should he. Some things would go as expected and desired. Others, not so much. He accepted this. "Whatever you do," he tells them now, "make it a good story."

I live that advice.

Experiences make more sense when they become stories. To turn experience into story is to transform it, and to begin to understand how it fits in with all the other stories that make up a life. Or a community. Or a chaotic world.

Stories are, for me, the best medicine. Especially the funny ones. I gauge the quality of my days by the number of belly laughs. A belly laugh before 9:00 AM means the day is off to a good start. A five-belly-laugh day is a pretty darned good one. A day when I get to spend an hour in an old meeting house or a library or a conference center with a bunch of people telling stories and laughing together, that's a gift.

Each storytelling session is different. It creates its own dynamics. Each session is, in itself, a story, never to be repeated. That freshness and vitality keeps me percolating.

My blog—an informal, online record—provides a place to store the stories until needed for telling and, as it turns out, for this book. In the blog I record the location, stories told, names of tellers, and unusual happenings. Sometimes the unusual happenings become a story.

In East Grafton at the Union Church, a respectable crowd (thirty-five or forty people) recalled the antics of a number of town characters—in particular Harry, Pudgy, Bud, and John. It was wonderful to see how one story led to another and how memories surfaced. All of these characters are gone now, fondly remembered, despite—or maybe because of—their eccentricities and cantankerous natures. That afternoon, they walked among us.

This was made all the sweeter because an anonymous person had sent an untraceable e-mail to the sponsoring group, calling me mean names, suggesting the program be cancelled, and threatening to disrupt it. The sponsors ignored it. If you're in the public eye, you risk catching the attention of people with hate to spew. As the fella said, "It's like winter in Maine. Not the most fun you'll ever have, but you'll probably live through it."

Debbie, librarian and former postmistress, spoke warmly about a character named Harry, who wheeled into the post office in a tear. A letter had been left in his mailbox by mistake! It was not his letter!

She looked the envelope over and noted that it was addressed to 197 Prescott Hill Road. Harry lived at 197 Mill Brook Road. She explained that the mail person must have seen the number and thought it was him, so delivered it accordingly.

"Yass," Harry said, irate, "but how the hell did they get my number in the first place?"

The story of Pudgy and the sand was well known to the crowd. It goes like this:

Pudgy and the Sand—A Cautionary Tale

Pudgy got into hot water at the dump for taking sand from the wrong pile. He dipped his bucket into the pile designated for public works instead of the pile for residents.

That very day, as he drove out of the dump, he dropped dead at the stop sign before he could turn onto the main road.

Locals saw his car blocking the way. They saw the shape of his body under the white sheet being loaded into the ambulance. It was sad.

Now in town they say, "Don't take sand from the wrong pile. Remember what happened to Pudgy."

Several East Graftoners remembered Bud and how slowly he drove. You didn't want to get behind Bud on a back road or your journey would take a while. One woman got stuck behind Bud on a back road. "I wasn't tailgating or anything. I'd guess we were going about ten miles an hour."

Eventually, Bud pulled over to the side and, as she passed, at about eleven miles an hour, he stuck his arm out the window and gave her the finger.

Good old Bud.

Rich said they used to get calls at town hall about a character named John. He was a wealthy man who lived rough, burning green wood in an open stove and fueling the fire with kerosene, so at times he was quite sooty. John loved to hitchhike. Every now and then town hall would get a call from some police department in another state. "Can you vouch for this fella says he's from Grafton? He's bumming around our town with $10,000 in his pocket."

Of course they could vouch for John.

Rich picked up John beside the road in the pouring rain. He was soaked to the skin with a plastic pumpkin on his head for a hat. Another time, John was out and about in town wearing a snorkel and carrying a whip. He said, "John, you can get in, but put the whip in the back of the truck." John obliged.

John came to Rich's house to use the phone. He was pretty sooty and puffing on his corncob pipe. Rich said he'd bring the phone out.

While he was waiting, John took a seat on a retaining wall and happened to pick a spot right above a yellow jackets' nest.

Rich said, "John, you're sitting on a yellow jackets' nest," and backed away as the bees swarmed.

John said, "They don't mean anybody any harm. They're just happy little people."

He didn't get stung once.

Debbie spoke fondly of a library patron who called the library shortly after he'd left the premises. She thought he said, "Did I leave my keys down at the library?"

"Your keys," she said. "How could you drive home without your keys?"

"I didn't say keys, dammit, I said TEETH."

The teeth were later discovered in his couch.

But the best thing that happened all afternoon was the arrival of an unexpected visitor.

At the beginning of our session, Debbie asked if anybody was here for the rabies clinic, which was being held down the road. Nobody was. In the middle of the session though, a man and a dog slid in through the back door. We greeted them warmly. "Come on in." The dog was happy to join us, but the man looked around, "Is this the rabies clinic?"

Someone quipped: "That's what happens when you have two things going on in Grafton on the same day."

SMILE WHEN YOU CAN

Things are apt to strike me funny that may not strike others the same way. My husband John Rule got kind of mad when his wire fox terrier, Bob, left a calling card in his shoe—a message that Bob, just a puppy at the time, did not appreciate being home alone all day.

I still smile when I think of John slipping his big foot into that size thirteen shoe, the expression on his face when the calling card squished under his weight.

Come to think of it, more than a few humorous situations at our house have involved animal excrement. When we first bought the house, we heated it with a wood stove. It was just a little house then. Later we added on and got a furnace. Sometimes on a cold night the wood stove would go out, so by morning it was darned chilly. We measured the chill by the thickness of the ice in the toilet.

John, bless him, got up first to stoke the stove. I was still under the covers when I heard a great thud. At the foot of the stairs, he had stepped barefoot on a large, cold dog turd. It sent him flying. My pealing laughter was entirely inappropriate. John could have broken his neck. He didn't.

Fast forward to another fateful day when John Rule rang his little bell once too often. He'd had abdominal surgery and was restricted to the upstairs bedroom and bathroom. If he needed anything, he was to ring the bell and I'd drop what I was doing and come to help. I was on call.

First couple of days, he rang the bell for food, drink, and medication. I did my best to be patient. As the days wore on, the sound of the bell became more and more annoying. About a week into his recovery, I heard the bell, dropped whatever important stuff I was doing, and rushed upstairs.

"What?"

There was John propped up in bed. There was Bob the dog sitting at the foot of the bed. "What's wrong?" I said.

"Bob looks upset," John said.

Bob looked how he always looked. He's a wire fox terrier. You can't even see his eyes.

"You have lost your bell privileges," I said to John and confiscated it.

That bell did not ring again until decades later when my mom came to live with us. About a year into her stay, she fell, broke her pelvis, and became wheelchair bound. She didn't seem to mind. She liked wheeling around.

Some people become enraged when cut off in traffic. I laugh and wave, grateful our vehicles didn't collide. I am not an especially skilled driver—overly cautious—which is why I never drive in Boston. Can't merge. Too timid. I'd just keep driving forever in whatever lane I landed in. I drive the way I've lived my life, along the path of least resistance, which translates to accepting my nature and, ultimately, following my passion.

This fear of Boston driving harkens to childhood. Once a year before Christmas, my parents would take us kids to the big city of Manchester to shop at a famous department store. You could find just about everything you wanted at Mammoth Mills.

To get to Manchester, we took I-93 south. Before the Mammoth Mills exit, the highway split. Two lanes went into the city, two lanes, according to the sign, took you directly to Boston. When that sign came into view my mother would grow fearful. She'd say something along the lines of "Oh my god, Bud, turn right!"

I knew if my dad somehow missed that crucial exit, we'd end up in Boston, never be heard from again. To this day, I'm afraid to go to Boston, which is just a hour and a half away, even if somebody else is driving. When a trip to Boston is in the works, I tidy my house. If I should die on the trip, I don't want people to find dirty dishes in the sink and underwear on the bedroom floor.

When a close call occurs on the road, I consider myself and the other driver fortunate to have come through unscathed. Survival makes me happy. It makes me laugh. My daughter, Adi, says, "Not everybody gets you, Mum." She is wise. I don't laugh to be malicious. It's just the way I see the world. Life is absurd. People are ridiculous. Especially me.

One year, my mom and dad said I could spend a windfall of ten dollars in pre-holiday Christmas money on anything I wanted. I couldn't believe it. Anything? Anything at all? I looked the Mammoth Mills merchandise over carefully and chose a powder blue stuffed poodle with a plush-covered wire frame and a zipper. It was a pajama holder. I could put it on my bed and keep my pajamas in it.

It was beautiful—possibly the softest, fuzziest, most beautiful object I'd ever seen. I knew, even at age six, that it was a silly waste of money. But I wanted it. And I could afford it.

I could tell my mother did not approve when I put the poodle in our basket. She said, "What in the world do you want with *that?*" But I didn't back down. And she couldn't really object, because she'd said I could spend the money on *anything*. She was always true to her word.

I can't remember if my brother Robert, two years younger, also had spending money, but I expect he must have. Fair is fair. He had likely picked out something too. We stood in line at the check-out, our merchandise on the counter for purchase. My dad, my mom, and me, with my little brother bringing up the rear.

After the cashier had rung up our purchases and bagged them, as Dad pulled out his wallet to pay, the cashier pointed. At first I thought she was pointing at me, but no, she was pointing at my brother—four years old. He had his hands behind his back and was balancing an enormous beach ball. Trying to sneak it out of the store, I guess. He wanted it bad.

My parents were mortified. I felt sick for the little guy, caught red-handed. Of course, he had to put the beach ball back. I don't remember if my parents yelled at him—probably not. More likely he got the silent treatment. They were mad. They were thinking, *Can't take you kids anywhere. You kids don't know how to behave among people,* even if they didn't say it out loud. Though they might have.

I felt ashamed. I don't know if Robert felt that way, too, but at the time, I believed he and I were in sync. I believed we felt alike because we were the only two in the world who were experiencing the same thing at the same time in the same little house on Corn Hill Road with our parents, the greatest parents in the world.

Later, much later, I learned that Robert and I—though we experienced many of the same things growing up—had, in fact, lived in different worlds. We live, as adults, in different worlds. And while this is painful, I have come to understand that this happens in families more often than anyone is willing to admit.

Always, beneath the laughter, there is sorrow. That's what makes laughter so potent.

One of Dad's favorite sayings was, "It'll go along like this for a while and then it'll get worse." He was not an optimist—but he loved to laugh. If what dad says is true, "It'll go along like this for a while and then it'll get worse," we better darned well find humor wherever we can. Dad's friend Stanley Ford may have put it best:

What Stanley Went Through

"How you doin', Stanley?"

"Not too bad," Stanley says, "considering what I been through."

"What's that?"

"Well, the last thing was a set of stairs."

Turns out what I really love to do—what keeps me going and heals me—is laughing in a room filled with other people also laughing. This has sustained me through my worst days and it has made my best days better.

Applause is nice too. I think we should all get and give one or two rounds of applause every day just to celebrate each other. Celebrate small accomplishments. Celebrate life. Go ahead, applaud yourself. Applaud being on the right side of the grass.

Some people play tennis or Yahtzee or the tuba. I play the audience. And the audience plays me. It works out good for the most part.

And so we come full circle. I started out as a writer, eased into telling, and now I turn into a writer again by committing to the page stories collected from hundreds of people at hundreds of story sessions over many years.

This book is made possible by all the folks, named and unnamed in these pages, who so generously shared stories so they can be passed on.

I pose a riddle to kids:

The more you give me away, the more I belong to you. What am I?

Kids come up with lots of imaginative answers—candy, toys, puppies, the flu. My favorite: Love.

The solution I'm looking for, though, is stories. But laughter will do as well.

Though it has taken decades to grow into the title, I am a storyteller. Set out to be a writer of literary fiction that would reveal the deepest truths of the human condition. That didn't work out. Turns out I wasn't all that keen on the deepest truths of the human condition.

Or maybe these little stories reveal more than you might think on first pass. Maybe, in fact, this is where the deepest truths of the human condition live.

Wouldn't that be something?

PART IV
Stories by the Dozen

Gathered over my whole life, but mainly over the last twenty-five years, here are some of the stories people have told me at sessions, over the telephone, or in lucky meetings on the street or at the grocery store. Some were e-mailed or mailed. Some came from interviews or home visits. Some I don't even know where they came from, they just appeared. Most fit into the category of yankee humor.

In the telling and retelling, no doubt the stories have evolved. I hope, though, that the story you read here is not so different from the original story that it's unrecognizable. I hope the heart of the story remains even if the details have changed.

I've included story origins and the names of tellers and subjects when possible, sometimes within the story, sometimes at the beginning. Stories marked "apocryphal" are ones I've heard many times from many sources. They are part of the yankee humor canon. They have some truth to them. They are beloved. They speak to who we are—deep down.

I've divided the stories into categories with much overlap. These are stories for reading, reading aloud, and—especially—for sharing.

CHARACTER AND CHARACTERS

I'll Always Remember Minnie

Sometimes I tell stories at churches from the pulpit. About a half hour in, Minnie—in her nineties with a touch of dementia—stood and observed loudly, "*She* ain't a preacher."

She was right.

Fred's Missing Smelt Net
Dick Wakefield

My father's youngest sister Dot was married to Fred Davis, a Moultonborough native. One of his sisters married a local store owner named Herbert Tilton. One evening, Uncle Fred stopped at Herb's store for the usual milk, bread, and paper. Herb said, "Davis! When you bringing back my smelt net?"

Fred said, "I ain't got your damn smelt net."

Herb replied, "You don't need to get testy. I'm asking everybody."

A Notorious Tightwad
Peter Randall

Dean Pettee was a notorious tightwad. One fall day he took his horse to the stable to see about boarding it for the winter. Spent most of the day negotiating the price with the stable owner.

After they agreed on the amount, Pettee started for the door, then stopped short and asked: "Who's going to get the manure?"

The owner said, "For the price you're payin' there ain't gonna be any!"

Godammit, Windy
Ken Randall

Windy Wilson of Sanbornton liked to talk. One day, Ken, passing on the road, spotted Windy and his father on the porch roof shingling. Windy, upon noticing Ken, climbed down the ladder and entered into conversation, talking a mile a minute.

After some time, Windy's father climbed down the ladder. He said to Ken:

"Do you need Windy for help?"
"No."
"Do you need him for advice?"
"No."
"Do you need him for consultation?"
"No?"
"Do you need him for anything at all?"
"No."

Father Wilson then turned to Windy, "Then godammit, Windy, get back on the roof."

The Flower Contest
Floyd Plummer

Ralph Sinclair of Newport was a great jokester. When the bank had a flower contest, Ralph poked a weed into a pot of soil and entered it.

To his surprise, he got a call to come down and collect his prize for "Most Unusual Flower." When he opened the prize package, he discovered horse manure.

Asked how he liked his prize, Ralph said, "I imagine it'll draw a lot of interest when I lock it up in my safety deposit box."

That Leo Corliss
Beverly Patton

Pearl Tucker lived next door to Leo Corliss in Alexandria Village. One day, Pearl asked Leo to take a look at her desk. One of the drawers was sticking shut.

Later that day, she was talking with a neighbor. "That Leo Corliss," she said with a twinkle, "he's been fooling around with my drawers all day!"

Jules Pellerin

Jules Pellerin was in the boat business on Lake Sunapee. Fella came in with a whitewater canoe pretty well stove up from an encounter with a rock on the Saco river. Jules patched it up as best he could.

Another fella is looking to buy it. "Does it leak?" the fella says.

"Do you want it to?" Jules says.

Another time a fella bought an aluminum boat cheap beside the road. He hauled it down to Jules. Somebody had painted it white. The paint was ugly and peeling. The fella wanted it restored to its former aluminum glory.

"How much will it cost me to get this boat stripped and restored?" the fella asks Jules.

"Not a cent," Jules says, "cause I ain't gonna do it."

The Collection

Dr. Bozuwa served as the family doctor in Wakefield for many years. Wakefield has more lakes and ponds than any other town in New Hampshire—seven of them.

A little boy getting bandaged up in Dr. Bozuwa's office noticed a collection of fishing lures and flies framed on the wall—at least thirty of them, all different. The boy said: "Dr. Bozuwa, you must really like fishing."

Dr. Bozuwa said: "I don't fish. All those I pulled out of people's heads."

Uncle Oscar Leighton
Susan Carr

Oscar Leighton, known as Uncle Oscar, was Celia Thaxter's brother and the son of Thomas Leighton. For decades, he piloted a boat between the mainland and the Isles of Shoals.

Oscar wintered at Hobkirk Inn in Camden, SC. He didn't learn to drive a car until he was ninety, after which he would drive from Portsmouth to Camden every year.

Having spent his life piloting boats, Uncle Oscar had a mariner's approach to parking. He never used the brakes. When he would arrive at the Hobkirk, he'd shift the car's gears down as far as they'd go would go to slow it, and then aim for the front steps or for the big tree near them—and pull safely into dock.

Uncle Oscar wanted to live to be 100 years old, but he died in an accident just shy of his 100th birthday. It wasn't a car accident. He fell on a space heater and set his beard on fire—a sad end to a long, full life.

Gom

Each fall, mid-November, the men of the family gathered at camp to close it up for winter. This involved draining the pipes, cleaning out the fridge, nailing down anything loose, a general battening down of the hatches. They worked hard all day, then, come evening, played cards and drank cider.

Next morning, a couple of the boys were hauling the dock out when Paul and Vin from across the lake tooled up in their fishing boat. Greetings were exchanged. Paul said, "None of my business, but roundabout two o'clock this morning I heard an awful racket over this side of the pond. Looked like a cop car or three, maybe a fire engine, sirens going, lights flashing."

"Oh yuh," Mike says. "That was us."

"Gom," Vin says—meaning, "What happened?"

Mike explains. He's a lawyer so he does a lot of explaining.

Seems Uncle Nub woke in the night to the call of nature and headed for the outhouse. He evidently forgot the boys had dug a new hole and moved it two rods east that afternoon. It was dark and Nub was in a hurry. Long story short, he fell into the old hole.

The boys heard him hollering, so they rushed out, shone a flashlight down the hole.

Nub was pretty well stuck and coated. Nobody volunteered to jump in with him, but somebody fetched a come-along and instructed him to cinch himself under the arm pits. Which he did. Quite a lot of suction was working against them, but they managed to haul him out.

Nobody wanted to touch him in the condition he was in, so they dragged him down to the dock (for his own good, despite vigorous protest) and rolled him into the lake.

Water's pretty chilly in November and Nub surfaced screeching bloody murder. Evidently the next-door neighbors thought somebody was being murdered, so they called the cops, hence the sirens and lights and the one fire engine for good measure.

Mike says, "Sorry if we woke you fellas up."

"No problem," Paul says.

Vin says, "Gom," meaning "We was just wondering."

Left or Right
Brenda Aldrich

In the seventies, a big truck crashed into the bridge on 117 and 18 in Sugar Hill. The bridge was a goner, so the town had to rebuild. A meeting was held to discuss the matter. The rebuilt bridge could go straight across the river, or it could tilt south toward Franconia or north toward Littleton. Which did the public prefer?

Maxine allowed as how she generally turned right toward Franconia when she left town.

Her husband allowed as how he generally turned left toward Littleton.

Police Chief Gary Cole had the last word though. He said, "Don't the two of you ever ride together?"

Bird's Eye View

Bob worked in heavy equipment—bulldozers, wreckers, big trucks, little trucks. He said, "We'd get equipment out of Pease and fix it for them. Jack, the boss—Gibson Motor and Machine—wanted to get the equipment back to Pease as soon as possible. He says, 'Christ, don't go sleeping on the job.' We said, 'Jack, you know damn well we aren't sleeping.'"

Jack had a glass eye. He took it out and put it on a lower rail of the scaffolding. He says, "Now I'm gonna keep my eye on you."

After Jack left, Vern takes the glass eye, climbs up, and sets it on the very top of the scaffolding.

When Jack comes back he's mad. "Where the hell is my eyeball?"

Vern says, "I put it up top. You can see more from up there."

The Time Prudence Got Her Foot Stuck in her Bra

Before I'd even started telling stories that afternoon, a woman sat down beside me and said, "I heard you collect stories."

I said, "I do. They're free and you don't have to dust 'em."

She said, "Would you like to hear the one about the time I got my foot stuck in my bra?"

Who wouldn't?

She said, "I'll tell it to you. But don't mention you heard it from Prudence in Milton."

Here's her story:

Whenever I get home from shopping or anything the first thing I do is take off my bra and hang it on the knob of my bedroom door.

I was having coffee with my daughter in the kitchen. She saw something in the paper she thought I ought to read. I had my coffee in my hand and walked down the hall to the bedroom to grab my reading glasses off the bed table.

I had my coffee in one hand, my reading glasses in the other. I went to kick the bedroom door closed and my foot got stuck in my bra.

My coffee went one way, my reading glasses went the other.

If I was a 38D instead of a 34B, I'd still be swinging.

Fred Lee

Fred Lee was a famous North Country character. Many stories are told about him. Some are probably true.

He worked some for the state. He was working on the Kancamagus Highway when a stranger in a big black car pulled over to the side of the road and yelled from the window, "Hey Mister, where's Lincoln?"

Fred said, "Far's I know he died a hundred fifty years ago."

Fred worked for many years at Loon Mountain, owned by Sherman Adams, formerly a legislator, governor, and chief of staff under Eisenhower. One afternoon, Adams called Fred into his office. He told Fred to shut the door and sit down.

Fred did.

Adams asked Fred how long he'd been employed at Loon Mountain. Fred said he'd worked there twelve years or more. Adams said, "Fred, I've decided to give you a raise of five cents an hour, just don't tell anybody."

Fred said, "I won't. I'm just as ashamed of it as you are."

The Test

A new guy moves into town to be caretaker for one of the big houses. At the general store he stocks up on supplies—milk, butter, potatoes, baked beans in a can. He also asks for a pack of Lucky Strikes.

The storekeeper loads all the stuff into a paper bag. When the new guy gets home he discovers a carton of Lucky Strikes instead of a pack in the bag.

He checks the slip—sure enough, he only paid for a pack.

The next time he goes into the store, he says to the storekeeper: "You didn't realize it, but last week you gave me a carton of Lucky Strikes when I only paid for a pack."

The storekeeper nods. "Oh," he says, "I realized it."

The Big Boss and the Little Boss
Norman Green

Norman's father worked nights in the boiler room at the mill. One night the big boss comes poking around, trying to make trouble the way big bosses do. He sees some packages in the trough wrapped in tin foil. Picks one up. Unwraps it. It's a six-pack of beer.

The big boss says to the little boss: "I will not tolerate men drinking on the job. Come Monday, any man caught drinking on the job will be immediately terminated."

The little boss says: "You understand we'll be closed on Tuesday."

COMMERCE AND FRUGALITY

He Went to See a Man About a Horse

In Chocorua, they tell about William James, brother to Henry, who had a home in town. A Harvard man, William was determined to master the art of yankee trading.

Off he went in search of a horse and a man with one for sale. "How much do you want for that horse?" William James asked.

"How much do you have?"

"A hundred fifty dollars."

"Well," says the yankee, "that's the price."

Mrs. Eisenberg's Chocolate Cake

Mrs. Eisenberg sent her husband to school with a chocolate cake for the PTA bake sale. At the table, he asked the volunteer how much the cake would sell for when the sale started that afternoon. "Two-fifty," she said.

So he paid her and took the cake home. ∽

First Come
Sue Anne Bottomley

The family home was on Beacon Street in Concord. In those days, there was a small grocery store at just about every intersection. Pa would walk a block on most days to do the shopping. This was during the Depression, in the thirties, when there were a lot of shortages. Pa never knew what he'd find at the store and what he'd bring home, but it usually wasn't much. Enough for the day's dinner.

One day, the kids were amazed to see Pa carrying home two armloads of provisions—bags of flour, sugar, lard, and meat. They said, "Pa, how did you manage to buy all this?"

Pa said, "I got there before the hoarders." ∽

Butter Barter
Apocryphal

During the Depression, money was in short supply, so folks bartered: eggs for flour, hay for soap, bacon for cordwood. A woman came into Hod

Hastings' store with a pound of butter that had a daisy embossed on top from the butter press. She said, "I'd like to trade this pound of buttah for a pound of buttah."

"Why?" Hod asked.

"Well," she said, "If you must know, after I finished churning the buttah, I looked and in the bottom of the churn was a dead mouse. I screamed, the kids come runnin', saw the cahcass, and refuse to eat the buttah. So I thought I'd trade this pound for another pound, because what you don't know won't hurt you."

Hod said, "I think I can help you, ma'am." He took the pound of butter to the back of the store, scraped the daisy off the top, and carved in an apple. Back at the counter, he handed the butter to the woman. "You are absolutely right, ma'am," he said. "What you don't know won't hurt you."

A Bargain at Any Price

Riverside Cabins went out of business. The land and buildings were auctioned off along with the contents. Lots of locals attended the auction. The prices were low—$2.00 for bedspreads, $1.00 for a curtain, $3.50 for the beside lamp with a base made from the leg of a deer (hair and hoof intact). Toasters were going for a quarter apiece.

Brig bought a toaster. He was pretty proud of it. His friend Wallace said, "Brig, that's an awful nice toaster. Only thing is, it's got no cord."

"That's okay," Brig says. "I got no electricity."

The Horse That Didn't Look So Good
Apocryphal

"That's a nice horse," the farmer said to the horse trader. "What'll you take for her?"

"Well," the trader said, "she is a strong, sweet-natured animal but she don't look so good."

"How much?" the farmer said.

They dickered and came up with a mutually agreeable price. The deal was done. The farmer went down the road with his new horse. But he was back fifteen minutes later.

"You suckered me," the farmer said. "That horse is blind."

The horse trader said, "I told you she didn't look so good."

On Wednesday

In East Alton, a big granite stone fell from a retaining wall. It was too big—2' by 2' by 6'—to be moved by hand, so the owner, Warren, asked Irving if he'd come with his backhoe and return the stone to its rightful place. "Sure," Irving said, "I'll be over on Wednesday."

True to his word, two years later, Irving and his backhoe showed up on a Wednesday. After the deed was done, Warren said, "Thanks a lot, Irving. I'll pay you on Wednesday."

A Little Something for His Sick Wife

The Maine potato farmer walked into a greenhouse in Swanzey Center. He explained his wife was feeling poorly so he wanted to bring her back a little something as a gift.

The proprietor showed him a beautiful big pot of red geraniums. "How much?" the farmer said.

"Seven dollars and ninety-five cents."

"She ain't that sick," the farmer said and bought a flat of petunias for $1.99.

The Rich Get Richer

A member of the Haverhill, Massachusetts, women's club, a descendant of Roger Williams (these things come up in conversation), worked in a resort in New Hampshire as a girl. This was in the days when wealthy folks stayed all summer. She waited tables.

One guest, a little old lady, was among her charges for breakfast, lunch, and dinner every day. This guest never ordered anything off the menu. Every morsel was served according to special instructions.

After a few weeks, the little old lady slipped the waitress a fifty-cent piece and whispered: "You can expect this every month, deah."

The Price of Strawberries in Maine

Driving down the busy road between Bangor and Ellsworth, Craig sees strawberries for sale. It's that time of year. The sign says, $2.00/quart, but the stand is on the wrong side of the road, so he keeps going. A couple miles farther along, he sees another stand, "Maine Strawberries, $2.00/

quart." But he's going too fast and is past the stand before he can put his turn signal on. Same thing with a third stand.

Finally, he pulls over. Fella has a picnic table in front of his house, loaded with strawberries. "Those look good," Craig says.

"Picked 'em myself this mornin'."

"I'll take two quarts."

"That'll be $5.00," the fella says.

"That's $2.50 a quart," Craig says. "I just drove by three different stands and they were going for $2.00."

Fella says, "Shoulda bought 'em."

Fair Trade
Apocryphal

In the spring of the year, the farmer was plowing his field with a hand plow behind a big bay hoss. About halfway through the job, the hoss dropped dead in the furrow. Something he'd never done before. And would never do again.

The farmer was disappointed, but he had an idea.

He rode his other hoss five miles up the road to his neighbor's.

"Charlie," he said, "you know that big bay work hoss I got down to my place?"

"I do," Charlie said. "That's a fine hoss. A fine strong work hoss."

"How would you trade your white hoss for my bay?" says the farmer.

Charlie thought about it. "I'd trade even," he says. And they shook on it.

"Well, Charlie," says the farmer. "I hate to tell you but my big bay hoss lays dead in the furrow."

"My white hoss died three weeks ago," says Charlie.

The Owl Collection

Mother's cousin Ruby collected owls—porcelain owls, paper owls, pictures of owls, embroidered owls, any kind of owls at all. She had a house full of owls. Sorting through one spring, she donated a couple of duplicates to the church fair.

Mother attended the church fair, spotted those owls, and bought them. For Ruby.

COMMON SENSE

Pretty Damned Good Judgment

A CPA from Vermont wanted an A-frame moved from one of his properties to another in the same town. He hired Stanley to do the moving. Stanley got the building on a flatbed and proceeded through the center of town. It was slow going, but he was making headway, and was just a half mile from his destination when the blue lights showed up in his rearview mirror.

Truck and building blocked the road. Traffic lined up in both directions. Folks emerged from their houses to see what the excitement was.

The state trooper looked the situation over. He asked Stanley if the owner had done due diligence and obtained all the proper permits for such a move.

Stanley, lying, said that indeed the owner had obtained all the permits needed, but he didn't happen to have the paperwork on him.

The trooper looked at Stanley. He looked back at the line of cars clogging Main Street. He said, "In that case, Stanley, I'll take your word for it."

Stanley said, "That, sir, is an exercise of pretty damned good judgment."

Ponder This
Mary Ruell

Ruben, the hired hand, showed up hours late to work.

The boss said, "Ruben, how come you're so late?"

Ruben said: "My alarm clock went off early. And besides that, I caught a ride."

Old Robbie Knows

The family debated the cost for the replacement roof on the barn at the former egg farm. Grown sisters and brother bickered over what do to and who should pay. Finally, Old Robbie, the patriarch, settled the debate. "No sense putting a new roof over an empty barn."

Signs R 4 Reading

At the Hannaford's, Don said, "You're Rebecca. You tell stories."

I said, "That's right."

He explained that he's a selectman in a nearby town. The select board received a bill, hand delivered by an irate out-of-towner. Seems the fellow's GPS sent him cross-country from one tarred road to another, but in between was a not-tarred road. Kinda rough. He got stuck, had to be towed, his axle bent, and so forth.

So, the select board, which ought to be watching after the town roads, got the bill. The irate out-of-towner even gave the board a photograph of his damaged car, right next to a sign that said: "Class Six Road, Closed Subject to Gates and Bars."

"I guess you didn't pay the bill," I said to Don.

"Nope."

Winter Arrangements

In October, the woman arranges with Dennis that he'll take care of her driveway come winter. She asks: "When do you start plowing?"

Dennis says, "When it snows."

Shut the Door Quick

A plumber gets called out to an old farmhouse. The toilet's leaking and needs attention. The owner comes to the door and gives the plumber directions to the bathroom: Through the front room and down the hall. First door on the left.

"Go in quick and shut the door behind you," the owner says. "Mother's taking a tub and she'll be ugly if you let in a draft."

DIRECTIONS AND TRAVEL

Making Good Time
Apocryphal

Doris recalled traveling to Boston to see a Red Sox game. On the way home, her uncle said to her grandfather, "I think we're lost."

Grampa replied, "Yuh, but we're making good time." ∽

The Bent Bolt
Kendra Totman

Kendra's dad was hauling a trailer from Maine to Dartmouth where he went to school. All of a sudden, he noticed that the trailer was banging around behind him, so he pulled over. One of the bolts had come out of the hitch. He walked back down the highway and found the bolt, but it was bent and useless.

What to do?

He abandoned the trailer on the side of the road and drove to the next exit. He found a country store but couldn't find anyone inside to wait on him.

Finally, he heard a voice coming from the rocking chair on the front porch. Kendra's dad hadn't even noticed the fella in the chair, he was in such a rush to get back to the trailer.

Turns out the fella in the chair owned the place. "Can I help you?" the fella asked.

Kendra's dad asked if there was a hardware section.

"Ayuh, back of the store."

"Do you have some pliers?"

"Ayuh, here you go."

"How about a wrench?"

"Ayuh." The owner handed him a wrench.

"Do you happen to have any bolts like this one?" Kendra's dad held up the bent bolt from the trailer.

The owner studied it for a bit, then replied, "Don't have any bolts like that. We only carry the straight ones." ∽

Honk

The yankee's car broke down in the middle of the intersection—steam rising from the hood.

An impatient person three cars back blasted his horn. So the yankee gets out of his vehicle, walks back, leans into the impatient person's window and says: "You could walk up there and try to get my car going, and I'll sit here and honk your horn, if you think that would help."

Does It Make Any Difference?
Apocryphal

Steve told the story of a couple he met while working in Massachusetts. They'd just moved up from the south, never been north before. Decided, on his recommendation, to try a day trip to Maine. They passed by the restaurant with the big blue whale (used to be Yoken's in Portsmouth) and stopped for lunch at a restaurant across from the store with the bear on the second floor (Weathervane across from Kittery Trading Post). Enjoyed their first lobsters.

In fact, things were going so well, they decided to push on to Portland. Got out the map and were looking it over. I-95 seemed the speedier route, but Route 1 might offer more sights. They spotted a fella emerging from the Weathervane, looked local. So the husband inquired, "Does it make any difference whether we go to Portland on I-95 or Route 1?"

The local replied: "Not to me, it don't."

Good Battery?

Paul from the Midwest married into New England. He and his wife were visiting Mount Holly, Vermont, checking out wood stoves. They parked on the main street and walked to the wood stove store, but it was closed.

As they returned to the sidewalk, a local said, "Do you have a good battery?"

Being a Midwesterner, Paul waxed friendly. He sure did, and jumper cables too, if somebody needed a jump. "Do you need a jump?" he asked.

"No," the local said. "I was just asking 'cause you left your lights on."

Slippery Slope
A Fella in Goshen

My wife and I had been driving for eight hours to get to her folks' home in Acworth. Much of the way we were fighting through a massive snowstorm.

Finally, we got to within two miles of the homestead on Charlestown Road and breathed sighs of relief: Almost there. Started up the big hill and the car begun to slip and slide, then came to a halt. She just wouldn't go anymore. Hill too steep and slippery.

So I got out to push and told my wife to gun it. After much grunting, groaning and strain, I finally managed to push hard enough for the car to go. She took off up the hill.

Then I saw the brake lights.

My wife had stopped fifty yards ahead so I could get back in. Now the car was stuck again.

I trudged up to do some more pushing. Put my shoulder to the trunk and really put my back into it.

In the midst of this debacle, my mother-in-law came spinning up the hill in a four-wheel-drive. Didn't recognize us. Drove right on by.

Depends

Claire called about an apartment to rent on Main Street. The landlord told her it was about half a block from the five-and-dime. "On the right or the left?" she asked.

"Depends what direction you're coming from."

How Do You Get To . . . ?

Fella says, "How do you get to Claremont?"

Other fella says, "Usually my son takes me."

She Married Him Anyway

Amanda's husband, before he was her husband, took her for a ride in his brand-new car from Fitz's in Manchester.

It was awful cold, twenty below zero. She noticed that the gas gauge was on empty. "Oh dear," she said, "I hope we don't run out of gas and have to walk in the cold."

He gallantly replied, "If we run out of gas, I'll walk—you keep the car running and stay warm."

Rabbit Track

In '72 or '73, David was teaching in Lebanon, New Hampshire. A big wind and rainstorm lasted about three days. The children had a hard time getting to school, but most of them made it.

Ruthie and her siblings lived in a foster home across the river in Thetford, Vermont. On the third day of the storm, the children needed a ride home after school. David volunteered. Piled them into the car and set off.

At the river, he discovered the bridge had washed out on the Vermont side.

"Ruthie," he said, "what did your mother do yesterday when she came to the washed-out bridge?"

Ruthie said, "She drove down that road there."

David took the road Ruthie indicated. He drove a mile. The road turned from tar to dirt. He drove another couple of miles. It turned into an impassable rabbit track. It was all he could do to get his vehicle turned around to head back.

"Ruthie," he said, "What happened when your mother tried to get through on this road yesterday?"

Ruthie said, "Same thing."

Mind Your Beeswax

Hubert was waiting for a train at the old Concord railway station. It was a round station. You might remember it. A beautiful piece of architecture. They could turn the locomotives around inside. The track moved 360 degrees. Tore the station down in the 1960s to make room for a shopping mall. Damn shame.

Anyway, Hubert was in line at the ticket office when somebody poked his shoulder and said, "Hey, Hubert, where you headed?"

Hubert gave a typical yankee response. "None of your damned business," he said. "And I wouldn't tell you that much if you weren't my sister."

Daisy (and Bub and Chester)
Apocryphal

Seems Bruce drove his vehicle off the side of the road and got it stuck in the mud. He asked at a nearby farmhouse, did the farmer have a tractor to snag him out? "No," the farmer said, "but I got a mule."

"No mule can pull that car out of there," Bruce said. "It's hung up bad."

Nevertheless, the farmer hitched the mule to the bumper, and yelled, "Go Daisy. Go Bub. Go Chester." Sure enough, the mule dragged the car clear.

Bruce was impressed. "But why," he asked, "did you yell out three names?"

"She's blind," the farmer said. "That way, she thinks she's got help."

Almost Home

A bridge connects Springfield, Vermont, and Charlestown, New Hampshire. For decades it was a toll bridge. Gary recalled a cross-country family trek that took a good three weeks. They drove all over—to holes like the Grand Canyon and peaks like Pike's. It was quite a trip in that old woody wagon, Gary and his siblings packed into the back seat. After all that time on the road, they were relieved to be almost home.

It was nighttime when they approached the toll bridge. One five-cent toll separated them from the Granite State.

But there was a hold up.

Gary's dad stopped behind a Cadillac with New York plates. The booth was lit and they could see the collector rummaging around in drawers. After a few minutes, he left the booth and walked across the road to a big house—presumably his.

The lights in the house went on and off, one after another, room to room, upstairs and down, as the toll taker passed through. Ten minutes later, he emerged, walked back across the road to the booth, and handed something to the driver of the Cadillac.

The Cadillac moved on and Gary's dad pulled up to the window. "What was that all about?" he asked the collector.

"Well," the old fella said, "that guy from New York handed me a hundred-dollar bill. Guess he didn't think I'd bother to make change."

Literally

Stranger: "Where's this road go?"
Local: "Don't go nowhere, just sits there."
And
Stranger: "Can I take this bridge to Claremont?"
Local: "You could but I wouldn't recommend it."
And
Stranger: "Do you know how to get to Piermont?"
Local: "Yup."

Don't, But If You Do

I was given directions to a church where I was to tell stories in a town I'll call Woodford.

My guide said, "If you go past the church by mistake, whatever you do, don't go over the one-lane bridge. But if you do go over the one-lane bridge, whatever you do, don't take the dirt road on the right that goes out into the piney woods. But if you do take the dirt road out into the piney woods and you get to the place where there's swamp on both sides, be sure to toot so they'll know not to shoot you."

I've told this story many times and thought it might be a bit of an exaggeration until a man said, "Becky Rule, you tell the truth. My brother-in-law was a selectman in Woodford and he told about those folks who live at the end of that dirt road."

I said, "Did he ever go over the bridge, take the right into the piney woods all the way to the place where there's swamp on both sides?"

"No," the man said. "They would have shot him."

FAMILY DYNAMICS

Grampa Stewart and L.E. Go Skiing

When my grandfather-to-be, Robert Stewart, was courting my grandmother-to-be, Lillian Ford, he visited the Ford homestead on a Friday night to play cards with the gang. It was midwinter and a time when roads were rolled for sleigh travel rather than plowed. The homestead sat at the top of a hill away back in the woods. Robert Stewart had snowshoed up the hill, not a short walk, close to two miles.

When the evening ended, Lawrence Elliot Ford, known as L.E., Lillian's big brother, offered to ski Robert Stewart down the hill to save some time. Some other visitors had taken a sleigh down the hill earlier. L.E. planned to drive that sleigh home. Seemed like a good plan.

Problem was, there was just the one set of old wooden skis about seven feet long and the skis had straps for just one set of feet. L.E. strapped his big feet to the skis, lit his pipe, and instructed Robert Stewart to stand on the skis behind him and hold tight.

Which my grandfather-to-be did.

Lucky thing there were multiple sleigh ruts in the snow from comings and goings. A pair of them, just about a foot apart, seemed perfect. By placing a ski in each rut, Robert and L.E. could make a straight run down the hill. They wouldn't even have to steer.

The slope was gradual, the moon bright, the skis fit just right in the ruts. Started out slow. Going along good. At about the halfway point, they began to pick up speed. Robert Stewart held tight to L.E.'s waist.

They negotiated a long slow curve with grace. And then, as they approached the last steep incline, Robert spotted something in the moonlight straight ahead. A dark mound in the snow seemed to fill one of the ruts. L.E. saw it too. He said, around the stem of his pipe: "Bob, we're goin' to have to lift our left feet."

The mound was a large, frozen horse flap.

They lifted their left feet.

They fell ass over teakettle.

No bones were broken, but L.E. lost his pipe, which was found the following spring by his mother when she was out picking wild strawberries.

Shortly thereafter, Grammie and Grampa were married. He and L.E. always got along good. ❧

Lunacy

Clarence and Merle went hornpouting one night. During the expedition they got into the sauce. The hornpout were biting good, and the sauce was tasty too. When they got out of the boat to head home (let's assume they were walking—not driving after having imbibed), they set the bag of pout on the ground, and Merle slipped and sat on the bag. The horns of the pout penetrated his backside in a number of places.

Back at the house, Merle told his wife of his injuries and explained he'd sat on a bag of pout. She didn't believe a word of it.

Next day, she confronted Clarence. "Clarence," she said, "were you part of this lunacy last night?"

Clarence explained that he had been and that, indeed, Merle had sat on a bag of pout.

"Oh," she said, "that's a relief. I thought he'd been drinking." ❧

They All Lived Together

The couple took in the wife's mother and the husband's father, since the two older folks needed some support in their golden years. All lived together, but not in harmony. The in-laws did not get along. Not at all.

After the father died, the mother-in-law was overheard to say at the funeral, as she stood by the open casket: "Well, John, I have to say, this is the first time I've been pleased to see you." ❧

The Depot Master

Judy Whitcomb Hall

Judy's grandfather, Oliver Patch Whitcomb, delivered milk to the Boston and Maine train station. The depot master would always ask: "Any news on the hill?"

Generally, there wasn't much, but one day, Patch said, "Roger had his hand taken off."

"No!"

"Ayuh. He put it on his wife's knee, and she took it off." ❧

Dog Dishes
Luci Barnes

Supplies were short during the Depression. Even though the family—six kids—lived on a farm, food wasn't that plentiful. Some relatives began showing up on Sundays expecting Sunday dinner. Which was okay for a few weeks but became a burden after a while.

What to do? Something subtle perhaps?

Whether it was Mother or Father who came up with the idea, it took the two of them to carry it out. After dinner, they put the dirty dishes on the floor for the dog to lick clean.

The dog did a fine job.

Then, the coop de grass, they picked the dishes up and put them in the cupboard.

The relatives from Maine never showed up for Sunday dinner again. ⌒

The Cat Is on the Porch

A woman in Effingham told this story with a New Jersey accent only slightly tempered by years of living in New Hampshire.

Her husband suffered a serious heart attack. From his bed in the ICU he implored her to take good care of his cat. His first morning in the hospital, he asked the head nurse to phone her up, and get her out of bed. He knew she'd have trouble waking up on her own—always did. His first words were, "Good morning, deah. Time to get up. How's my cat?"

He remained hospitalized for several weeks. On his bedside table, at his request, was a picture of his cat. "Not a picture of me," the woman said, "a picture of the cat!"

Well, bad luck comes in threes—or sometimes twos. While the husband was recovering in the hospital, the cat died. The doctor said to spare the sick man any shocks and the woman didn't want to lie, so she put the corpse on the porch. It was winter; the corpse froze solid. When the husband called and asked after the cat, she truthfully said, "I just put him out."

Next time he asked, she said, "He's on the porch. I'm looking right at him."

This went on for weeks, until at last the husband was well enough to come home. The doctor said the husband must be told about the death of his cat while still in the hospital. Just in case.

Oh, it was hard, the woman said. She tried three times to break the news and failed.

Now it's the day of the husband's release. Her last chance. She bursts into tears and manages to choke out the words, "Deah, your cat has died."

"Oh well," he said, "That cat never liked me anyway."

Hell on Wheels
Paul Yelle

Paul from Campton recalled his mother trying out the new three-wheeler. She took it for a turn. "Wish I had a speedometer," she said.

Father said: "You'd need a calendar at the speed you're going."

Pachelbel's Canon Would Be Nice
Bruce Hardy

Bruce said his dad's best friend took piano lessons from his mom in the sixties. The spinet on which she taught was in the bedroom—only place in the house it would fit—so that's where the lessons took place.

At a dinner one evening, Bruce overhead this comment from Dad: "Stub, you been taking a lot of piano lessons from my wife in my bedroom. You better goddamn well know how to play."

Enough is Enough

Nancy said she gave birth to three baby boys, one after another. When her fourth child, a girl, was born, friends asked what her name was going to be. Nancy said, "We're calling her Quits."

In a related story, the young couple gave their son what some in the family considered an exotic name. "Eric," Cousin Matty says, "what kind of a name is that?"

Dad says, "It's a four-letter word for him."

All for Want of a Union Suit

Barbara in Colebrook told this family story of her grandfather Josiah Piper, who married the local schoolmarm when they were both middle-aged and set in their ways.

One of the first edicts from the schoolmarm after the wedding was that Josiah had to give up his union suit for a night shirt. Josiah didn't want to, but he did.

Around that same time, a fox was coming around at night and bothering the chickens. Night after night a chicken or two would be lost to the fox.

Josiah loaded his shotgun and set it by the front door. In the middle of the night, he heard a ruckus in the henhouse, jumped out of bed, grabbed the shotgun, ran to the henhouse, stuck his head and the barrel of that shotgun through the little door. If there was a fox in there, he was gonna get it.

Just then, Josiah's hound dog snuck up behind him and stuck his cold nose where the sun down shine, causing Josiah to startle. His finger slipped, the shotgun fired, and seventeen chickens died.

Not Such a Big Deal

At the library festival in Goshen, I got to talking with Mrs. Barker, one of the town's prominent citizens. We got on to the subject of children. I said: "Mrs. Barker, did you come from a large family yourself?"

She said, "I come from a family of twenty children."

"Twenty children," I said, amazed.

"Well," she said, "we're all grown now."

Ed and the Spoons
Warren Angus Wilbur

Ed Perkins wife says, "Ed Perkins when I married you I had a half a dozen silver spoons. Now, you old bastard, I ain't got but six."

A Hollow Threat

Uncle Frank took Johnny and Jimmy swimming in the Contoocook River. When it came time to go home, Johnny refused to get out of the water.

Frank said, "You get out of that water right now, Johnny, or next time I take you swimming you wunt come."

How We Do
Apocryphal

To maintain civility, the feuding couple talked only through the cat.

"Cat, would you ask Ethel to pass the salt?"

"Cat, tell Lawrence the toilet's stopped up."

"The daughter's coming to visit Thursday night, Cat. Lawrence might want to know."

"I'm going into town to pick up a hundred pounds of chicken feed. Ask her if we're in dire need of anything else, would you, Cat?"

While Lawrence was in town, Ethel noticed the neighbor at the back wall, dismantling it into his pickup truck. She lit out across the field. "What are you doing?" she says, testy.

"What's it look like I'm doing, Ethel? I'm getting a load of rocks off this falling down wall."

"That's not your wall," Ethel says. "That's my wall."

"Lawrence said take 'em. He said he was putting in strawberries."

"Strawberries," Ethel says. "I'm allergic to strawberries!"

When the neighbor returned to his house, he said to his wife, "When Lawrence got home, I bet that poor cat caught hell."

Roots

John Rule, Adi Rule, and I have visited Ireland a few times over the years. The first time we went in search of ancestors and visited my great aunt Annie at the family homestead. We learned that Annie's father, my great-grandfather, had been born on an estate, complete with castle, in Portumna, and that the stone remnants of his thatched hut could still be seen.

So John and I struck out one evening across a golf course to get to an overgrown road that led to the hut. It was around the time of the summer solstice, so even though it was after 9:00 PM, it was still light out.

A couple of locals were playing golf. They asked what we were up to. "We're here researching the family," I said. "Looking for relatives."

"You Americans," the Irishman said, "You're always looking for your relatives. I spend most of me time avoiding mine."

FARMING, GARDENING, WORKING THE LAND, AND WORKING IN THE WOODS

He Turned out Good
Apocryphal, maybe

In Weare, they tell the story of Buzz Boyd, a farmer who needed to take on some extra help one summer. He was clearing some acreage in the back forty.

As it happens, there was a young man in town who needed some extra money since he was going away to college come fall. He was going on a Rhodes Scholarship, that's Rhodes, with an *h*.

Buzz hired the young fellow. After a couple of weeks, a friend of Buzz's stopped by to ask how Young David was making out.

"Well," Buzz said. "The boy's willing. And he may be smart. But he don't know nothing."

Young David went on to become a Justice of the Supreme Court of the United States. A New Hampshire native son—but apparently not much of a woodsman. ~

Not Making Much Progress
Alden Farrar

The farmer was making good progress until his tractor got stuck in reverse. Unplowed twelve acres. ~

On the Barrens

I was walking some blueberry barrens in Maine when I spotted two men at a distance. They were looking at the ground and working with something that appeared to be a hockey stick—or maybe a hoe. I was pretty sure they weren't playing hockey. Thought maybe they were burying a body.

But as I got closer, I saw they weren't digging. One of them was touching the rag-wrapped end of a pole to tall plants. Very gently. Very slowly. The other was doing the heavy-looking-on. I jumped to a conclusion. There was poison on that rag. When I got close enough I said: "Killing weeds, huh?"

"Yup," they said.

I looked the field over. Thirty or forty acres of blueberries and weeds as far as the eye could see. "Gosh," I said. "Big job."

The one doing the heavy-looking-on said, "We do our best."

Just One Question
Robert Arsenault

Brothers Harold and Stanley Wentzel were second only to Pat Herr, Vice President in charge of Brown Company forestry. It was big operation.

A would-be assistant by the name of Jon Bork came in with all sorts of credentials, master's degree, and such. Pat Herr introduced him, listed all his impressive qualifications.

Stanley Wentzel had just one question about the applicant: "Can he file a buck saw?"

Of Beans and Zucchini
Apocryphal

An old-timer watched his new neighbor planting beans. At the end of the process, the old-timer said: "You might's well put up a tombstone and give them a decent burial."

Same new neighbor put in fifteen hills of zucchini. End of July he had zucchini coming out of his ears. Another neighbor suggested he put the extras out by the road with a free sign, so he loaded up a wheelbarrow and parked it by the road with a big sign: Free for the Taking.

Come evening, the zucchinis were in a pile on the ground and the wheelbarrow was gone.

A Wild Ride
Warren Angus Wilbur

Young Georgie raised a flock of White Plymouth Rocks, pullets. Bandits came in the night and stole every one of them.

He bought another dozen. The bandits stole those, too.

Georgie was some mad. He bought a dozen more. This time he was determined to nab those bandits. He and a couple of buddies staked out the henhouse. They fortified themselves with a few six-packs of beer, spread clean hay on floor to be comfortable, and waited amongst the chickens.

The first and second nights of the stakeout, nothing happened. But on the third night, they were awakened by what they thought was an earthquake followed by a windstorm. How that henhouse shook. How the wind did blow through the walls as it lurched back and forth.

Only later did they realize there hadn't been an earthquake or a windstorm. The bandits had picked that henhouse up, thrown it in the back of the truck, and set off down the road.

GHOSTS AND CEMETERIES

Sorry to Disturb You
Jim Blodgett

Jim is the great-grandson of Winfred Scott Littlehale of South Sutton. Winfred collected animals—foxes, rabbits, snakes—and made pets of them. Among his favorites was an albino porcupine.

Winfred died in 1904 and was buried in an unmarked grave, said to lie between two big rocks in his back field, with holes poked in the ground so his pet snakes could visit.

Jim set out to find his great-grandfather's grave. He used a metal detector, thinking it might find hinges on a casket or some such. The detector didn't detect much, but when he checked out two particularly big rocks in the field, what should appear just ten feet away, but an albino porcupine.

Jim doffed his hat and said, "Sorry we disturbed you, Great-Grandfather."

Bad News

Overheard at a diner by a woman new to New England:

First yankee: "I see Ezra Bartlett got his name in the paper."
Second yankee: "Oh, yuh. What for?"
First yankee: "He died."

Is There a Form to Fill Out?

A woman called town hall wondering what the procedure was for purchasing a cemetery plot.

"Well, I can tell you this," the clerk said. "You can't just come in cold."

Welcome Home
Elise and Thom Conlon

The Conlons run the Dudley House Bed & Breakfast. I met them at a reading at Fox Tale Books in New Durham. They told a story that gave me goose bumps.

In their search of small New England towns for a B&B to buy, they walked into the Dudley House, and it felt like home. They knew immediately it was the one and snapped it up.

The owners left them a history of the place. Going through the history, Thom noticed something strange about the family tree. Back a few generations, the Dudley family tree had a lot in common with Elise's family tree—that is, they were the same people.

Unwittingly, the Conlons had indeed come home.

And They Won't Be Pleased One Little Bit

In Goffstown, during a discussion of the deteriorating road through the cemetery—a hilly cemetery, a steep hill—the voters seemed undecided. Should we spend the money to repair the road or leave it be another year or two?

Superintendent of Cemeteries Leo Root spoke eloquently to the question. He said, "You can decide what you want, but if that road keeps falling apart, those people buried up on the hill will be coming back to greet you."

Some Things Don't Change

Richard met up with his old friend Arlo. They hadn't seen each other in a while.

Arlo says, "Hey Richard. How's your wife?"

Richard says, "Still dead."

Funeral Tie

Apocryphal, maybe

At one session, Marion delivered this story. She moved with a walker and had oxygen on wheels, so it wasn't easy for her to come to the front of the hall. She told the story with such sincerity, I knew it must be true.

Marion's father-in-law died, so naturally she went to the calling hours. There was her mother-in-law standing at the head of the open casket. Marion went over to her.

"How's he look?" the mother-in-law said.

"Good," Marion said.

"What do you think of his tie?"

"It's nice," Marion said. "It's a nice tie. Elegant."

The mother-in-law said, "I bought that tie for him three Christmases ago. He never wore it. By god, he's gonna wear it now."

Plots

At the annual meeting, I sat between the town historian and a newcomer to town. During dinner we discussed cemeteries. The newcomer says, "I've been thinking about buying a plot for me and my family."

The historian says, "You used to be able to buy a four-body plot for fifteen dollars. These days it'll cost you $1,500 or $2,000 depending on whether you want the upper or lower cemetery." Then she added: "Course you can get scattered for nothing."

Which begs the question, why do plots in the upper cemetery cost more than plots in the lower cemetery?

Better view.

Jaffrey to Jasper and Back

A New Hampshire native lived in Jasper, Georgia, for many years because of work. During that time, she got a call from a Jasper public servant who asked if she might be interested in buying a plot in a new cemetery they were opening up.

"No," she said, "I would not! I already have a plot in Jaffrey, New Hampshire, and I can't wait to get back to it."

Frugal to a Fault

My mother had her first cancer surgery when she was seventy years old. Before she got her diagnosis, we'd scheduled a trip to Red's Shoe Barn for a new pair of shoes. After the operation, I suggested that as soon as she felt well enough, we head to Red's and get those shoes she needed.

She refused. She said, "I won't live long enough to wear them out."

She lived to be eighty-four. But we never did take that trip to Red's.

HOLIDAYS

If the Turkey Was a Horse

Karen from Rhode Island is, by her own admission, not much of a cook. One Christmas, it was her turn to host the family Christmas party. Her sisters came by on Christmas Eve to help with the prep. They peeled and sliced and chopped and put a stuffing together for the turkey.

After they left, all Karen had to do was put the huge turkey in the oven to cook overnight. She got the bird in the big pan, but something didn't look quite right. She wasn't sure which end was up. So she called her mother to ask how to position the turkey. Mother, who had always lamented Karen's lack of interest in cooking, told her, "Breast side up."

Karen thanked her. She returned to the turkey but couldn't figure out which was the breast and which was some other parts. She maneuvered the turkey this way and that, but it didn't seem comfortable in the pan. So she called her mother again, "How do I know which way to put the turkey in the pan?"

Mother, irritated, said, "I told you, breast side up, for crissakes."

Karen gave it another try. She didn't want to screw up her first turkey. She still couldn't figure it out. The turkey was flopping all over. She didn't want to call her mother again, because her mother didn't seem to understand that "Breast side up" wasn't cutting it. Finally, she devised a plan.

She called her mother. "Ma," she said, "if the turkey was a horse, would it have its hooves in the air or be standing up?"

Secret Santas
Nancy Coutts

Nancy swore her third-graders to secrecy regarding the names they picked out of the hat for Secret Santa at the Christmas party. The gift exchange was their idea and she succumbed under pressure. She duly wrote names on thirty-six little slips of paper and had each child draw one. "But," she said, "don't tell anyone who you picked."

They promised not to tell.

Then came recess.

The children returned to the classroom agitated. Miss Coutts had written her own name on every slip!

We Cry for Pie
Janet Brown

At the conclusion of the holiday dinner, everyone tucked into the much-anticipated apple pie. After one bite, Mother said: "Oh, I'm sorry, this isn't as good as I usually make."

The daughter-in-law snapped, "That's because I made it."

A Practical Joke between Brothers

True story—names changed because some of these people are still kickin'.

The brothers liked to play tricks on each other. Bill ran a Christmas tree farm. Owen was known for his frugality. Yup, he was a cheap son-of-a-gun. One fall, Bill says to Owen, "You want me to save you a Christmas tree?"

Owen says, "How much?"

Bill says, "Free to you, Brother."

Owen likes that price.

Bill says, "I'll give you a good one with a root ball so you can plant it in the backyard after."

Owen likes that idea.

Come Christmastime, Bill delivers a nice spruce in a bucket, complete with burlap-wrapped root ball. He drops it off on Owen's porch where it sat for a week or so in the freezin' cold. Trees don't mind freezin' cold. They're used to it.

Did I mention that Owen, at that time, had twin babies and a Labrador retriever?

On Christmas Eve, Owen hauled the free tree into the house, bucket and all. He and his wife decorated it nice. The babies loved the blinking lights. Owen took snapshots of the two of them sitting under the tree in their reindeer jammies.

Christmas morning, the stockings were emptied, the gifts unwrapped, the turkey cooking. "What's that smell?" Owen said to his wife. "Baby need changing?"

"No," she said. "The babies are fine."

Later, as they're setting the food on the table: "What's that smell? Did the dog have an accident? Smells like the dog had an accident."

Owen looks in the usual places. Comes up empty.

Over dessert, Owen says, "I smell . . ." He sniffs. His nose leads him to the Christmas tree, the gift from brother Bill. Yup, the root ball of that free tree was packed with cow manure. On the porch, frozen, it gave off no odor. But in that warm house as the root ball melted the odor intensified.

I, for one, enjoy the fragrance of cow manure. But maybe not in the house during Christmas dinner.

Wonder what Owen's going to give Brother Bill next Christmas.

A Case of Mistaken Identity

Jimmy Cannon was known to drink heavily, which one Christmas Eve he did.

He drank so heavily, he couldn't make it home from the bar, so as he walked past the crèche on the town square, he decided to have a little nap. He crawled into the hay and went to sleep.

Next morning, the town constable roused him: "Jesus Christ!" the constable shouted.

"No-no-no-no," said Jimmy, "Jimmy Cannon!"

INGENUITY

Stumper
Jerry Grogin

Salmon Portland Chase served as senator from Ohio, as Secretary of the Treasury under Abraham Lincoln, and, eventually, Chief Justice of the Supreme Court. He was born in Cornish, New Hampshire.

Another Cornish man, Dick Lovejoy, had the honor of attending Annapolis, known for its rigid discipline and hazing rituals. When asked any question by an upperclassman, first-year students had to answer. If they were wrong, they had to do a number of pushups on the spot. If they were right, they got to ask the upperclassman a related question. If the related question stumped the upperclassman, the freshman was off the hook for the rest on the year—no more questions, no more pushups.

At the dining hall, an upperclassman asked Dick this stumper: "Whose photograph appears on the $10,000 bill?"

Dick said: "Salmon Portland Chase."

Astonished, the upperclassman said: "How did you know that?"

Dick started to say, "I come from . . ," but stopped himself. Instead he asked the upperclassman, "Where was Salmon Portland Chase born?"

And stumped him.

It Worked!
Larry Boutwell

Poor man had a flat tire. He couldn't get the wheel off no matter how hard he worked at turning the lugs, leading him to curse something awful.

The minister stopped by the roadside to offer his help. "Instead of cursing," he suggested, "you might offer a humble prayer to the Lord."

So the man did.

Then he took up the wrench, tugged on the lug, and by golly it came off slick as a bean, prompting the minister to say, "Well, I'll be goddamned!"

And the Winner Is
Perry Sawyer

Perry's brother entered his team of oxen in the pulling contest at the fair. When he got home, Father said, "How'd you do?"

"We come in next to top."

The neighbor, Hugh Dunning, also had a team of oxen. "How'd Hugh do?" Father asked.

"He come in next to last."

"How many teams in the contest?" Father said.

"Two."

KIDS

Camouflage
Steve Lombard

"Did you hear about the kid who dropped his gum in the chicken house?"

"No."

"Took him all day to find it."

A Family Story Passed Down Through Generations
Bob Gentile

Someone spotted the chimney fire in the homestead and roused the family. Mother and Father said to the four young brothers, "We've got to get out of the house!" They could hear the sirens of the fire trucks and police in the distance.

Young Jimmy said, "Mother, what pants should I wear?"

A New Baby
Barbara Stevens

Barbara remembered sending her little boy, Bobby, to the neighbors' with a casserole after the new baby came home from the hospital. The neighbor gratefully accepted the food. "Would you like to see the baby?" she asked Bobby.

"Naw," he said, "we get a new one at our house 'bout every year."

A Dozen Chicks

A mother in Grantham said when her son was small, he raised chickens for 4-H. One night she heard an awful ruckus. When she approached the chicken pen, she saw a fox making a getaway. Oh no! She counted the chickens. What a relief. The twelve chicks were still in the pen.

The next morning, she told her son what a close call the chicks had. "But don't worry," she said, "I did a head count."

"Mom," he said, "that's no good. Foxes leave the heads."

Where's Caleb?

Mary in Gilmanton said Mrs. Jones owned a dairy farm up the road and the six little neighbor kids (I think Mary was one of them) walked up to the farm to see some newborn kittens. Five of the kids walked back home, but one stayed to help Mrs. Jones shuck peas.

Mother, of course, noticed one of her children missing. "Where's Caleb?" she asked.

"Oh," said a sister, "he's up peeing with Mrs. Jones."

Eagle Eyes

Olive was proud of her little girl, Alice, and how quickly she was learning the Lord's Prayer. Yup, Alice recited it back to her, word perfect, until the line, "and deliver us from eagles."

If you've ever seen an eagle up close on the branch of a pine tree, turning its beady eye on your Chihuahua named Chico (which I have), you know what Alice was talking about.

The Littlest Yankee

Everett and his grandson were riding through town in the pickup when Everett saw a person he knew on the side of the road, so he waved. The person didn't wave back.

"That wasn't very nice," Everett said. "He didn't even wave back."

Little Colin, just five years old, said, "He nodded."

Don't Count Your Chickens

Grammie was playing the board game The Game of Life with her five- and eleven-year-old grandsons. The younger boy said to his brother, "You're going down!" Grammie said, "Don't count your chickens before they're hatched."

The little one said, surprised and delighted: "We have chickens?"

Skunks Under the House

Anne moved to Everett, Massachusetts. She liked her new home and her next-door neighbor, Ray, who was handy, helpful, eighty-plus years old, and originally from Maine.

Spring comes and so do the skunks. One or two take up residence under Anne's house. She would like them removed but doesn't know how. So she consults the neighbor.

"Ray," she says, "where do you suppose all these skunks come from?"

He says, "Must be they come down from Maine."

Seems when he was a boy, he encountered a lot of those Maine skunks.

"How'd you get rid of them?"

He says, "Hang on, I'll be right back."

He returns from his house with a souvenir baseball bat—about a foot long—and a fireplace glove.

"When I was a boy," he says, "we'd crawl under the house, conk 'em in the head with the little bat to daze 'em, and drag 'em out by the tail. Relocate 'em down the rud."

"And that worked?" she said.

"Oh, yuh, worked good."

Anne feels the need to probe a little deeper. "Ray," she says, "after you conked the skunk, grabbed him by the tail, and relocated him down the road, when you went back to the house, what did your mother say?"

Ray thought a minute. "She said, 'Ray, go out back, strip naked and bury your clothes.'"

First Trip to Fenway

Chet was so excited. His grandfather was taking him to his first real live Red Sox game in Boston at Fenway Park. It was a long ride down and hard to park, but they finally found their seats in the bleachers and Chet gazed out over the ball field. "Grampa," he said, "it's in color!"

Peaks Island

Alison fondly remembers her uncle Leslie Michael Stanton, who lived much of each year on Peaks Island, Casco Bay, Maine. He was, she said, the last of the dory fisherman and she treasures a photograph of him at the helm with his hands on the wheel.

As a child, she spent summers learning about lobstering and the ways of the sea. One of her earliest memories is of her first visit to Peaks. She played on the beach. Her mother said, "What do you think of the water, dear?"

She replied, "It's salty, Mama."

A Hit

Sonia told about a retired major-league player (she couldn't remember his name) who coached T-ball. Her son was assigned to his team.

Lee was not the most competitive kid. He was the daydreamer in left field picking dandelions. She worried that the coach would be too demanding.

On the contrary, one practice, instead of using the T, coach lobbed pitches at the kids. He kept lobbing until each kid got a hit. When her son stepped to home base, he missed the first 36 pitches, but finally connected.

Afterwards he said, "Mom, did Coach really pitch for the Red Sox?"

"Yes," she said.

"Well," Lee said, "I guess I must be pretty good!"

Hooky Runs in the Family
Dick MacLeod

Sometimes, instead of waiting for the school bus in front of the big rock, Dick waited behind the big rock—and the bus would sail on by. This gave him a day to himself. So long as he remembered to get home by 3:00, he was all set. (The little devil!)

It was kind of a family tradition, his daughter said: "My mother never went to school on a Friday."

Dick said: "I took off every Monday."

THE LAW

Chief Russ

In Temple, folks got talking about a chief of police from years past—popular guy who generated a lot of stories. In one, Chief Russ shows up at town meeting. He gives a report. The department was moving ahead, he said, and had bought some new equipment including a new fingerprint machine.

During the question period, he was asked how that new fingerprint machine was working out. Chief Russ allowed as how he really couldn't say. Somebody stole it.

Welcome to Milford

Mr. and Mrs. Keller had just moved into town. John accidentally ran a stop sign, got a ticket, paid his fine, and all was well, until one morning the police showed up with an arrest warrant.

Another John Keller in a nearby town had done some serious law breaking, skipped his court date, and was WANTED.

After careful a reading of the paperwork, the police decided it was a case of mistaken identity and went away—though the Keller's five-year-old was quite upset because they'd tried to take her daddy. And lord knows what the neighbors thought about the cruiser in the yard of the new people.

A few hours later, the police showed up again. The second shift hadn't gotten the memo about the two John Kellers. More chaos ensued. Once again, John avoided arrest, but he came close.

At bedtime, Mrs. Keller said: "We might as well stay up, because when the next shift comes on, they'll probably be back."

Sure enough, about 11:00 PM floodlights and sirens bombarded the house, no doubt waking the neighborhood. Again, John talked his way off the hook.

He went to work the next morning a little bleary-eyed. Meanwhile, the chief called Mrs. Keller to apologize. He was especially sorry their little girl was upset and wanted to make it up to her. Would Mom and daughter like a ride around town in a cruiser so they could meet some of the nice police officers and the little girl would realize they were, in fact, kind and well-meaning?

"Sure," Mrs. Keller says. "That would be fun." And it was.

Except, John got a call at work from a concerned neighbor. "The police were back at your house," the neighbor said. "I don't know what's going on, but this time they hauled off your wife and your daughter."

All's Well That Ends Well, Even If It's Topsy Turvy

The town of Washington has a chief of police with a dry sense of humor.

At a storytelling session, a fella related the sad tale of how he and his wife went out shopping and, coming home on Route 3, crested a hill to find a flock of turkeys in their lane.

The fella swerved and, long story short, the car ended up upside down in the ditch. The shopping—everything from toilet paper to lettuce, tomatoes, and carrots—got upended too and spilled all over the car.

The fella and his wife could hear the gasoline gurgling so they extricated themselves from the car as soon as they could.

They weren't hurt too bad, just a little bunged up.

Soon the rescue and police showed up. The fella and his wife were, naturally, shaken, so they paid close attention when Chief Marshall walked over to them, looking grim.

"I've got bad news," he said.

"Oh?" they said.

"Your salad has been tossed."

Actually, the funniest part of this story was that, as the husband told it, the wife corrected him on a few details, including the punch line, which the husband delivered this way: "The chief said we had a mixed salad."

"No," she corrected, "the chief *said*, 'Your salad has been tossed!'"

In the Pokey

A prominent citizen had too much to drink and caused a ruckus in the village one evening. She ended up in a cell in the basement of town hall next to the police chief's office.

When she sobered up a little and realized she'd be spending the night, she asked the chief if he'd go to the general store next door and get her some Kotex.

He said, "I'm sorry, Marge, but you'll have to eat corn flakes like everybody else."

Here in Effingham

A police chief from away was brought in to explain why Effingham needed a second police officer. The fellow pointed out that neighboring towns had much larger police forces. One had five officers, another had fifteen.

During the Q&A that followed, a native offered a comment: "Effingham don't need as may police officers as those other towns."

"Why's that?" asked the police chief from away.

"Here in Effingham," the native said, "we're better armed."

Three Cops

Some years ago, Roger Maxfield was selectman in Loudon. At the time, the police force was made up of three officers and they all drove their own cars.

The purchase of a police car came up for discussion. Levi Ladd, a construction guy with a practical nature, raised the question: "What are you gonna do with three cops and one car?"

Roger said, "Two in the front, one in the back."

Gawldum Kids and Gawldum Signs

Bob Ramsey was a well-known chief of police, known also for having a temper. He tried to keep order in town as best he could, but sometimes the job got frustrating.

Where the ledges dropped off to the lake, three or four No Parking signs lined the road. Every weekend that summer, kids ripped those signs down and threw them into the lake.

Pastor Fisher was driving by and spotted Bob to his hips in the water, pulling out signs. Again. The pastor rolled down his window and was about to make a wise-ass comment, when Bob's wife intervened, "If you value your life, Reverend, you'll keep on going."

A Little Hellion

Peter "was a hellion, even as a little kid." His mother was home with a passel of kids when the sheriff knocked on the door. "Is there a Peter Couples residing here?"

Mother said indeed there was. "What's the problem?"

The sheriff explained that an eye-witness claimed to have seen said Peter Couples burglarizing a house in the neighborhood.

Mother called Peter in from another room. He was four. She asked for an explanation.

"Yes," he said. "It was me. They weren't home and I needed a peanut butter sandwich."

Keis, Nelson
Buddy McDougal

This is not a Hebron story, it's an East Hebron story. My old friend, Nelson Adams, he's from East Hebron, same as me, told me what happened. Most of you know him—if you don't know him, too bad.

Some of you remember Chief Barnard. He was the chief of police for Hebron and East Hebron for years. He pretty much had the territory covered from Bridgewater to the Plymouth line. All except Groton. Groton had its own chief.

Chief Barnard got word over the horn that a couple of bandits were coming his way. They had stolen a car in Concord, and it looked like they were heading for Plymouth.

The chief called up his deputy, who at the time happened to be Nelson Adams. The two of them drove to the top of Hoyt Hill. You can see all around from the top of Hoyt Hill.

They waited and waited. It was nighttime. Getting later and later. Talked about town affairs, or whatever it is that two policemen talk about when they get together.

After a while they spotted two pinprick headlights coming fast up the valley. "I think that is the two fellas we want," Chief Barnard said.

"Yup," Nelson said. "I think we can be pretty certain that's them. What are we gonna do, Chief?"

The chief thought a minute. Then he said, "Keis, Nelson, we set right here and don't move, in five minutes they'll be in Plymouth."

What the Kindergarteners Had for Supper
Mary Jane Ogmundson

At circle, the kindergarten teacher asked the children what they'd had for supper the night before. Mary said hamburgers. Joy said macaroni and cheese. Billy said venison stew made from the deer hanging in his daddy's barn.

The teacher said, "Billy, that can't be right. It's March."

Linda said, "It's true, Mrs. O. There's five of 'em hanging in the barn. And two of 'em belong to my daddy."

His Intentions Were Good

A retired state trooper told this true story of his rookie days. He was out patrolling, one of his first patrols in the North Country, got onto some back roads off back roads, and came upon a cabin afire. The smoke was billowing out the top of it.

He called in the alarm: "I don't know exactly where I am, but send back-up," something to that effect. Then he popped the trunk, pulled out a massive fire extinguisher, kicked in the door of the cottage, and proceeded to spray everything in sight with the white, powdery fire retardant.

When the extinguisher extinguished itself and the dust settled, he surveyed the scene: Two old guys sitting on a bench, all white, making small coughing sounds. They regarded him balefully.

The cabin wasn't a cabin at all. It was a sap house.

LIARS AND TALL TALES

Plaid
Dick MacLeod

Dick is one of the founders of the famous Loon Mountain Scottish Festival. He once painted the shutters on his house in the tartan plaid of his clan. When asked how he made all those stripes, he explained that instead of shaking the can to mix the paint, he held it very still, straight up and down, and the paint striped on its own. ∽

One Helluva Kick
Andy McAvoy

The dad was playing a game with his three sons. They took turns kicking the football over the roof of the house to him, and he kicked it back. When he tired of the game, he hid the ball. The boys complained: "Kick it back, Dad!"

"I did," he said. "I must have kicked it so hard it never landed."

Later, on a trip to Nantucket, he hid the ball in his in-laws' backyard. The boys discovered it and were puzzled. Dad said, "I told you that was one hell of a kick!" ∽

Do You Know the Way to UNH?
Apocryphal

Some UNH boys got to drinking one night at a party in the woods, which was all right except when everybody went home, one poor soul was left behind. He'd fallen asleep, and when he woke he was thirsty, hungry, and he didn't know where he was.

He started walking on the gravel road, thinking it would lead to civilization sooner or later. He walked and walked. Came upon a farmhouse and had an idea. He picked up a dried cow flap in the field and went to the door. "I wonder," he asked the lady of the house, "if I might beg a glass of water to drink with my breakfast." He held up the cow flap.

Why, no young man would be eating a dried cow flap on her watch, the lady said. She ushered him in and made up a plate of bacon and eggs.

The young man went on his way. At noon time, hungry again, he still hadn't located civilization. So he tried the same thing at another farmhouse. "Might I have a glass of milk to go with my lunch?" he asked the lady of the house—and held up a dried cow flap.

"That's no lunch for a young man!" she said. She prepared a nice sandwich.

He went along down the road. Supper time, he tried once more. This time, I'm guessing, he was going to ask directions. This time, too, instead of the lady of the house, the gentleman came to the door. The boy asked the farmer if he might beg a cup of coffee to go with his supper and held up the dried cow flap.

"That dried cow flap is no good for supper," the farmer said. "Come on out to the barn and I'll get you a fresh one."

Magic Lantern
Apocryphal

When Charlie's wife went into labor, the neighbor helped out. She and Mrs. Charlie did most of the work, but Charlie also helped by holding the lantern. After a couple hours labor, Mrs. Charlie was ready to deliver. A little head popped out. "Oh," said the neighbor, "you've got a beautiful baby daughter."

Charlie and Mrs. Charlie were pleased. "But wait," says the neighbor lady, "hold the lantern close. Here comes . . . yes . . . it's another one. Oh, Charlie, it's a beautiful baby boy. But wait, we're not done yet. Another girl."

Just then, the lantern went out.

"What happened to the lantern, Charlie?"

"I put it out. Had to. The light's attractin' 'em."

Dang that Rooster
Beverly Patton

Grandmother had an aggressive rooster. One day he spurred her for the last time. "Head's off for that rooster!" Grandma said, "At least we can have him for Sunday dinner."

But the rooster got the last laugh. He cooked up so tough "you couldn't even cut the gravy."

Tut Tuttle's Cow and the Drawbridge
Apocryphal

A few of us in Kingston tried to piece together the story of Tut Tuttle and the drawbridge. Near as we could figure, one of Tut Tuttle's cows was feeling poorly, so Tut administered an enema of warm soapy water poured into the bell of a trumpet gently inserted where it would do the most good.

The cow got nervous during the procedure and ran for it. Ran right for the drawbridge, and, well, with all that internal pressure, the horn she blew.

It being a foggy day, the fellow running the drawbridge failed to see Tut Tuttle's distressed cow. He thought the blare was a signal to raise the bridge for a passing boat.

So he did.

Tut Tuttle's cow ran right off the edge of the bridge and plunged into the water below.

Which didn't do her any good.

Tut was so mad. He said the bridge-keeper should be fired if he couldn't tell the difference between a maritime signal and a cow with a trumpet up her bum.

The Biggest Liar in the State of Maine
Warren Angus Wilbur

Merle says, "Paul, this is a compliment. You are the biggest liar in the state of Maine."

Paul says, "I ain't. But as soon as you go back to Massachusetts, I will be."

Neither as It Turns Out

Waiting in line for a hot dog at the Nottingham Senior Picnic, I got chatting with a man in line behind me. "What do you do for work?" he said.

"I'm a professional liar."

"Oh," he said, "are you in the House or the Senate?"

LOBSTER AND OTHER EDIBLES

Just an Inch or Two in the Bottom

The flatlander complained to the Mainer about how long it took to get the pot of water boiling for lobsters.

"Jeesh," the Mainer said, "you don't boil a whole bucket of water. Just put an inch or two in the bottom of the pot and let 'em steam. You want to cook 'em, not drown 'em."

Go West Young Lobster.
Apocryphal

A seacoast couple sent a dozen live lobsters to some friends in the Midwest who, on a visit earlier in the year, declared lobster "ambrosia."

A week went by and the couple received no thank you call or note. Then another week passed. Worried that maybe the lobsters had gotten lost in the mail, they called to inquire if they'd arrived safely.

"Oh," the friends said, "this is awkward. The lobsters arrived all right, but they must have spoiled on the way—they were brownish green instead of that nice bright red like the ones we had at your house. So we threw them out."

Don't Worry Ma'am
Apocryphal

On the coast, you can go down to the pier, pick out your lobster, and they'll cook it for you on the spot. Sure enough, the lady from the Midwest wanted to try lobster. She picked one out.

The Mainer grabbed the lobster and held it over a pot of boiling water. "You're not going to put that living animal into that boiling water, are you?" the lady said, appalled.

"Don't worry, Ma'am. They're used to it."

Cod Balls

There's a nice man, whose name I can't remember, whom I met on Star Island. Every time our paths cross—and they cross once a year or so—he reminds me of a cooking class we attended on Star. The instructor demonstrated how to cook cod balls the way they did in the 1700s.

One of the students piped up: "Did they use any other parts of the fish?"

Something Decent To Eat

At the church supper Ronald selected a piece of his wife's apple pie from the pie table. His granddaughter said, "Grampa, why do you always pick Grammie's pie when there are all those other pies to choose from?"

Ronald said, "Cause I want something decent to eat."

His Eyes Were Bigger Than His Stomach

Ken grew up on Peaks Island in Maine. One day he traveled with his father to Boston. It was quite a trip from the boat to the bus in Portland to the train station then on the train to Boston.

They got there all right and stopped at a deli for lunch. Ken spotted a big turkey leg in the case. He wanted that leg. The deli man said, "That kid'll never eat that whole leg." Ken's father had his doubts too. But Ken swore he could, begged for the leg, got the leg, and dug in.

Sure enough, the leg got about half eaten and Ken could eat no more. Father said there was no sense wasting a good half of a turkey leg. So the leg went into a paper bag. Ken had to carry it to Fenway Park and the Red Sox game, then to the train station, then all the way to Portland on the train, then on the bus to the landing, then on the boat to Peaks Island, and from there home.

By the time the day was done, Ken said, "I was awful sick of that turkey leg."

Family Potatoes for Dinner

Daniel sold hay, eggs, and vegetables from a farm stand by the road. He had the eggs in cartons—large, medium, small. He separated the potatoes into bins—big ones, medium ones, and one bin of mixed sizes, ungraded.

A lady commented that the eggs and potatoes looked pretty, except for that one bin of mixed-size potatoes.

Daniel explained: "Ma'am, those are family potatoes—parents and little kids. I refuse to separate 'em."

Beautiful Blue Eyes
Apocryphal

A lady from Warner walked into an ice cream shop, spotted Paul Newman at a table, and, yankee-like, pretended not to notice him. Walked right by. Chin up. Ordered an ice cream, got her change, walked right past the man with the beautiful blue eyes, again pretending not to notice.

Out on the sidewalk, her change was in her hand, but no sign of the ice cream.

Back into the shop she went. She said to the clerk: "I'm missing my ice cream."

Paul Newman said, "It's in your purse."

Beans

Seems there was a bean supper each Saturday night at the hall in Chatham. Ethan enjoyed attending. He lived right across the road in Stow, Maine, but when he enjoyed a good bean supper, he made a point of spending the night at his sister's house in Chatham.

Didn't want to risk breaking the law against transporting gas across state lines.

The Legend of Mooseturd Pie
Apocryphal

If you don't know the legend of the Mooseturd Pie, here it is. Sometimes it is called by other names, but the gist remains.

In the logging camp, absent a professional cookee, one logger had to do all the cooking. Feeding those lumberjacks was a colossal job and Sis got stuck with it. By tradition, the first man to complain about the grub had to take over. After about six weeks of thankless toil over a hot wood stove, Sis decided he'd had enough.

He burned the pancakes. Nobody complained.

He hot-peppered the beans. Delicious, the loggers declared.

He boiled the venison. Nobody said a word.

In desperation, he took to the woods, collected two quarts of moose droppings, and baked them into a pie. Deano liked the looks of that warm pie. He took a big bite. "That pie tastes like moose turds," he shouted. "But it's good."

He Cannot Tell a Lie, Nor Could He Eat the Pie
John Scudder

Reverend Hill loved pie. Marcy Abel loved to bake and thought it would be nice to bake her favorite rhubarb pie for the reverend.

During one of the reverend's visits to her home, she presented him with a delicious looking pie she'd baked that morning. She told the reverend that he must take the pie home and share it with is family. He took it willingly.

The pie made it home safely and, after supper, the Hill family got ready to enjoy it. Reverend Hill took the first bite. The first forkful went into his mouth and *pffftt*, almost as quickly, was spit out! It was awful! Just terrible!

Mrs. Hill tried a bite and confirmed that it was horrible. Evidently Mrs. Abel had put salt into the pie instead of sugar.

The pie went into the garbage can.

That Sunday after church, Mrs. Abel asked the reverend how he liked the pie. The reverend did not know what to do. He didn't want to hurt her feelings, and being a man of the cloth, he couldn't lie.

After some thought he replied, "Well, all I can say is that it didn't last very long around our house."

Alvin and the Bake Sale Cookies

Bob Bristol served as selectman for many years. He also raised golden retrievers, which he sometimes brought to work at town hall. A bake sale was planned, so all day folks brought goodies to town hall and set them on a table in preparation for the next day's sale.

Bob's dog, Alvin, unbeknownst to Bob, sneaked downstairs and ate a good portion of the baked goods, waxed paper, plastic wrap, and all.

When the damage was discovered, Bob said nothing.

But he did admit, some time later, that at home on the evening the baked goods disappeared, "Alvin fahted the most dreadful fahts."

MISUNDERSTANDINGS AND MISCOMMUNICATION

A Nice Country Setting

The woman from away was moving her family to Vermont. She'd landed a good job in administration at a hospital, and wanted to buy a modest house, she told the realtor, with a nice country setting.

"Paved or unpaved?" the realtor asked.

The woman from away thought he was talking about the driveway.

Three Cups

A young man reminisced about his family ties to Berlin. He did not grow up there, but often visited his grandparents.

In a family story, three of the St. Onge brothers made the high school hockey team at the same time. Some of their equipment was provided, but some they had to provide themselves. Money was tight in this family of fifteen children, so they were a bit rueful when they got home from school and said to their mother, Joan d'Arc St. Onge, "Mémère, we need three cups."

Joan d'Arc St. Onge went straight to the cupboard and took out three little cups with saucers.

Dragass

Twin sisters Angel and Cathy from Dalton came out of the hills for stories at the Mount Washington Hotel on a Saturday night.

A year before, when I visited the Wash, Angel told me the following story—which I retold that Saturday.

"Did I get it right?" I asked.

"Well," Angel said, "you got the gist."

Here's the story, or at least the gist of it:

When Angel and Cathy retired, they moved into the old family camp in Dalton. That first spring, they tried out the lawnmower, but it didn't start. They asked their neighbor, who was handy, what to do. He said: "All you need is some dragass."

"Dragass?"

"Yuh, go down the hardware store and pick up some dragass."

"Dragass?"

"Right."

"How do you spell it?"

"D-R-Y-G-A-S. Dragass."

So they bought some, put it in the tank, and sure enough, the neighbor was right. All that old lawnmower needed was a touch of dragass.

Percy Ain't a Poit

I was invited to be the first speaker at the new historical society building in Stratford Hollow. It used to be a church, but they ran out of parishioners, so the historical society inherited the building.

The members of the society immediately started sprucing things up. One of their first tasks was to sand and varnish the pews. Unfortunately, they used the slow-drying varnish, which was fine with me because I was standing up front. Let's just say the girl with the blue angora sweater in the third pew left a little something behind.

At our writing workshop, I asked the assembled what the population of Stratford was. They looked at each other, and one man piped up: "All of us."

Which wasn't precisely true. There at the back of the hall, hovering in the doorway, was a slight man in overalls and a baseball cap. I looked at him. The assembled turned and looked at him. A woman in the front pew motioned him in: "Come on in, Percy. You're not late. We're just getting started."

Percy shuffled in and took a seat in the front pew. We got started. We wrote. We talked about stories, and poems, and our lives. We wrote some more. We read aloud. We critiqued one another's work. After about an hour and a half, I called a halt. "We'll take a five-minute break," I said. "Go ahead and use the bathroom if you need to, but come right back. We've got another hour to go. And if you don't come back my feelings will be hurt."

Percy stood directly in front of me, and I could tell by the look in his eyes that he was about to make a break for it.

"Percy," I said, "you are coming back after the break, aren't you?"

He looked at me. He said, "I ain't a poit, nor a writer. I just stopped by to fix the furnace."

Not a Lawyer

Elizabeth's father dressed rough around the house and around town. He was apt to be seen in a raggedy flannel shirt and jeans strung up with bailing twine.

When Elizabeth's brother and his wife were closing on a house, Dad tagged along to meet the realtor. They sat around a table and Dad peppered the realtor with questions. Making a joke (kind of), the realtor said, "Who does this guy think he is, a lawyer?"

There was an awkward pause. "Actually," the brother said, "he's a judge."

NATIVES

Don't Let Moose Fool You

Moose and Edwin were longtime fishing and storytelling buddies who lived in Sandwich. One time, during a discussion of natives, Edwin pulled a newcomer aside and confided: "A lot of people think Moose is a native. He's not a native. He was born in Tamworth."

How To Become a Native

You become a native when the last person dies who remembers you moving in.

There's Some Question About Brucie

At the historical society annual meeting, a man told about researching his family genealogy. His grandparents had fourteen children. Someone said, "Were they all New Hampshire natives?"

"Well, there's some question about Brucie," he said, "Brucie was born in Maine. But, a-course, Grampa never left the state."

In Three Words or Fewer
Maxine Aldridge

When a tourist asks Maxine, owner of Harmon's Cheese & Country Store in Sugar Hill, the difference between Vermont and New Hampshire maple syrup, she says, "The Connecticut River."

Virginia Man
Aprocyphal

Randall was born in Virginia, but his parents moved to Keene, New Hampshire, when he was an infant. He lived in Keene, raised his family there, took a great interest in the community where he served on many boards and committees. When he died, the headline on his obituary read: "Virginia Man dies at 101."

How Long You Lived in Town?

Newcomer asks an old-timer how long she's lived in town. "Forty-seven years," the old-timer says. "They're just getting used to me."

Aggie 'Bout Had the Situation Covered

Norma (or—as we say in some parts of New England—Nawmer) told about her aunts Rebecker and Aggie.

The house caught fire.

Aggie ran for the door yelling, "Fire! Fire! Help! Help!"

Rebecker, breathless behind her, said: "What'll I yell, Aggie?"

True Story of Different Aesthetic Sensibilities

An old mill on the river looked, to the rich man from New York, like it would make a great house, renovated of course. At a cocktail party, he mentioned the project to a friend who was a professor. The professor said his architectural students were available to design houses for free as part of their course work.

The rich man jumped at the chance! One of the students redesigned the old mill as a home, and the rich man was delighted with the design. A local contractor took on the job of taking down much of the old mill and rebuilding it. The rich man returned to New York.

Months later, he came back to the mill site to see what had been accomplished. He became irate. "That house doesn't look anything like the design in the plans I gave you."

The builder says, "I know. I didn't like 'em."

Low Flyers

Jack Hanover

Jack has a place on Winnipesaukee. One of his yankee neighbors had a porch. He ran a screen between the porch rail and the floor to keep his grand kids from falling off the edge. But, when the fella from away asked the yankee how come he had just the bottom half of his porch screened in, the yankee said, "Around here, we have low-flying mosquitos."

By Hook or Crook
Apocryphal

A well-dressed man in a big car with New York license plates pulled into the driveway of a Maine farmhouse. He marched up to the door big as brass and knocked. He asked the farmer: "Does your wife hook rugs?"

"She does."

"May I see them?"

"Why not."

The New Yorker walks room to room scrutinizing the beautiful hand-hooked rugs. "I'll buy all you have," he told the farmer.

Farmer says: "You got a wife?"

"Yes."

"She ain't crippled up?"

"No."

"Get her to hook you some."

Yup, There's a Name for It
Don Hamlin

Don was sitting at Panera Bread in Hollis one day when he saw a near accident caused by one aggressive, horn-tooting driver out in front of the store.

"Massachusetts driver," said the native, disgusted.

"No," Don said. "The car had New Hampshire plates."

"Transplant," the native said.

POLITICS AND TOWN MEETING

Five Gold Eagles
Dan Rothman

A New Boston resident wrote to me after I'd given a presentation on town meeting at the historical society. Here's the story exactly as he wrote it:

When you asked for a story about a New Boston town meeting, I half-remembered a very old story I'd read somewhere. I'm quite sure I would have remembered the other half if I wasn't lulled to sleep by the *clickety-clack* of Candy Woodbury's knitting needles. Now that I'm home, I found the story on my very own website, on my page about New Boston churches.

New Boston's first meetinghouse was rather plain, and in 1810 some patriotic citizens thought it might be nice to decorate the cupola with a gold eagle. They wrote to Boston to find out what it might cost, and at town meeting shared what they'd learned: A wooden eagle carved from hickory and gilded with gold leaf would cost five dollars. Coincidentally, at the time, the one-dollar coin was also called a "gold eagle."

Before the townspeople could vote on this purchase, a farmer named Joseph Dunbar rose to speak. "Gentlemen—and others—I always reckoned the voters of New Boston were big fools, and probably always would be, but if they are willing to give five honest-to-goodness gold eagles for one gilt one, they are a darned sight bigger fools than I supposed."

A Moderator's Gotta Do What a Moderator's Gotta Do

Walter Peterson, a beloved Republican governor and legislator, also served as moderator in his hometown of Peterborough for twenty-seven years. Moderators, of course, must be nonpartisan. Peterson was leading a workshop for newly-elected moderators when a sticky question came up. "What do you do if a liberal raises his hand to speak at town meeting?"

Peterson said, "Some days my eyesight's not so good."

He Chose Wisely

They say James Cleveland, longtime congressman from New Hampshire, was challenged on the point of not being a native by a political opponent. Cleveland responded: "Yes, it's true. I did not move to New Hampshire until I was two years old. At the time I thought it would be most beneficial to stay near my mother."

The Shy Road Agent

In many towns, the road agent is elected, which means he or she will, upon occasion, be asked to address the legislative body. Gil was an elected road agent. Young fella. Kinda shy. He tried best as he could to keep out of the fray at town meeting.

Folks were complaining about the state of the roads. One voter proposed adding $10,000 to the road agent's budget so he could hire some folks and get more work done in the coming year.

"Would an additional $10,000 improve the state of the roads?" the young road agent was asked.

"Well," Gil said, blushing, "it wunt hurt 'em."

He Should Know
Julia King

At a candidates' forum in Bartlett, the moderator, Norman Head, asked the road agent, Travis Chick, how many miles of road the town currently had to plow. "Fifty," was Travis's short reply.

The fire chief, Pat Roberts, was sitting next to where Travis was standing. He leaned over to a friend on his other side and whispered, "Don't he know you have to come back?"

Without missing a beat Travis corrected himself: "That's a hundred, 'cause you have to come back."

No Need to Complicate Matters

At town meeting, the road agent assured the voters that the Inky Swamp Road would be paved in the coming year.

Cleve, who lived on the road, asked if the road agent was planning to "stripe it."

"No need," said the road agent. "Cleve, all you need to know is drive on the right and pass on the left."

Defibrillate This!
Deb Schulte

The New Castle town historian passed on this town meeting story. The town had put in a request for a defibrillator for the EMTs. Discussion included questions about the EMT's qualifications to run the defibrillator and, of course, cost. Seemed kinda pricey to a lot of folks.

An older gentleman named Bill explained that he had a modest home. Would the selectman tell him how much the defibrillator would cost him in property taxes in the coming year?

Selectman said, "On your house, Bill, it'd be about $20.00."

Bill said, "My wife's worth $20.00."

The article passed.

A Tie

At the Wilmot town meeting, some years ago, a suggestion was made to erect a new and updated veterans monument. Seems they were a few wars behind. Discussion ensued. The monument was a fine idea, but should it be erected in Wilmot Center or Wilmot Flat? The vote tied at 150 for the Center, 150 for the Flat.

So they didn't build it.

Subject to Gates and Bars

Dick recalled a town meeting in 1975. The town fathers wanted to close a road, subject to gates and bars. One of the locals objected strenuously and gave an impassioned speech about how his father had driven that road, and his grandfather. His great-grandfather, by golly, drove his team of horses down that road, and it should be kept open and maintained.

At the conclusion of the speech, another local spoke up, "Sit down, Walter, and go find a job."

Take Your Turn

At Belmont High School, Mr. Fournier told about his days as town moderator.

A fellow in town named Elcid Moody was quite a philosopher and always had much to say at town meeting. Mr. Fournier enforced the rule that once you spoke on an article, you couldn't speak again until everybody else who wanted to speak had said their piece.

Well, Elcid spoke on a budget question. Several others spoke. Elcid got in line to speak again. He was about to step up to the mic when he noticed a woman standing behind him, so with a gallant flourish he said, "You go right ahead, ma'am."

She did.

"Move the question," she said.

Two Road Agents
Margaret Perry

In Alstead, there was considerable dissatisfaction with the condition of the town roads, and with Alstead being a rather large town, some thought the town ought to hire two road agents, one for the east part and one for the west part.

The proposal made it onto the warrant, and the matter was duly brought up for discussion at town meeting.

After a couple of remarks, a man stood and, in effect, settled the matter. "I cannot support this article. I should think one road agent is bad enough."

New Plow

The road agent put in a plea for a new snowplow. Yup, he said, it was needed. No sense putting it off. The old plow has had it.

But one old-timer had his thinking cap on. "Wa'n't that the same snowplow we had last year?"

"Yup."

"And wa'n't last winter the winter we didn't get any snow?"

"Yup."

"If it was good enough last year and we never used it, why ain't it good enough this year?"

The Ladder Truck

At town meeting, a warrant article called for a shiny new fire truck—a ladder truck in fact. But a wise man objected. He said, "There's three problems. First, we don't have enough money. Second, we don't have a building big enough to store it. And third, we don't have anybody smart enough to drive the back half."

Fix the Door at Least

In Rumney, some years ago, the discussion at town meeting highlighted the need to fix up the town hall. Seems it had fallen into disrepair. Some said yes, repairs were needed. Others said it had been standing strong for over a hundred years and would go another hundred easy. No need to spend money "at this time."

Joe Kent, the moderator, declared a short recess to cool hot heads before returning to the debate. When some members of the legislative body stepped outside for the break, the town hall door fell off its hinges into the snow.

How this affected the vote is lost to history.

A Good Old Truck

In hopes of persuading voters to support a new town truck, the road agent elaborated on his request. "Yuh," he says, "it's been a good old truck, 285 thousand miles on it. But the last twelve was towed."

The Last Word

The new police cruiser (this was some years ago) was going to cost the town something around $5,000. One of the citizens stood to protest what he thought was an outrageous expenditure. He went on for some time, turning a little purple in the face. "You don't like the new cruiser," called a voice from the back of the gallery.

"No, I don't!"

"Then don't vote for it."

You Get What You Pay For

Discussion of the replacement for a bridge washed away in the flood led to the question, "Can't we build it for less money?"

"Yup, but it won't reach the other side."

Truer Words Never Spoken

On the proposed new zoning ordinance, the old-timer said: "If we'd passed this twenty-five years ago, most of you wouldn't be here."

They Didn't Think It Through

In Randolph, the legislative body voted to save money by replacing the town cruiser with a vw Rabbit.

"How'd that turn out?" I asked.

"Not so great. The chief of police was too fat to fit behind the wheel."

Sadie's Holding Tank
Jackie Heath

For many years, the little library in Holderness did not have a bathroom. Finally, an article was put on the warrant to see if the town would vote to fund one.

The town meeting went peacefully, with attendees voting in the regular stuff, fire trucks and so forth.

When discussion on the proposed bathroom came up, things became somewhat heated. Why fix it if it ain't broken? There'd never been a bathroom in the library before; why do we need one now?

Mr. Perkins got up and said that his sister Sadie had been a librarian there for thirty years and she'd never needed nor expressed a need for a bathroom.

A fellow from public works spoke to Mr. Perkins' point: "That Sadie Perkins must have had a helluva good holding tank!"

How Do You Take Your Bourbon?

The building of a sewer system in town was a contentious issue. It was going to be expensive. But not building it was going to be even more expensive. The state threatened a fine of $1,000 a week until a set of plans had been developed and the project set in motion. The town had a water system and everybody on that system had to have town sewer.

The legislative body realized this project must be undertaken, but they weren't happy about it. George Pitts summed up the frustration many felt: "I told you it was a mistake to put in town water!"

His neighbor said, "George, don't you drink your bourbon with water?"

George said, "You know darned well I drink it neat."

Don't Let the Door Hit Ya

Many years ago, Mrs. Mudge, who was never happy, gave a fiery speech to the select board about how the tax rate was getting so high people like her were going to have to move out.

The road agent was on hand. Usually a man of few words, Fred, nevertheless, had something to say on the topic. "Mr. Chairman," he said.

"Yes, Fred."

"You tell Mrs. Mudge we got some trucks available if she needs help gettin' out."

Those Smarty Pants
Dean Marden

In Hanover, town officials got the bright idea of charging $10.00 for a head tax. Dartmouth students—and there were a lot of them—had to pay up. They did. Which made them eligible to vote in local elections and at the town meeting.

The students, annoyed by the tax, petitioned an article and showed up in sufficient numbers to pass it. The article authorized the construction of a building a foot square and a mile high.

Next time around, the head tax was repealed.

Unanimous

The position of constable was historically an elected one. It still is in a few towns, only now we call it chief of police. This particular year, nobody ran. But a fella named Joe got two write-in votes.

This was at a time when voting occurred and votes were counted during the morning of town meeting. This no longer happens, as it is too time-consuming, but for a hundred years, give or take, it's how all town positions were filled.

Joe was not well-liked in town. He was arrogant and bossy. Some people thought he was a New York City cop in the witness protection program.

When the votes were counted, townspeople present were dismayed at the prospect of Joe as town constable. Joe, as it happened, was not present at the meeting. The moderator said, he wouldn't tell Joe he'd been elected if, and only if, everybody else in the room promised the same.

They did.

Joe never knew he'd been elected.

And the next year, the town eliminated the position of constable.

You Can't Beat an International

Fred Chaney of New Boston was fire chief for many years and known to be opinionated. In 1964, the town felt it might be time to buy a new vehicle to replace the 1937 truck.

Fred spoke up. He wasn't happy with the cost of insurance for the new truck. He nitpicked about the specs. A big controversy erupted—new truck, no new truck. The discussion waged on, hot and heavy.

Finally, Fred rapped his stick on the floor. The room went quiet. Fred said: "I could support this truck if it was an International."

That'll Do

Debate raged over a warrant article to raise and appropriate $2,000 to have the village sprayed against mosquitos. Some worried about the health risks of the chemicals. Others, like Catherine, just couldn't stand another mosquito infestation.

She said: "I was holding a cookout, had company over, and the mosquitos were so thick we had to move everything inside. I couldn't even enjoy the outdoors around my own home. It was terrible!"

Eugene spoke up. "Mr. Moderator, I'd like to propose an amendment. Amend down from two thousand to a dollah ninety-eight. Buy Catherine a can of bug dope."

A Grave Concern

In Brookline, a newcomer asked a question and it received such a perfect answer that every year at the town meeting, somebody asks again. It's tradition.

Newcomer says, "I see we're expending $500 a year for a sexton. What's a sexton?"

Grover Farwell replies, "I'm the sexton. And I'm going to bury you."

Good Question

At the Unity town meeting, some folks thought the one street light on the main drag was costing too much in electricity and ought to be turned off as a money-saving measure.

"But if you turn off the light," a resident queried, "and somebody drives through at night, how would they know they've been here?"

Note: To check the veracity of this story, I asked at a session in Unity whether or not the town had a streetlight. "No," somebody said. "But we used to."

Voter Turnout

During one special town meeting, great effort was made on both sides to bring out the vote. Carlton had no car, but somebody fetched him.

After Carlton had cast his vote, Mazie—who'd been in line behind him and might have cast a glance at his ballot—said to the one who'd done the fetching: "If I were you, I wouldn't bother giving him a ride home."

Mr. and Mrs. Smith

Mrs. Smith made a presentation of some length regarding a warrant article she supported. Then came time for questions and comments.

Mr. Smith had a comment. He addressed the voters: "Don't believe her. I'm married to her and she's never right."

Mrs. Smith said, "I married him fifty years ago. And, it's true, I haven't been right since."

Election Day Brownies

My friend Jean Lane always baked brownies for election day. She baked Republican brownies and Democrat brownies.

"What's the difference?" someone inevitably asked her.

She said, "The Democrats are the ones with the nuts."

Pikatzo
Frank Case

At a Raymond school meeting, discussion escalated about whether the district ought to hire a part-time art teacher. One voter rose and said with conviction, "Raymond ain't never had no Pikatzo, and it ain't never gonna have no Pikatzo."

The voter's wife said, "Not if we don't hire an art teacher, we ain't."

A Short Recess
Richard Gale via Jack Hutchinson

In Deerfield, the PTA was at odds with some of the decisions made by the school board. Tension was high and had been for months. After much debate at school meeting, the president of the PTA posed this question to the school board chair: "Madam Chairman, the PTA wants to know if the Board of Education appreciates the PTA."

The school board chair looked to the moderator.

The PTA president persisted: "Madam Chairman, I want an answer."

The school board chair whispered something in the moderator's ear, then announced, "I've asked the moderator for a short recess. I want to confer with the board."

The PTA president responded: "I want the moderator to promise that when we reconvene, I will have the floor." It was agreed.

Short recess.

Reconvention.

The PTA president reiterates: "Madam Chairman, the PTA wants to know if the Board of Education appreciates the PTA."

The chair responds: "I've conferred with the school board. Their message to you is that the Board of Education appreciates the PTA just about as much as the PTA appreciates the school board."

No Maps

Rod announced that he'd done some research and discovered there were no maps of the water and sewer system in town. This was a serious oversight. Where, he demanded, was this information to be had?

Ira, town surveyor since 1904, went to the mic. "I know where all the pipes are."

Rod was undeterred. "But what if you should retire, or—god forbid—what if you should die?"

Ira said, "Then it ain't my problem." ~

Richard vs. the Town Clerk

Richard spoke in favor of the noise ordinance. He spoke with feeling about dogs barking at night and disturbing his much-needed sleep—in particular, the town clerk's dogs. They were a nuisance.

The debate turned personal. The town clerk defended her dogs and herself. "If you'd stay home on the farm, Richard, instead of spending nights in the village with your lady friend, you wouldn't be bothered by my dogs." ~

Tear Down Those Sheds

Auctioning off of pews and horse hitches or even horse-and-buggy sheds was common when town halls and churches were being constructed. The money helped fund the construction.

Two hundred years later, give or take, the rustic sheds between the church and meeting house on the town square struck a concerned citizen as an eye sore. She went to the selectmen. "Those old sheds should be torn down. They're hazards and they're ugly."

The selectmen said, "We don't have anything to do with the sheds. They belong to the church. You need to talk to the pastor and the church folks."

So, the crusader attended a meeting of the church committee. "Those sheds spoil the looks of the common and nobody uses them anyway," she said.

"They don't belong to the church," the committee chair told her. "They belong to the founding families. They were auctioned off as horse-and-buggy shelters for when folks went to church or town meeting. You'll have to talk to the owners."

The determined woman said that, indeed, she would, if she could have the owners' names. "I'll give you a list," the chair said, "but there's a problem. They're all dead." ~

One Too Many

Turnout for town meeting is fairly predictable, but sometimes when a special meeting gets called on a controversial matter, a whole lot of people show up. If it gets too crowded in the hall, fire officials have been known to shut the meeting down and send everybody home.

At one such meeting, the fire chief started counting heads, grumbling that the room appeared to be over its posted capacity. "I think we've got a problem," the chief said to the native.

"We wouldn't have a problem," the native said, "if you'd just go home."

There's a Big Rock in the Road

An irate resident shows up at the meeting of the select board. He walks up to the table and sets a big rock—must have weighed a hundred pounds—in front of the board. The resident said he was sick of the town refusing to fix his road. It was shameful. He said, "I've been driving around this rock for two years and the town's done nothin' about it."

"You ain't drivin' around it anymore," said the chair.

Right to Know and Record

In that distant time before cell phones and digital cameras, if someone wanted to record town meeting, they needed a video camera, which could be quite an operation. So, the recording of meetings was the exception rather than the rule.

Ginger let it be known she intended to record town meeting and, according to the Right to Know laws she often quoted, town officials couldn't stop her.

Sure enough, she showed up early, set the camera up on a tripod at the back of the hall, plugged in her equipment. Did a test run. Everything worked fine.

Unfortunately, when the meeting started, she couldn't get the camera to work. She pushed every button, switched every switch, checked the connections. Dead as a doornail.

Ginger was visibly disappointed.

After the meeting, the moderator had a quiet word with the select board chair. "Willis," he said, "I know Ginger had the right to record the meeting. Too bad her camera didn't work."

"That reminds me," the selectman said, "I gotta put that fuse back in."

Town Meeting in Frenchboro

When we can, we go to the Frenchboro Lobster Festival on Long Island off the coast of Maine up near Bar Harbor. Frenchboro is the only town on Long Island. Its population as of the 2010 census was sixty-one souls. On the verge of telling a town meeting story at the festival, I asked the crowd if they held town meeting in Frenchboro.

Fella says: "Every day."

Got Plenty of That out in the Barn Soaked into the Floorboards

For years, I thought this story could only be told, never written. Some stories are like that. Aural. They work for the ear but not for the eye. I think maybe, now, I've figured out how to write it.

More than fifty years ago, a group of civic-minded individuals from the North Country heard about a new program to help people facing the end of life. It was a program called hospice. These days, just about everybody knows about hospice and how helpful it can be. My mother benefited greatly from five months of home hospice care at the end of her life. Most families have been touched or will be touched by the hospice experience.

But in the North Country fifty years ago, no one knew a thing about it.

This civic-minded group petitioned warrant articles in several small towns to raise money to get a local program started up. With twenty-five signatures (used to be ten) anybody can bring any matter before the town meeting for a vote.

Here we are at Columbia town meeting more than fifty years ago. The moderator and legislative body have gone through a number of articles already, voting yea or nay. Finally, we get to the petitioned article in question and the moderator reads it out: "Article Fifteen. To see if the town will vote to raise and appropriate five hundred dollars for hoss piss."

The farmer in the back says, "I'm voting no."

Fire Hose

Voters at town meeting debated whether to purchase a hundred feet of new fire hose. The fire chief said yes. The chair of the budget committee said no. So they compromised: Wait 'til there's a fire and see how much we're short.

SMALL TOWNS AND NEIGHBORS

No Mystery Here
Tom Keegan

Hap from Elkins had some chickens come up missing.

He said to his neighbor down the road: "Be sure not to let your chickens out. They might come home."

The Census-Taker

The census-taker went door to door on Main Street. He'd knock and knock. If nobody answered, after a while he moved on.

At one house, he knocked and knocked. No answer.

He was about to move on when he heard a high-pitched voice from a second-floor window across the street. A woman leaned out of the window. "Nobody lives there but me," she said, "and I'm over here."

Sugar Bear

Judy lived in Marlow with her first husband and their dog, a border collie named Sugar Bear. The first husband insisted that the dog run free. Judy and her first husband and Sugar Bear lived next door to a native and his three grown sons.

One foggy morning, Judy stepped out on the porch in curlers and a robe to call Sugar Bear. She couldn't see a thing and was worried the dog might be in the road. "Sugar Bear," she called. No Sugar Bear. Then louder. "Sugar Bear!" No dog. Finally, "SUGAR BEAR!"

"Comin'," boomed a deep man's voice from next door.

To this day, Judy doesn't know which of her neighbors answered the call.

No Big Rush

Gretchen and her husband bought a house in Warner upon retirement. They were, in fact, coming home to a town she remembered fondly from childhood. Her grandparents' house stood just down the road from her retirement cottage. The homestead had long since passed out of family hands, but Gretchen kept an eye on it just the same.

When new owners put on a fresh coat of paint, trimmed the maple trees, and planted a flower garden out front, she took a vicarious pride in the old place looking so good. "One of these days," she said to herself, "I'm going to stop in and congratulate those new folks on the fine job they're doing with Gram and Gramp's old house."

Time passed and Gretchen's neighborly intention slid to the back burner. Until one weekend when company came and Gretchen wanted to serve a nice pancake breakfast but—horror of horrors—had no pure New Hampshire maple syrup. She happened to think: *The folks who own Gram and Gramp's house sell syrup.* So she skipped down the hill, introduced herself to the owner, a born and bred yankee himself, bought a quart of hi-test, and congratulated him on his upkeep of the homestead.

"How long have you been living here?" she asked.

"Oh," he said, "we been in this house 'bout twelve years."

"Twelve years!" she said. "Can it be that long? I've been meaning to stop in and say hello since you first moved in. I'm mortified that I didn't stop by sooner."

"Don't worry," he said, "we wa'n't waiting for you."

One Man's Trash

At a neighborhood barbecue, Tim is proud of his new lawnmower. It needed some work, he says, but after tinkering with it a couple of Saturdays, it's running smooth.

"Where do you think I got it?" he asks his next-door neighbor.

"The dump," Lars says.

"Good guess," Tim says.

"No guess," Lars says. "I'm the one who put it there."

The Riot

"Heard there was a near riot Saturday night."

"Ayuh. Two fellas out in front of town hall."

"What were they doing?"

"Standing around."

Tracking Down Edith Ann's Number
Eileen from Monroe

I had to reach Edith Ann to let her know the trailer for towing the Alumni Band in the parade was all set. Looked her up in the phone book. No luck. Called Norene, who's in her late seventies and one of the younger band members. Right away she gave me Edith Ann's number.

When I commented I'd been unable to find her in the phone book, Norene said, "Oh, that's because you're new in town. You didn't know to look under Forrest."

"Who is Forrest?" I asked. I was sure Edith Ann was not married.

"Her father," Norene explained.

"Isn't he deceased?"

"Oh yes, for about thirty years now. But we all know to still look for him in the phone book."

Tit for Tat
Chris Divine

Bette got locked into the dump. She unloaded her wagon, but when she got to the gate it was closed and locked. She went back to the dump master's little house: "I'm locked in."

"Dump's closed from 12:00 to 12:30," Pete said. "It's my lunch hour."

"You need to let me out."

"I'm on a break. I'll let you out when I finish my break."

Bette had to wait. She wasn't happy.

A week later, she returned to the dump with a lock and chain. After unloading, she passed through the gate and proceeded to apply the lock and chain. Pete said, "What are you doin'?" (Only with more colorful language.)

"I'm finished dumping so I'm locking the gate and going home."

Home she went.

What Passes for Fun in Piermont

When I asked for Piermont stories, the locals were stumped. "Nothing funny about Piermont," Helga said.

Somebody else piped up, "Nothing ever happens in Piermont."

"What do you do for fun?" I asked.

"Pay taxes."

Check the Checklist

A supervisor of the checklist was stunned on voting day to see that one of the town's leading citizens was not on the list of eligible voters, though he'd lived in town all his life and his parents and grandparents before him. A new statewide computer system had towns sucking names off lists from other towns. Say, for example, Sharon Roy registers to vote in Canterbury. She gets looked up on the system and is found in Colebrook, so the computer automatically sucks her off the Colebrook checklist and relocates her in Canterbury. But what if she was a different Sharon Roy? What if there were two of them?

The aforementioned supervisor noticed that Joe was missing from the checklist. She drove to his house. Found his wife in the kitchen. "Nona" she said, "did you know Joe moved to Milton?"

Nona says, "What's he doing settin' in the living room then?"

Peace and Unity

I heard this story in Plainfield. Martha and Enoch were in their seventies when they tied the knot. The preacher read the vows, "Repeat after me. 'I, Enoch, vow to live with Martha in peace and unity.'"

Enoch says, "I'll agree to live in peace but damned if I'll live in Unity."

Those Damn Women

In Marlborough during the 1970s, a group of women met regularly to discuss books among other things. These women decided they'd like to do more for the town. So they went to the town fathers to offer their services on committees and so forth. "Just let us menfolk take care of the town," the town fathers said. "You ladies go plant flowers in the square."

This did not sit well.

Soon the ladies found a cause. Town meeting and school meeting were traditionally held on Saturday, back to back. This didn't seem to allow enough time for deliberation, so the ladies lobbied to have one of them moved to a Tuesday evening. They succeeded. Which made the town fathers mad. Evidently, they didn't want to have to work an extra evening. "After that," the storyteller said, "we were referred to as 'those damn women.'"

"Are there any other of 'those damn women' here tonight?" I asked.

"Most of us are dead," she said.

Welcome to the Neighborhood

The town turned out for the funeral of a popular resident who'd moved to town from Massachusetts after his retirement and lived there a good twenty-five years. He served on many town committees and had several terms as selectman.

When it came time for people to speak of him, an old-timer stood up, kinda misty-eyed. "Gosh," he said, "Jake was almost like one of us."

No Abatement for You

A couple had moved from the city to an old house in Windham. The taxes were steep, so the husband went to the selectmen to try for an abatement. "We've got three easements on the property," he explained. "We got a gravel road that runs right through it and a power line that's an eyesore."

Selectman said, "If it's such a lousy piece of property, what the hell'd you buy it for?"

Not a Park

Jim said his aunt and uncle owned a nice house with a big lawn under maples near the covered bridge in the middle of town, a tourist attraction.

He was driving by one day and spotted a car with out-of-state plates parked out front of the house. The family belonging to the car had laid out a blanket and were having a picnic on that big lawn.

He stopped and said hello. "You must be friends with the sheriff," he said to the strangers.

"Why do you say that?"

"If you weren't he'd shoot you for trespassing on his lawn."

A Matter of Perspective
Ruth Keith

We drove out to visit a friend, miles and miles on a long dirt road. About eight miles from the friend's house, we saw a new house had been recently built.

When we finally got to our friend's, we asked her about her new neighbors.

She said, "Yep, they's a-crowdin' me."

Just One Rule

A woman moved from New Jersey to a small town in the Lakes Region. She called town hall to find out about getting a permit to burn brush. Town hall referred her to the fire department. "Chief," she said, "what kind of forms do I have to fill out to burn brush on my property?"

"No forms."

"Well, is there a permit procedure or a fee?"

"Nope."

"Well," she says, "what are the rules?"

"It's an all-volunteer fire department," he says. "The only rule is if you're going to burn, we'd appreciate it if you'd do it after five o'clock when the firefighters are home from work."

Which Way to the Holiday Inn?

Woman came screaming into town hall yard. She burst through the doors, accosted the a local. "Can you direct me to the Holiday Inn?"

"Holiday Inn?"

"Yes. The Holiday Inn, here in Springfield. I've been driving three hours and I'm late."

Of course, there is no Holiday Inn in Springfield, New Hampshire. No inn at all. Nor any hotels or motels closer than New London. Turns out she thought she was in Vermont.

WATER AND WATERWAYS

The Big Lake

The fella from away said of Lake Winnipesaukee upon seeing it for the first time: "That's a lot of water."

To which the local replied: "Yup, and that's just the top of it."

The Locals Say Umbaygog

Lake Umbagog is a huge shallow body of water near the Canadian border. A woman, whose name should not escape me but sadly does, told about one of her relatives taking a couple of friends ice fishing on the big lake.

The three men crowded into the cab of the pickup truck. The bed was loaded with fishing gear, lunch, bait, and so forth. As they drove across the ice to a prime fishing spot, three empty plastic milk jugs on a rope—thirty-five, forty feet long—bounced along behind them.

One of the friends asked about those milk jugs. "What are those for?"

The driver said, "If we go through the ice, they'll float, so the ones who come to fish the truck out will know where to find us."

First Things First

Ada and Urban's camp is across the lake and down a-ways. I can see it clearly with binoculars from our dock. One afternoon, I got a call from Ada: "Get in your kayak and paddle down here quick," she said, "if you want to see a bear in our big pine tree."

I threw on my life preserver, climbed into the kayak and paddled across the lake and down a-ways as fast as I could. As I drew closer, I could see Ada in the window, her arms raised, hands pressed to the glass. Her mouth was open. She seemed to be yelling something, but I couldn't hear what.

Then I spotted a couple other neighbors, Pudgy and Joe, on Joe's beach, sitting in lawn chairs, looking in the direction of Ada and Urban's camp next door. They were yelling something too, but I couldn't make out what.

In the big pine tree, I spotted it—a young bear, black as oil, clinging to the trunk about twenty feet up. A couple of other boats had anchored just off Ada and Urban's dock. Those folks were watching the bear too. And on the other side of the picnic table I glimpsed Urban with a camera, snapping away.

I paddled in as close as I dared. Wanted to get a good look before the bear ran off. When I let up on the paddling and the kayak stilled, I could finally make out what Joe and Pudgy were yelling. They were yelling, "Urban, go in the house and put some pants on!"

The Tide

Hermit Island is a big camping area on Casco Bay, near Bath, Maine. People come from all over to set up their tents on sites overlooking the ocean or even right on the beach. The thing about Hermit Island—it's not an island. It's the tip of a peninsula—or as they say in Maine, a spit. From the tar road, you drive on a raised gravel road across a tidal flat to get to the Kelp Shed, where you check in and are directed to your campsite.

A woman from an inland state, maybe Kansas, drove in one evening around sunset. She was given a map of all the little roads on the island. X marked the spot where she should set up her tent. She went off and all seemed well until the next morning when she came tearing into the Kelp Shed demanding to talk to somebody important. Apparently, somebody important showed up, and she launched into her complaint. "I paid for a waterfront site," she said. "But out in front of my tent it's nothing but mud as far as the eye can see."

"Well," somebody important said. "There's the tide to consider. You know about the tide."

"Of course I know about the tide," the woman said. "I'm talking about mud."

"Well, ma'am," somebody important said. "The tide comes in and the tide goes out. The tide went out. You have to understand, ma'am, every day the tide goes out. You know about the tide going out? Right?"

"Of course, I know the tide goes out," the woman huffed. "I didn't know it took the water with it."

Mount Washington, the Boat

Julia's family has owned a camp on an island in Winnipesaukee for generations.

At a wedding in Putney, Vermont, a man approached her and asked for a dance. As they were dancing, he said, "I know who you are. I know your dad. I know your summer home. And I know how to get there."

She was only slightly alarmed. Then he said, "I captain the *Mount Washington*."

An eavesdropping Vermonter quipped, "That's a job that goes nowhere."

Minnie Sees the Ocean

Aunt Minnie from the Midwest always wanted to see the ocean. In old age she got the chance because her nephew was stationed at Pease Air Force Base in Newington. Minnie flew to New Hampshire and the nephew drove her to Rye Beach to see the ocean for the first time.

As they stood on the sand looking at the water, the nephew noticed that Minnie seemed a little down in the mouth. "What's the matter, Aunt Minnie?" he said.

"Oh," she said, "I had an idea it would be bigger than this."

WEATHER AND FASHION

Generations Connect

Years ago, I did a long residence at the Indian River School in Caanan, New Hampshire. It's a cooperative school serving several small towns in the region. The students interviewed community members about the history of their town. We shaped the interviews into a staged reading. It was quite a production, with drawings depicting the towns' histories, original music performed by the youngsters, and young actors portraying the interviewees and telling their stories.

One boy portrayed Richard O'Day and told about the Hurricane of 1938 in O'Day's own words. He said, "It was quite a blow. Sounded just like a freight train going by the house the wind was so strong. During a lull, we thought it was a lull, my brother and I sneaked out on the back porch. The wind off the lake was so strong we was flapping in the breeze. We had to hold onto the railings to keep from blowing away."

As the boy finished his monologue, there came a voice from the audience—the real Richard O'Day. He said, "Ayuh, that's just the way it was!"

The Doll House
Helen Kenison

Helen weathered the '38 storm, but her family's cottage by the lake was blown away. She was a child at the time. She had a doll house in that cottage—hand made with little curtains in all the windows.

When the family went back to view the wreckage after the big blow, Helen found a small piece of one of the windows from that doll house. She said, "I forgot about losing the cottage; my doll house was gone!" All these years later, Helen still misses that doll house.

The Window Did Not Break
George Arouchon

George was a young boy at the time of the '38 hurricane. His parents, Syrian immigrants, ran a barber shop on Tremont Street in Boston.

When the hurricane hit—unexpected as it was—George's father saw that the wind was lifting slate tiles from the roof of the church across the street and sending them flying. He protected the large plate glass window on the barber shop by wielding a broom and batting the tiles away.

When Mother heard what Father had done, she cried "Where was George?"

Turns out young George stood shoulder to knee with his father wielding a broom of his own and helping to protect the store.

Ed and the Doll Carriage

Ed was born on September 9, 1938. Just a couple weeks later, on September 23, came the hurricane. According to the family story (Ed, of course, has no memory of this), the river rose to the point that their house was threatened, so Mother held the infant in her arms, Father held onto Mother, and the family crossed fast-moving water to climb to the neighbors' house on higher ground.

The neighbors were two maiden ladies who welcomed the little family with open arms.

The wind blew so hard they worried the center chimney would blow over, so—to be safe—infant Ed was tucked in a wicker doll carriage, which was placed under the grand piano.

The center chimney did not blow over.

But for as long as those ladies lived, when one of them spotted Ed around town, she'd say, "Ed, have you slept in my doll carriage lately?"

What to Do in a Hurricane

Vea Jenks, from a penciled note she sent me with the inked inscription "This was something my mother had"

During the Hurricane of '38, an old farmer arose and began to dress.

"What you doin', Herman?" his wife called from their bed.

"Dressin'," the old farmer said. "This house may soon be blowed clear to the village. I don't know about you, but I'm a-goin' in my pants."

Hurricane at the Beach

Recalling the hurricane, a woman said she was seven at the time and charged with babysitting a one-year-old. This was in Squamscott, Massachusetts. There was no warning about the storm coming. It was upon them before they thought to look for it.

She had wheeled the baby in a huge carriage (seemed huge to her) to the beach where they watched the crashing waves.

On the return trip, pushing that heavy carriage up the hill to the main road, she was stunned to see her father in the car pull over beside them. "What impressed me," she said, "was seeing my father home in the middle of the day. He never came home in the middle of the day."

"It's a hurricane!" he said. "I'll take the baby and you push the carriage home."

"Even at seven," she said, "I knew that was wrong. We should have both got into the car and left the carriage. But my father didn't want to lose that good carriage."

Don't Even Think About It
David Howard

Aunt Polly come down with walking pneumonia last spring.

"My own damn fault," she said. "Peeled down too soon."

A Lesson in One-Upmanship
Paul Currier

At Procter's Store in Enfield, a half dozen old boys were shooting the breeze about how cold it got out their way during this latest cold snap. One said five below. Another said ten below. Fifteen below at 5:00 AM, said the third.

Chester said, "All I know is it was so cold the smoke froze in the stove pipe." But the winner was Junior, who said, "I had to look four clapboards below the sill to find the mercury."

The Big Sleep
Ken Randall

Ken recalled being in the ticket office at the base of Mount Washington one long-ago September when four young women wearing high heels and shorts announced their plan to climb the Ammonoosuc Trail.

As most hikers know, the difference in temperature and weather conditions between the bottom of Mount Washington and the top can be dramatic. Ken didn't think the young women were dressed or equipped for the wintery weather they'd find at the top. But they were determined.

Finally, he said, "Do me a favor, and if you start getting sleepy, just lie down beside the trail and go to sleep with your arms and legs crossed."

"Why?" the young women asked.

"If you get sleepy, that's a sign of hypothermia. So when you go to sleep, it'll be the Big Sleep. If you've got your arms and legs crossed, it'll be easier to wrap you up and haul you off the mountain in a gurney."

At Last Something Worth Mentioning

Skip's dad worked at the lumberyard in all kinds of weather. When he was very small, Skip didn't talk. He seemed to be a smart little boy, he just didn't talk.

Every day he'd wait at the window and watch for his dad to come walking up the hill, home from the lumberyard down the road.

His mother swears Skip spoke his first words with his nose pressed to the frosted glass. Here comes Dad, home at last on a cold, cold day during a long cold spell. Skip says, "The icicles on his beard are a little longer today."

WILDLIFE, HUNTING, AND FISHING

Two Willies and a Tom

Willie told about going fishing with his father (Old Willie), and Uncle Tommy, who'd had a stroke and couldn't use his right arm or leg. The three went fishing in the stream, early April, ice barely out. Sure enough, poor Uncle Tommy lost his balance on account of his weak right side and down he went into the rushing water.

He lay on his back, floating best he could, yelling, "Help me, Willie. I can't swim."

Old Willie yelled back, "Tommy, stand up."

Seems the stream was only about two feet deep.

When Tommy stood and clambered out of the water, he was some cold. Old Willie told Young Willie to run back to the camp and get some matches, so Tommy could warm himself at a campfire before he caught a death of cold.

Young Willie started for the road, but Old Willie called, "Go through the woods. The camp's only about 350 yards away as the crow flies." And he pointed the boy in the right direction.

Young Willie run into the woods. He run and run. He slowed down when things began to look kinda the same. This went on for some time. Finally, he began to yell, and followed the whistle of his father back down to the stream.

Old Willie says, "Where's the matches?"

Young Willie points: "350 yards in that direction."

Did You Get Him?

Dewey said all the roads in Alexandria used to be gravel. It was pretty common during partridge or deer season to spot game on the side of the road, roll down the window, and let fly. Course, there are laws against that now.

One day in the freezing rain, a fella (who may or may not have been Dewey himself) spotted a big buck just off the road as he was driving up Hemp Hill. He stopped, grabbed his gun with one hand, and went to roll the window down with the other, but it was frozen shut.

Dang!

"Did you get the deer in the end?" I asked.
"He was still standing there when I drove off."

An Expert Opinion

Kenneth in Claremont told about the fella with a skunk in the cellar that refused to leave. Called the Game Warden, who said, "Leave the cellar window open and spread a trail of bread crumbs leading outside."

Fella did.

Next day he had two skunks in the cellar.

How Natives Catch Fish
Mimi Lisbon of Wolfeboro

You probably already know the one about the fellow who was out ice fishing, and, boy, he was hauling in fish hand over fist!

Well, the other fishermen just shook their heads in frustration as they watched, because no matter what they tried they were catching nothing.

Finally, one of the group called out, "Say old man, what are you using for bait?"

To which the old fellow replied "Peas."

"Did you say *peas*? That ain't no bait I ever heard of."

"You ain't never heard of peas as bait before? Thought everybody knew 'bout that. Still, just this once, I'll share my secret with you, but you have to promise not to spread it all over town."

"We won't tell nobody. You have our word."

"There's nothing to it. All you need to do is open a can of peas and dump them into your fishing hole, then, when a fish comes up for a pee, you grab him!"

Undeterred
Lisa Rollins

Lisa from Ashland sent me this story. She says it's not a horned pout story, more of a lantern story—but I call it both. Here's what she wrote:

About thirty-five years ago or so, my father Ben Rollins, along with his best buddy Kent Smith, Sr. (god rest his soul), and few other buds were out late one night smelt'n.

Each man carried his smelt dip'n net, pail, and lantern. Dad was a pipe smoker too, always smoked George Washington tobacco and on special occasions, Half & Half.

As they were walking down a path next to a stream running into Big Squam, each of the men stepped over a low-lying wire fence. This fence was right at the end of a dock they were walking onto, waiting for the smelt to "run."

As they stepped over the fence, each called out to the guy in back of him to "watch out for the fence." Apparently, Dad didn't hear the warning.

He fell into the drink along with the net, pail, lantern, and pipe. Went straight to the bottom, then popped back up like cork with the net, pail, and lantern in his hands. The lantern was still lit. And his pipe was still clenched between his teeth.

After hauling him out of the drink, the boys rushed him home for a change of clothes and a couple a shots of whiskey. Later they returned to the smelt'n spot, scooped up a nice mess of smelts, and brought 'em home.

Nothing tastes much better than freshly caught smelts fried crisp at about one o'clock in the morning.

Three Short Trout
Merle Straw

As a kid, Merle loved to visit his grandparents in Guilford, Maine. Merle and Grampa went fishing one morning. They got their limit—and maybe a little over. Worked up an appetite and went directly from the trout stream to a local restaurant.

Setting down to lunch, Merle said to Grampa, "Why don't you take your hat off?"

Grampa did. And there plastered to his bald head were three short trout. He'd hidden them in his hat and forgot.

Good Sport

In West Gardiner, Maine, outside the Rod and Gun shop, a protest sign read: "Hunting is no sport."

A local commented, "Course huntin's not a sport. If it was, we'd give guns to the deer."

Sneaky

In the blueberry barrens near our camp in Franklin, Maine, the dogs and I were walking. It had rained the night before, then come off cold, so the water froze in the ruts and potholes creating skims of ice.

About a mile out we heard roaring, revving, and crunching. The ice in the ruts and holes was cracking under the tires of a vehicle driven way too fast on the rough, narrow road. Around the corner came a four-wheel-drive pickup truck. The truck pulled up beside us. I could see the two men inside. They were wearing blaze orange and had their rifles on the seat between them.

The driver rolled down his window. He put his finger to his lips, winked, and whispered: "You didn't hear us coming, did you? We're deer hunters."

Enough for One Day
Bob Chadbourn

Carl and Pete were up Pittsburg way moose hunting. Pete shot a big one, run about a thousand pounds, give or take, but when Carl and Pete grabbed on either end to haul that moose out of the woods, it was just too heavy.

Luckily, a couple of loggers, Marcel and Rene, were working nearby. They had a horse and a scoot, and between the four of them and the horse and the scoot, they got that moose back to the truck.

The hunters were so grateful, they wanted to give the loggers a reward. Carl had just a ten-dollar bill. So did Pete. What the heck. They handed the $20.00 to the loggers, who stared at the money a full minute. Marcel says to Rene, "No more logging today."

Robin and the Mouse

Don told the story of Robin the logger who worked with Don's brother, a forester. Robin was a big strong guy, over six feet tall and 300 pounds. He meant well but was hard on equipment. Each morning, Robin would leave his bag lunch on the seat of the truck while he worked.

One day a mouse was spotted in the truck cab eating Robin's lunch. The forester said, "Robin, don't leave your lunch in the truck. Mice'll get in there and the next thing you know they'll be chewing the wires."

Robin meant well but he forgot. Left his lunch in the truck again. When he went to grab it, the mouse was in the bag. He tried to grab the mouse, but it got loose and ran off. Robin vowed to get the little bugger. (Only he didn't say bugger.)

Later that afternoon, he was running the crane and spotted the mouse sitting on a pile of logs. Robin grabbed a claw-full of logs, swung them around, dropped them on the mouse.

The mouse ran off. Again.

Some say the mouse was smarter than Robin. Some say dropping a claw load of logs on a mouse is the definition of overkill.

Taking This One Alive
Apocryphal

This story dates back to the Works Progress Administration (WPA). A worker invited friends from New York to come up to Maine and learn something about bear hunting.

The three of them got out in the woods and this fellow told his friends he'd go on ahead and do a little scouting.

By and by, they saw their guide tearing through the woods with a bear close on his heels, "Get out of the way, boys. I'm taking this one back to camp alive."

If She Don't Die

Some of the workers at the mill used to fish in the river right outside the building. They kept their poles in their lockers and, when they had a minute, they'd throw a line in the water. One guy, Emile, got lucky. He hauled in three huge trout, one after another. "You're not going to eat those trout, are you, Emile?" a coworker asked, concerned about pollution.

Emile said, "I'll give one to my mother-in-law. If she don't die, I'll eat the other two."

A week later, the coworker said, "Hey, Emile. I saw your mother-in-law at church."

"The fish were good," Emile said.

As Good an Excuse as Any

That afternoon little Jamie had trouble keeping his eyes open. He was asleep with his head down on his desk. The teacher couldn't allow that. She woke him up. "Jamie," she says, "you can't be sleeping in school."

"I'm awful sorry, Mrs. Johnson," Jamie says. "We was up all night burying moose bones."

Alden and the Squirrel
Alden Farrar

My ancestor that I was named for went out hunting and there on a high branch was a squirrel, just chittering away. So old Alden loaded up his muzzleloader, and I guess he overloaded it because when he went to shoot at the squirrel, which was still up there chittering, the muzzleloader bucked and knocked him on his back. When Alden come to his senses, stretched out on the ground, muzzle loader still in hand, the squirrel was still chittering on that high branch. Alden said, "Chitter damn you chitter, you wouldn't be chittering if you were on the other end of this thing."

Do You Have To?

Gob and his brother Walter were fly fishing on the Squam River. Walter made a mighty cast, but the line flipped back on him and that Golden Demon embedded itself deep in his arm. Across the river, as luck would have it, is Doc Paul. He gets his bag, wades across, and swabs Gob's arm with disinfectant. "I'll have to cut the hook off before I pull the fly out," he says.

"Doc," Gob says, "do you have to? That's the only one I've caught a fish on all day."

YANKEE ATTITUDE AND WISDOM

Trip to Boston

Denise, who grew up in northern Maine, told how her brother Richard Peloquin gained the respect of his much cooler high school peers. At his fortieth class reunion, Mike O'Neil, the coolest kid in Key Club, reminded Richard of the time he drove a group of them from the high school all the way to downtown Boston (a place none of them had ever been before) for a field trip.

All those years later, Mike was still impressed. "Richard," he said, "you were just seventeen years old, a kid from the Maine woods, and you got us to downtown Boston without a hitch. How'd you do it?"

Richard said, "I used a map."

Revenge

The woman moved into town. Right off she spotted Mike on the side of the road having a beer. She reported him to the police! Said he was breaking the open can law. (Even though it was a bottle.) Mike said nothing, but a while later, after dark, he parked his truck out front of her house.

And left it there 'til morning.

Big Spill

Clyde was telling Francis about the disaster at the hardware store. One of the shelves that held the cans of paint collapsed. The cans fell and the tops popped and it was a big mess.

Francis said: "It must have been terrible—all those gallons of paint spilled on the floor in the store!"

Clyde said: "T'was mostly quarts."

The Conversation
Apocryphal

Asked about his children, the yankee said, "Two girls and a boy."
"Tell me about them."
"Just did."

Know What You Don't Know

Connie's father said of the hired man, "I taught him everything I know and he still don't know nothin'." ❧

The Cog Will Take You Up and Bring You Back

Martha and Gordon's son-in-law climbed Mount Washington. At the general store, he announced that he was exhausted from the climb, but it was worth it for the view.

One of the customers looked at him kinda squinty, "Din't ya know they had a train?" ❧

The Highest Peak

Years ago, Gordon climbed Mount Katahdin. It was a sunny day. He and other climbers were lying around at the top, enjoying the sunshine. One hiker said that Mount Katahdin was the highest in the Northeast.

Gordon corrected him: "Oh no. Mount Washington is the highest."

The Mainer replied, "Mount Washington don't count. It's got a road to the top." ❧

How Dare They?

Norman told of the time *Life* magazine did a piece on his home town of Whitefield. The reporters interviewed Mrs. Johnson, who'd lived in town all her life and could fill them in on highlights and history.

When the article came out, she was hoppin' mad. "They called me Old Mrs. Johnson," she said, indignantly. "I'm only ninety-two." ❧

What Do You Mean by That?

Glenn's grandfather, an opinionated person, had this to say to his equally opinionated grandson: "You're seldom right, but this time you're wrong." ❧

On the Ice in Newfoundland

Apocryphal

The humor of Newfoundland is similar to yankee humor and probably has the same roots. For example: Two old guys in Newfoundland went ice fishing. They worked hard chopping the holes. In the midst of the activity,

Joe headed for shore. Knocked at the door of a neighbor's house. "Come on in, Joe," the neighbor said. "How about a glass of screech?"

Joe didn't say no and enjoyed the beverage. After a while he allowed as how he best get going and could he borrow a rope. "A rope?" the neighbor inquired.

"Yup," Joe said, "Amos fell through the ice."

Fresh Out
Jean Whatley

Christian, in his early teen years, took a summer job in the meat department at Heath's Super Market in Center Harbor. He was placing wrapped meats in the display case when a woman, who appeared to be of considerable means and was fashionably dressed, asked if there were any dog bones.

"Excuse me just a moment, Ma'am," says Chris. "I'm not sure. I'll have to ask."

Just at that moment Ole Thomas, who'd worked at Heath's meat department some twenty years came upon the scene. Chris asked, "Tom, do we have any dog bones?"

"Nope," says Tom. "Ain't slaughtered any dogs today."

Now That You Mention It
Apocryphal

Beulah took care of the cranky old yankee's place for twenty-five years, give or take. Finally, she decided to say something. "All these years I've been working for you, keeping your house clean, cooking and so forth, and you never once said, 'Beulah, you're doing a good job.'"

The cranky old yankee says, "Never said you wa'n't."

Same Story Different Characters
Anne Lunt

Mrs. Skillins, wife of Bert Skillins, was a dyed-in-the-wool yankee, frugal in every way. Every Saturday morning for decades Sarah came to the house to pick up the laundry. She returned the clothes cleaned and pressed on a Monday. This went on when the children were growing, when they went off to war or college, and eventually off to marry and have children of their own.

At last, Sarah confronted Mrs. Skillins. "I've been taking care of your laundry for thirty-eight years, and you never once said 'Thank you' or 'You're doing a good job.'"

Mrs. Skillins was taken aback, "I go on hirin' you, don't I?"

We Don't Need No Stinkin' Bridge
Apocryphal

This is a classic. The warrant called for $100,000 to build a bridge across a brook. Old Zeb jumps to his feet in protest. "That's ridiculous. Why I could pee halfway across that piddling little brook!"

The moderator bangs the gavel, "Sir, you are out of order!"

Zeb says: "Damn right. If I wasn't I could pee all the way across."

Just Wondering

The tourists climbed Mount Monadnock and encountered the fire warden who manned the lookout up top. "How many fires do you spot from up here in a year?" a tourist asked.

"Varies."

Just Wondering II

"Think it'll ever stop raining?"
"Always has before."

Three Questions
Apocryphal

A fella from away inquires of the yankee out front of the general store, "Do you know where East Chemung is?"

"Nope."

"Do you know where Orchard Lane is?"

"Nope."

"How about Havenwood Circle?"

"Never heard of it."

Fella from away, "I guess you don't know much, do you?"

"Maybe not. Then again, I ain't the one that's lost."

What's Hay Up Your Way
Bob Ramsay

Tom Hutchins ran the water-powered sawmill in Alexandria. He and a couple of his buddies took the train from Bristol to Boston to catch a ball game. There he was standing on the sidewalk gawking up at the tall buildings. Along comes a city slicker who pegs him for a hay seed, and says, being smart: "What's hay up your way?"

Tom says: "Dried grass you damned fool."

Smelt Fishing
Jenni Shone

Jenni had a bum knee and her husband wanted to do some smelt fishing. So she brought a book, sat in the car with the heater on, and read while he fished.

At the dock, Bob joined a group of older guys also fishing. "Who's that in the car?" they asked.

Bob said, "That's my wife."

"Oh," one old guy said, "we usually leave 'em home."

The Dip

At first it was a dip, then a pot hole. The pot hole started out the size of a bushel basket, progressed to washtub capacity, and grew larger and larger through the spring. When the big rains came, it filled with water. That's when the neighbor put up his sign: "No fishing."

The Trip
David Griffin

David Jenkins went to New York City on a trip. When he got back to Auburn, New Hampshire, he didn't seem all that impressed with the Big Apple. "New York's just like Auburn, New Hampshire," he said, "'cept more people."

Friend
Apocryphal

Friend Johnson was a logger and retired railroad man who lived in Colebrook. One day, as Friend was enjoying a Moxie on the porch of the general store, a shiny car with New York plates pulled up out front.

"Say, Friend," said the slicker, "do you know how to get to Errol."

"How'd you know my name was Friend?" Friend said.

"Wild-ass guess," the slicker said.

"Well," says Friend, "why don't you take a wild-ass guess about how to get to Errol?"

Steep? I Guess It's Steep

When asked by a hiker if a certain mountain trail was steep, the local replied: "If anything, it leans forward a little."

A Tough Climb

The hiker from away asked a couple of locals about the difficulty of the trail to Round Pond. "It's steep in parts," one said.

"I'd call it tough," said the other. "It was a tough climb. A-course we were carrying a boat."

Say What You Mean, George

Kay told a cautionary tale about her Uncle George, raised in Cornish. It had snowed heavily during the night and the going was tough as Uncle George slogged the long miles to the one-room school house where he was a student.

Along came a neighbor driving a sleigh and gliding right along smart.

"George," called the neighbor, "would you like a ride?"

"I don't care," George said.

So the neighbor went right along down the road.

Okay by Me

The city slicker says to the local, "I'm trying to get to Manchester."

The local says, "I've no objection."

Big House, Little House, Back House, Barn
Bill Gleed

At the Robert Frost Farm in Derry, a man from the Midwest expressed surprise that the house was attached to the barn. "Where we come from, we put the barn out in the field where we do the work," the Midwesterner said. "Why the heck do you folks attach the barn to the house?"

The historian replied, "February."

I'm with Iris

In Lancaster, we got to discussing how sometimes talk can get a little heated when it comes to small-town politics. One woman said, "At the last town meeting, I may have come on a little strong, Iris. I'm sorry. I didn't have all my facts straight."

Iris seemed to think that was all right. She appreciated the woman's honesty, not to mention her finally getting her facts straight.

The woman went on: "I could have been more moderate in my words."

Iris said, "Life is too short to be moderate."

Thanks for the Reminder

The day after I turned fifty, I was telling stories at a retirement village. I announced to the crowd, "Yesterday I turned fifty." I could see they weren't impressed. Thinking quick, I added: "Yup, yesterday I turned fifty. I guess I'm about halfway there."

Thinking quicker, a lady piped up, "I'm ninety-nine. Guess I'm about all the way there."

If It's Good Enough for Jesus

A story from North Hampton: During the days of gas rationing, Mother Beatrice Ayer (of the Boston Brahmin Ayer family) was able to transport herself to church each Sunday in a donkey cart.

One Sunday, a black limousine pulled up behind the cart, and an Auntie sniffed: "My deah, is that any way for an Ayer to go to church?"

Beatrice replied, "If it is good enough for Jesus, it is good enough for me."

Acknowledgments

Thanks to the many storytellers over the years who've so generously shared their stories in person, in letters, in e-mails, over the phone. I hope this book does them justice. The storytelling community in New Hampshire is strong; I'm lucky to be part of it. We help each other! Thanks to New Hampshire Humanities for sponsoring so many of my storytelling programs over the years.

To the Chesley Writers, thanks for your encouragement and for inspiring me with your writing and dedication. Kirsty Walker at Hobblebush, thanks for believing in this book and making it beautiful. Todd Kramer, your art caught the essence of the work in a way that I couldn't imagine was possible. Well done. Dana van der Bijl and Adi Rule, the precision of your work to make the words and punctuation just right is greatly appreciated. John Rule, Adi Rule and Kris Seavey, my little family, thanks for putting up with all the nonsense and for your unwavering support. On we go.

About the Author

Rebecca Rule is a full-time writer, humorist, and storyteller. In the program that inspired this book, "That Reminds Me of a Story," she tells some of the best (and funniest) stories she's collected over the course of twenty-five years of spinning and gathering yarns at libraries, historical societies, rotaries, clubs, church groups, campgrounds, and charitable organizations. She says she likes collecting stories because "they're free and you don't have to dust them." Whenever she performs, she invites audience members to tell stories of their own in the spirit of oral history, and she pledges to pass the stories on. Stories are our identity. They hold our history, our culture, our heart—and they live on in the telling.

For ten years, she hosted the NH *Authors Series* on NHPTV. She currently hosts *Our Hometown*, also on NHPTV.

She's the author of a dozen books, including N *is for* NH, an ABC book with photographs by Scott Snyder. Other books include *The Iciest Diciest Scariest Sled Ride Ever!*, a picture book illustrated by Jennifer Thermes; *Headin' for the Rhubarb*, a NH Dictionary (well, kinda); and *The Best Revenge*, named one of five "Essential NH Books" by *New Hampshire* magazine and "Outstanding Work of Fiction" by the NH Writers Project. *Sixty Years of Cuttin' the Cheese: Joel Sherburne and Calef's Famous Country Store* takes a look at the beloved institution of the general store through the eyes of an amazing (and very funny) man who's worked in one for sixty years and counting. *Moved and Seconded:* NH *Town Meeting* focuses on the changes in town meeting over the years, the characters that make town meeting so fascinating, and why it's such a unique and enduring institution.

Awards and special recognition include an honorary doctorate of humane letters from New England College "for contributions to New Hampshire culture and literature," and an award from NH Humanities for demonstrating "what it means to create, teach, lead, assist, and encourage human understanding."

In his list of 100 things to do in NH, Steve Taylor lists at #1: "Attend an evening program where writer and teacher Rebecca Rule tells stories that embody the best of rural New Hampshire humor and mirth."